UGLY

ANITA BHAGWANDAS

UGLY

GIVING US BACK OUR BEAUTY STANDARDS

BLINK
bringing you closer

Published by Blink Publishing,
an imprint of Bonnier Books UK
4th Floor, Victoria House
Bloomsbury Square
London, WC1B 4DA
Owned by Bonnier Books
Sveavägen 56, Stockholm, Sweden

www.facebook.com/blinkpublishing
twitter.com/blinkpublishing

Hardback: 978-1-78870-475-5
Trade paperback: 978-1-78870-476-2
Ebook: 978-1-78870-477-9
Audio: 978-1-78870-598-1

British Library Cataloguing-in-Publication Data.

A catalogue record for this book is available from the British Library.

Design by www.envydesign.co.uk

Printed and bound in Great Britain by Clays Ltd, Elcograf S.p.A

1 3 5 7 9 10 8 6 4 2

Blink Publishing is an imprint of Bonnier Books UK
www.bonnierbooks.co.uk

To Mum and Dad:
thank you for everything

CONTENTS

BEFORE UGLY

'Anita Bhagwandas is really ugly.'

THIS WAS AN ANONYMOUS comment left on a digital feature ten years ago, as part of which I was pictured alongside my more conventionally attractive colleagues. Reading it stung. More than stung – it was lacerating. Despite knowing that internet trolls seek pleasure in torturing and the target is largely irrelevant, my mind immediately flipped into a familiar overdrive: did I know them? Had I hurt them somehow, or was a random person so abhorred by the horror of my face that they felt compelled to tell me? In my mind, it was all of the above – particularly the latter.

'Trolls will be trolls,' friends consoled when I told them of the incident. The website editor said: 'These things happen to public-facing women all the time, particularly women of colour,' when I asked her to take the comment down and she did. This was apparently just a sad fact of our modern technological age and the consensus was to forget all about it. Except that I couldn't. I couldn't let the word 'ugly' go. My brain slung it around, like a pizza chef tossing elasticated dough into the air and catching it again. It also hurt because this was not new information to me; I'd always felt resoundingly unattractive when it came to my appearance. And now, here was the proof for everyone to see publicly. Had the troll criticised my writing, called me 'weird-looking', maybe even the customary 'fat bitch' or any other similar insult I've received, then perhaps I wouldn't have been quite so rattled but here was an online confirmation from a stranger of how I really felt about myself. This was indisputably the truth: I was *ugly*.

There's something uniquely powerful and destructive about the word *ugly*. I've had a complex relationship with that emotive word for my entire existence. I doubt very much I am the only one. Growing up a plus-sized, dark-skinned Indian girl in Wales in the 1990s and 2000s, I wanted to look like anyone other than myself. It started with my dolls; I coveted their flaxen hair as I brushed it, wishing my frizzy, unwieldy locks looked the same. The girls in teen magazines like *Mizz* and *Bliss* that I adored and main love interests on my favourite TV shows all had 'girl-next-door' appeal – think Joey Potter in *Dawson's Creek*, Marissa Cooper in *The O.C.* or Rory Gilmore in *Gilmore Girls* and their wholesome, effortless, unarguable good looks. All of it made me feel profoundly self-conscious – I genuinely believed people were staring at me because I was so deeply unappealing and odd-looking, so vastly different from what I was very clearly being told was beautiful. Even being average or invisible would have felt like a form of acceptance rather than the searing ugliness I felt. That visceral feeling of being so deeply uncomfortable in my own skin felt physical, as though my insides were clawing their way out of my body, like a zombie emerging from a moss-covered grave.

This discomfort followed me from my teens to university and forwards into adult life – a constant imaginary friend that just won't let you move on and is always there to remind you of your lowly place in the world. Like many who lack all confidence, I developed a strong line in self-deprecation – the kind that makes you aggressively defiant and assume somebody must be obliterated on tequila if they dare pay you an appearance-based compliment. At work, I self-defined as the LOL-wielding office goth but inside, I felt like the unattractive underdog, outwardly jovial despite my caustically low self-esteem with a secret fear that my looks were holding me back, professionally and personally.

As an adult, I've tried diligently to 'fix' my 'ugly' problem. As the saying goes, God loves a trier and, trust me, I tried hard – so I'm *definitely* going to Heaven. To fix my appearance from the outside, I've embarked on multiple extreme diets, cleanses and detox retreats; I've taken appetite suppressants and spent endless hours researching various weight-loss surgeries. I have obsessed over beauty products, techniques and treatments, hoping they might make me feel more beautiful. To fix my internal issues, I've undergone hypnosis and done years of talk therapy; even my degree in philosophy came back to appearance ('What is the existential definition of beauty in classical art?' my dissertation pondered). Yet, no matter how much time and money I spent, the malaise still lingered, hovering like an unwelcome Dementor ready to snatch my self-esteem at any opportunity. I did *all* this work, unpicked *all* my issues and, while there were some small shifts in my mindset, still that feeling of ugliness, of wrongness, deep within my core was quick to surface when activated. When my then boyfriend cheated on me, 'ugly' was the reason my heartbroken brain gave me for the betrayal (rather than the reality of him simply being a sack of shit). When I narrowly missed out on a dream job despite being overqualified, 'not looking the part' was my default reasoning (rather than the nepotism so often at play in these decisions). However hard I tried to fight it, like a gradual decay, feeling ugly left nothing untouched; it popped up everywhere, as envy within my friendships, self-doubt in my relationships and toxic perfectionism in my work. Everything was contaminated by its malevolent, self-harming hold. Ugly, to me, has felt like a tattoo you can't ever erase; you're branded with it for life no matter what you change or try to.

To say that navigating 'ugly' shaped my life is an understatement. It affected everything, including my career trajectory, that eventually led to me becoming a beauty editor. In my mid-twenties, I was working as a features assistant, but beauty was my second job: I was spending all my money on beauty products, reading about it obsessively and writing about it for anyone who would let me – I even started a (terrible) beauty blog. I knew I wanted to be a beauty journalist more than anything else, and I didn't just love beauty, I was *compelled* by it (subconsciously did I have something to prove to myself? You bet!). I made the switch to beauty journalism and it was everything I'd hoped for and more: I met my make-up artist heroes and had the appearance of a very glamorous, enviable life. More importantly, I was able to write for and connect with the women that, like me, magazines and the beauty industry had largely ignored. Those issues cut so deeply for me, and for them too, that it didn't seem fluffy, or superfluous in the way some might see beauty journalism. But I felt a dark side to my chosen path. Unsurprisingly, being surrounded by constant perfection, from models to the classically pretty and perfectly coiffed beauty editors I compared myself to meant that internally I felt worse than ever. My perceived ugliness was more than mere inner turmoil, I believed it to be an immovable fact. I had forcibly put myself into the very world that I'd felt so alien from. Why? To finally be part of something that had eluded me my entire life – beauty. I hoped that being around so much of it meant that it would finally rub off on me, but instead, I felt uglier than ever.

Working on the inside of the beauty industry, I started to notice some changes – or, at least, to a point. Around 2010, social media like Instagram and Twitter gave people a voice and more control over what magazines and brands were creating for them, eroding the carefully crafted elitism and exclusion that formed the basis of the narrative in women's media that I'd been chipping away at from the inside. Campaigns started to become more inclusive on a surface level (though they still rarely featured disabled people, anyone genuinely plus size or with dark skin) and the beauty product launches I attended daily finally, for example, offered shades of foundation in my skin tone and informed me that instead of trying to fit in, I should feel 'empowered'. I didn't. Now, consumers were increasingly being told to 'love the skin you're in' or feel like you're 'worth it' – both applaudable sentiments. But I'd felt invisible and therefore ugly from my earliest years of playing with my blonde-haired Barbies: a few size-14 models on a catwalk weren't going to eradicate all of that conditioning. It's not a magic switch that flips your self-perception to 'beautiful' after so long of being told you're the opposite.

In recent years, I've admired elements of the body-positivity movement, giving the original fat-acceptance movement of the 1960s a new voice. But I could still see a clear divide: how could some achieve a state of body neutrality, acceptance or even self-love like those body-positivity influencers whose confidence I so admired, and others – myself included – just couldn't? If things were becoming more inclusive and we were seeing different forms of beauty and body shapes, why hadn't anything I'd tried to fix my self-loathing worked? Why did I still feel like this? *Something* I hadn't yet identified was keeping me lodged in this web of self-hatred. I was angry at myself too – I was well versed in the feminist theory and cultural criticism on how the capitalist patriarchal agenda has used beauty standards against women as a means of controlling our bodies and our behaviour – deep down, I think we all know that. Logically, I knew I now had permission to embrace my looks, but ugly was so deeply ingrained in me that it wouldn't let me go. More than anything else I wanted to be finally free of its clutches, but there was obviously a missing piece to this exhausting puzzle.

So, I started to ask: what *is* beauty exactly and who gets to define it? In other words, what was at the heart of the standards I didn't feel I measured up to and – more importantly – who set them? Beauty standards are a societally agreed set of ideals that, through culture, become a benchmark that people are required to meet to be considered beautiful, pretty, attractive. In Western society, in the last century in particular, the dominant beauty ideal for women has been slim, able-bodied, white and blue-eyed – the Eurocentric or Western beauty standard. But the thing with beauty standards is that we accept them as a fact, but they aren't – who decided that this was the only way to be beautiful and that everything outside of this was ugly? And how exactly do they create that destructive and harmful void – 'the ugly gap' – between how we actually look and how we *think* we should look?

I started researching historical beauty trends to try and get a sense of where these standards come from, just for my own interest. As soon as you do this, you can immediately see how beliefs and assumptions about beauty have changed wildly across decades and eras – so how can something be 'fact' if it changes so often? As the British actor and comedian Dawn French once said: 'If I had been around when Rubens was painting, I would have been revered as a fabulous model … Kate Moss? Well, she would have been the paintbrush.' Just in my lifetime thus far, I've seen the shift from the size-zero body ideal I grew up with in the early noughties to the extreme hourglass shape of the Kardashians we have today, which shows signs of teetering back again with a noughties fashion revival and reported return of 'heroin chic'. How will we look back at our current beauty standards from the vantage point of the future? Current practices, like our obsession with lip filler or cosmetic surgery, could so easily end up as unbelievable curiosities in beauty history – up there with Elizabethan lead-based make-up and Victorian diet pills containing parasites – much sooner than we think in our fast-paced, trend-led world.

Plenty has been written to justify the evolutionary reasons why we are attracted to certain appearance markers that signal health and/or fertility. And yet evidence that there is an ideal beauty backed up by science is pretty scant – and what there is only takes a little probing before it starts to crack. Take the persistent idea of facial symmetry equalling an ideal beauty. It originated as a mathematical concept in Ancient Greece and since then science has told us that an asymmetrical face could be seen as a sign of weakness and off-putting biologically in a mate, so the more symmetrical our faces, the more attractive we are. But the studies on this have often included a very small number of participants. More recently, researchers at the University of Antwerp analysed the data around beauty symmetry and found that this theory doesn't really hold up when you analyse larger quantities of people.[1] And when we look at people widely held as attractive, like model Rosie Huntington-Whiteley and Hollywood actor Ryan Gosling, we realise that they often have a visible asymmetry to their faces. A 2014 study which compared 3D scans of 5,000 teenagers alongside their medical history also found no correlation to health and symmetry of the face.[2] It makes me wonder *why* I've spent most of my adult life trying, and failing, to make my eyebrows match and look symmetrical, when it means *nothing*.

Researching beauty standards didn't offer all the answers I was searching for, so I turned to the concept of ugly, which has been illuminating beyond belief. We all know that calling somebody ugly is the most cutting and definitive of all insults. Once it's levelled as a blistering attack it's like a rocket destined for space, with no way to recall it or retract the impact it has on us. We feel the word ugly – and its implied meaning – to our deepest core because it is immediately 'othering' – a term used to describe the practice of designating someone, or a group of people, as 'not one of us'. This practice is often particularly directed towards marginalised groups, to reinforce their deviation from the norm or ideal.

The word ugly has been so seamlessly integrated into our culture that its meaning feels like a universally agreed fact, but it has picked up meanings and attributes over time. In English, the word ugly is believed to be medieval in its historical origin, coming from the Old Norse *uggligr*, meaning 'to be feared or dreaded'. Other definitions of ugly such as Greek *dyseides*, Latin *deformis*, Irish *dochrud* and Sanskrit *ku-rupa* suggest that it means 'ill-shaped'. Another Germanic origin defines the sentiment of ugly as 'hate, sorrow'. Over time its meaning has become more explicit – in 1755 influential writer 'Dr' Samuel Johnson created the first English dictionary using both 'ugliness' and 'deformity' as interchangeable terms linking them with having a poor moral compass too.[3] Over time, disabled people in America were subject to the 'Ugly Laws' in place from 1880s–1970s, aimed to prohibit visibly disabled people from visiting public spaces – they were fined or sent to poorhouses as a result.[4] It wasn't until the 1960s that laws started to be passed to actively protect the rights of disabled people in the US. In the UK, the Disability Discrimination Act came into force in 1995.[5]

Throughout history, it's also evident that the price of ugly has been far less perilous for men than women (and those of other gender identities). In Roman mythology, Vulcan, the god of fire, was considered so ugly at birth that his own mother threw him over a cliff; though he survived, prospered, and went on to marry Venus, the beautiful goddess of love (back off, Richard Curtis, that rom-com plot idea is *mine*.) Back in the mid-1700s, there was even a group of white men who turned ugliness into the first 'Ugly Face Club' in Liverpool. Members had to be male, bachelors and have features that were ugly, though Ugly Clubs – as these social fraternities were generally known – were not welcoming to disabled people. For them it was a way to bond, sit in coffeehouses and drink ale.[6] Women, however, have always contended with 'ugliness' as a problem to solve and a disadvantage for a good marriage. Winston Churchill's infamous quote encapsulates this double standard to perfection: 'My dear you are ugly, but tomorrow I shall be sober and you will still be ugly.'[7] And, when I sat down to start this chapter, I googled 'ugly', to see the top hits, which were 'ugly face' followed by 'ugly girl' – and before you ask, 'ugly boy' was not on the list.

One of the biggest contributors to our definition of ugly I uncovered? Freakshows. The concept of laughing at somebody unusual, or 'abnormal' had long been seen as sport. They became particularly popular in the Victorian era. Often freakshow acts were compared to animals as an underhand way of dehumanising them and reducing their worth to sub-human, like Fedor Adrianovich Jeftichew, a 19th-century Russian man also known as Dog-Faced Boy because of his hirsute face (the result of a medical condition called hypertrichosis.) Another example is Sara (Saartjie) Baartman, who was part of the Khoikhoi tribe of South Africa, nicknamed the 'de Hottentot Venus' (Hottentot was a colonial Dutch-given slur to describe the Khoikhoi people.) Baartman and women of her tribe had steatopygia, a genetic build-up of fat, which could result in very prominent buttocks and elongated labia. She spent years starring in European freakshows and being ordered to perform 'tricks' wearing nothing but a loin cloth. She died in 1815 aged just 26, though the cause isn't known exactly, but the dehumanising treatment didn't end there: her brain, skeleton and sexual organs were obtained and remained in display jars at the Musée de l'Homme (Museum of Man) in Paris until 1974 and weren't buried in South Africa until 2002. Freakshow line-ups would also include those who were heavily tattooed, non-white, intersex, bearded ladies or had any visible disabilities. They endured peering crowds, prodding and mocking as part of a system of exploitation that had become a pillar of Western entertainment.

Patterns in shifting beauty standards are more than just

historical oddities, they are warnings that can provide the missing piece between knowing we deserve to feel good about ourselves and truly understanding why we still don't. As I read about the concept of ugly through the ages and the accompanying social history of the time, I felt a small shift in my 'ugly' mindset – like a train gearing up to change course to another track. That's when the pennies dropped, like one of those arcade games where the coins tip painfully slowly over the edge. Penny 1: 'ugly' must serve somebody's agenda because its definition changes so often and so drastically. Penny 2: 'ugly' isn't fact, it's a construct. That means that ugly can – in theory – be rewritten because it was created by somebody in the first place. Why hasn't it already? The systems that benefit from us feeling ugly prevent this change from happening, because it serves their agenda to keep us feeling sad, lacking and preoccupied with our appearance.

Almost as far as we can go back, we can find evidence of women contorting themselves to fit trends, to correct what the beauty standards of the day told them was 'wrong' with their bodies. Seeing how long this has been going on and examining why it happened can give us insights into how those ideals became a boundary in the first place, dividing ugly and beautiful into distinct camps. Centuries of conditioning have made us believe that to be beautiful, admired, successful, rich and happy we must fit between certain aesthetic parameters, which are changing all the time – and hide a host of inconsistencies. As Dr Hannah McCann, a cultural studies lecturer at the University of Melbourne, said in the literary journal *Overland*: 'To suggest that there are universal ideals of beauty that transcend culture completely fails to comprehend the way that ideals of beauty have been constructed in order to be sold.'[8] Since the beginning of consumer culture, there have been companies offering to take our money in return for their 'help' in contorting or changing ourselves to fit into these narrow frameworks of beauty.

You might think, considering the progress made in women's rights and liberation in the last century, we would have broken free of some of the restrictive cultural norms placed on our bodies, yet we still have much of the same malaise as the Victorians did, just in modern guises. As stated in *The Beauty Myth: How Images of Beauty Are Used Against Women*, the game-changing book addressing patriarchal beauty standards: 'The more legal and material hindrances women have broken through, the more strictly and heavily and cruelly images of female beauty have come to weigh upon us.' Although the book was written in 1990, (and its author has now strayed into widely discredited territory), it's through beauty standards that the patriarchy still retains subtle but unmistakable ways to limit us. A woman can be a CEO, a prime minister or a scientist, but she is inevitably still judged and valued by her appearance first, in a way that doesn't happen to men, or is written off as a forgivable quirk (hello, Boris Johnson's unbrushed hair). The more space women take up in society, the more freedoms and equalities we have, the more we are heard: the more malevolent beauty ideals become.

In 2020, research by the British government found that a huge 61 per cent of adults (and 66 per cent of children) felt negative about their body image most of the time. Six out of ten women felt that 'diet culture, post-partum pressures, being bombarded with images of photoshopped, edited and sexualised women as well as the aging process and the lack of visual representation of older women … causes them to suffer with poor body image,' the report said. Seventy one per cent of disabled people (compared to 60 per cent able-bodied) reported feeling negative about their body image, while also 'feeling ignored, judged and isolated about their appearance'. None of the transgender people taking part in the above research felt 'very positive' about their body image and 23 per cent reported feeling mostly 'very negative' about their looks (compared to 12 per cent of cisgender participants). One transgender woman said: 'I have gone from hating my body due to dysphoria to hating my body due to pressures on women to conform.' BAME (Black Asian and Minority Ethnic) participants said their 'body image was negatively impacted by lack of representation across media and advertising especially plus size BAME women, particularly those with dark skin and unrelaxed afro-textured hair.'[9] These findings also show how truly miserable we still are about our appearance, like our mothers often were and perhaps their mothers too, and just like women in the history books I'd read about also were. In this age of wellness and an increasing focus on mental health we are still being made to feel we don't measure up and that our worth lies in conforming to beauty norms. We've been told we can be ourselves and look how we want, but how much has *really* changed?

This question underpins our current beauty narrative and its conflicting ideals. While there has been a move to acceptance of a slightly wider beauty standard across magazines, advertising and the beauty industry in recent years, it still feels dismissive, limited and hierarchical. If our social media body-positive ad campaigns are to be believed, it's just cis, white, heterosexual, able-bodied women struggling with their appearance. Our current version of inclusivity often cherry-picks 'representation' without acknowledging that it's still very limited. You really don't have to spend long asking what is making us feel so negatively about ourselves before you start to realise that beauty standards are woven into everything we touch, believe and consume, even categories we think are progressive. Like an invisible foe, they sit on our shoulders, constantly keeping us oppressed by reinforcing gender stereotypes, colourism, classism, ageism, ableism, sizeism and many more. We are told what is beautiful at every turn; to deviate, makes you a dissenter – it makes you ugly. But what I learned as I researched this book is how so many of our beauty standards have their origins in some of the darkest recesses in human history. As I aim to show you in these chapters, what we are told is 'beautiful' is often based on some very ugly truths. Without acceptance and knowledge of this, we'll never truly be free of their toxic reign – or be able to hold those accountable who still perpetuate the damaging narratives.

Each day, we unknowingly adorn ourselves in these historic beauty standards, as we look in the mirror, get dressed and do our make-up. This book is a journey to uncovering some of those origins and the systems of oppression that hold them in place, piecing together how they could still be affecting how we feel about ourselves now, centuries later. I am not a historian or an academic – and even work from those brilliant fields can come to us with biases, embedded in the historical record and still present in how we discuss it today. I am also very aware that I can't possibly cover everything or represent everyone's own lived experience – my editors must be already wringing their hands over my never-ending research – but hopefully within each chapter everyone can find something that will help you to think more clearly about the mechanisms behind contemporary beauty and unpick something you previously believed about your appearance.

A note on gender and this book: beauty standards affect people of all genders and gender identities, of course, but have a particular impact on women and people who are transgender, non-binary, or gender-non-conforming, because the patriarchy still exists and exerts control over those of us who deviate from cisgender heterosexual traditional masculinity and femininity. There is a historical legacy of 'appearance norms' that affects us all, but especially those of us who identify or present as women, as well as those who experience oppression for their perceived womanhood or femininity, such as gay and trans men. Throughout this book, I've used the term 'women' (rather than 'womxn', for example) and phrases like 'female' and 'feminine' because these words reflect the gender stereotypes and constructs that have defined our binary mainstream culture, government policy and beauty standards throughout much of history (particularly post-colonisation, as academic Dr Oyèrónkẹ́ Oyěwùmí has noted).

Gender binaries are a huge part of how we are sold beauty and beauty ideals too; just look at the way fragrance is marketed to men or women. We're told that sweet floral scents are for women, and woody, smoky notes are for men, but anyone can wear any scent. They've been gendered for us and now we associate them with how men and women 'should' smell. Another example is how long hair on women has traditionally been perceived as more 'feminine'. I've used the terms 'woman' and 'man' because that's predominantly how history has been contextualised – even if I personally see the world in a much more inclusive way. My use of 'women' includes transgender women – and while I can't speak to this or the non-binary experience, the beauty standards and general consensus of 'ugly' inevitably impacts on both those assigned male and female at birth, as well as intersex people. The heterosexual, cis gaze has been so dominant that our current beauty standards still largely reflect that history. This binary, gendered view of beauty in the mainstream has of course excluded many and adds an extra layer of intersectional intricacy as we begin to unpick beauty standards.

What does cut across everyone's realities though is our

increasing dissatisfaction with our appearance. Male beauty myths and constructs could fill an entire complex tome of their own – and this is a vital discussion to have. However, I do believe the power of 'ugly' can wound women in a very specific way (and some women more than others). As I have been writing this, Lee Canning, a member of the Abolish the Welsh Assembly Party, tweeted a picture of former leader of Plaid Cymru Leanne Wood with the words: 'the ugly face of nationalism'.[10] Imagine, just for a moment, that this charge was levelled at a man, with his picture, instead of a woman. Somehow its potency and severity seem a little less piercing, right? This insult 'ugly' just doesn't have the same impact or roll off the tongue quite so viciously when addressed to a man. While men deemed unattractive by the beauty standards of their day have nonetheless enjoyed great power, wealth and influence, a woman's appearance has always been and still is her currency and marker of value in society. Women have to be decorative to be of worth. Part of the blame for this belongs to the 'male gaze' – this is a term first used by John Berger in *Ways of Seeing*, and later coined and popularised by Laura Mulvey specifically in reference to narrative cinema – although the term is often used outside of feminist/film/art theory circles. That exists everywhere we look, from male-dominated industries like advertising to the largely male-directed films we watch – it's truly inescapable, as you'll see.

What has also become clear to me is that, despite all the apparent progress, the Western gaze remains hugely dominant – and the legacy of colonisation and slavery has left a lasting impact on what we see as ugly and beautiful today. Often those standards were demanded through force, pressure to assimilate and censorship – and still are. A poll carried out by the Dove Self-Esteem Project in 2020 found that more than half of Black children have been sent home from school, for wearing their hair in a protective style or naturally.[11]

Revolutions in representation and waves of feminism have come and gone – and yet we are still here, loathing how we look. Beauty is *still* a currency, as it was before women could vote, work, or determine their own futures, although now that currency extends to how we're perceived on social media or reality TV. We're taking in messaging about beauty standards at every hidden turn and like a shapeshifter, they manifest in new and unsettling ways to cut us down in our prime. If you're reading this, I think that, like me, you're probably exhausted by feeling this way – and just want to feel OK, or at least not hate how you look in the mirror each day. That isn't too much to ask and we should all be allowed to feel like that. But I realised that the reason that I hadn't been able to make a significant shift in my mindset to embrace my appearance – or at least, not to fear the word 'ugly' so much – wasn't the lack of trying but rather the lack of context and understanding of why I felt so bad, or crucially, had been made to feel so bad. I don't believe we have to throw away all our beauty products, renounce capitalism (where would we even start?) and go off-grid to disengage from everything around us to achieve this. It's a nice idea and it might work, but ultimately, it's unrealistic. There are facets of beauty that are good and beneficial too: like the number of women the beauty industry employs, the buzz of a new lipstick colour or the beauty bonding rituals of communing at a spa with friends. But beyond this, I believe it's imperative for us to know what is truly controlling our beauty standards, to be able to decipher what we're really buying into when we're told a cream will fix all our problems, or when we're continually shown what 'beautiful' looks like (and it's filtered to perfection).

For so long, we've been taught we must do anything we can to run from ugly. Except, what does that mean and who made the rules about what we think of as ugly? I believe that it's time to finally unpick and be sceptical about what the word 'ugly' truly conceals through examining how history – everything from pop culture, politics and royalty to industrial changes – has had a hand in creating and upholding the standards defining ugly. Learning about the origins of ugly means we can see exactly how it's been created, and who profits from it being upheld: spoiler alert, it's definitely not always women. And it is particularly trans women or women of colour, who often have beauty withheld from them or weaponised against them by some white women operating under the same beauty standards. Those white women may themselves be oppressed under the patriarchy, and held to unreachable beauty standards – but can still ultimately profit from gatekeeping womanhood, whether by attacking trans women or portraying Black women as angry and masculine, for example. We have spent too long kept from being able to accept and love ourselves. It affects every facet of our quality of life, from our ability to enjoy beach holidays to feeling OK about getting older, but it's truly also a matter of life and death: more than half of children aged 11–16 in England and Wales have been bullied about the way they look,[12] Reddit forums and news stories are full of people considering suicide because of their looks[13] and anorexia (though a complex condition and not just linked to beauty standards) has the highest mortality rate of any psychiatric condition.[14] There is so much more at stake here than a social media post telling us to 'love ourselves and do some self-care'. We don't, and shouldn't, have to suffer, or compromise our lives, for beauty anymore.

Looking back at how much of my time and joy has been squandered, fearing ugly, and in pursuit of unachievable and unrelenting beauty standards feels honestly, quite devastating. By uncovering the way that beauty standards have dictated our lives for centuries I hope we can finally take the power back from ugly and redefine what beauty really means to us.

AN UGLY START

'Everyone is like a butterfly, they start out ugly and awkward and then morph into beautiful, graceful butterflies that everyone loves ...'

– Actor Drew Barrymore

SORRY, DREW, BUTTERFLIES are bullshit, but maybe I'm biased ...

Life in grey South Wales was generally fairly uneventful but a seismic life-changing event was about to happen: I had been invited to my first princess party. The idea of wearing a fairy-tale dress and feeling like a real princess for the day made me feel giddy. On arrival at my friend's house, I dutifully queued up to receive my pink princess costume from the sparkly outfit rail, marvelling with excitement at all the other girls wearing them. Even dour little Rhiannon waiting next to me looked like she was about to do a happy wee. Finally, it was my turn. I looked up at the lady doling out the outfits, waiting expectantly for her to hand me the princess dress of my dreams. She looked me up and down, then turned back to her rail and said, 'You're too big for it. Here's a butterfly outfit,' before thrusting some trousers into my hands, along with a flaccid-looking cape contraption. A rush of heat came over me as I slunk off into the corner to put them on, sadness and crap wings in tow. Moments later, the photo on the previous page was captured.

My heart sank as I looked down at my outfit and the princesses around me, wondering why I was different – aside from not being white, that is. Being a child, I didn't have the words to identify the feeling but still, decades later, I can feel its searing intensity. I now recognise it as shame; it was the first moment that I felt 'different' from those around me, in a way that I could identify was considered negative and unfavourable. After that I lost interest in the party; the elastic wing/cape ensemble dug into my wrists and I was miserable. But I didn't tell anyone, including my parents. Instead, I went home in the car with an entirely new set of feelings about my appearance. I nursed those emotions, buried them deep, and a thorny seed of anguish was planted: ugly had entered the building.

My rational, now-adult self can see that perhaps the dress-wielder was tired and overwhelmed by a hoard of tiny sugar-fuelled girls clamouring for their princess moment. But my inner child still feels the pain of that experience, even though it was an offhand comment from somebody who meant nothing to me. All it takes is something seemingly innocuous…

Being othered for my appearance planted the seed of ugly that continued to grow into a painful and dysfunctional relationship with my looks as an adult. From that moment on, every time a classmate said my frizzy hair was horrible or my arms were hairy, that feeling I'd first experienced at the party grew. Shame has a way of doing that, it feels unspeakable and all-consuming. That initial incident was a spark that billowed into an entire lifetime of malaise about my appearance that felt like it was intrinsic, as if I was born with its cloying burden.

Except, I wasn't. None of us are born loathing the way we look, it's something we learn. But even before we learn what's beautiful and what's ugly, we're subject to scrutiny over our appearance and its changes. Everyone coos over a cute, squidgy baby: the dimpled cheeks, the leg rolls, the squish – it's adorable, right? But if that cuddly babe becomes a chubby toddler, and then evolves to be a chunky child? Suddenly, it's a problem and a way for us to be marked as different. There's even a Reddit thread for parents with 'ugly babies',[1] seeking support and publicly hoping that their offspring will grow into their 'big' noses and 'large' heads, or that their eye and hair colour might magically lighten over time (Eurocentric beauty standards never fail to show up). Other threads are dedicated to posting pictures of other people's 'ugly' babies for jest with captions like: ('put me back in', 'the face only a mother can love', 'Quasimodo, is that you?'). I love a well-placed funny as much as the next person, but before we can even walk or talk, there are swathes of people putting a 'value' on how we look. Of course, we can't account for every dark corner of the internet (seriously, where would we even begin?) but the sad fact is that these online forums aren't so far removed from society's value system based on appearance and it starts young.

As children, when we hear words like 'fat', 'ugly', 'stupid' or whatever is levelled at us, those words are coming from *somewhere* – after all, we don't start life with this vocabulary. When incidents like butterfly-gate occur – which they often do at an alarmingly young age – we receive the message that physically, our appearance isn't 'acceptable' in some way. A friend was called names all through school for having a bigger than 'average' nose. (How is that even quantifiable? Is there a secret nose scale we're judging them against?) Another mentioned that her 'gappy teeth and sticky-out ears' were a subject of familial ridicule (#Bants) until she underwent jaw reconstruction and had her ears pinned back. Which sounds exceptionally painful. And it might have been unnecessary, in a society more accepting of a broader range of appearance.

At an impressionable and vulnerable age we're told implicitly and explicitly how we should look and its importance. Even notable performers, the people we might assume were born with self-confidence, have been subject to agony over their looks. Singer-songwriter/actor Lady Gaga said: 'I was bullied in school, I felt ugly and my only escape was music.'[2] Writer and director Lena Dunham posted that: 'Throughout my teens I was told, in no uncertain terms, that I was fucking funny-looking. Potbelly, rabbit teeth, knock knees – I could never seem to get it right and it haunted my every move.'[3] Actor Uzo Aduba said in an interview: 'I grew up in a small New England town where the beauty ideal was very traditional and seemingly flawless: blonde hair, blue eyes, legs for days. In my mind, that meant anyone who didn't look that way was considered unattractive. I started to doubt everything about myself, from my curvy build to the gap in my teeth. I never felt beautiful.'[4] And even Queen Bey (singer-songwriter Beyoncé) says she felt it: 'Of course I've had an ugly period. When I was around 10 or 11, my mother gave me this ugly haircut and I was really, really chubby. So chubby that my family used to all lay me down flat so they could zip up my jeans. It took four of them and I would lie there on the bed while they all got to it.'[5] You get the gist, although the painless answer to Beyoncé's problems might have just been some bigger jeans! But even global adulation, it seems, doesn't erase the hurt and memories of being made to feel ugly earlier on in life.

It's disturbing to think how early we can learn to feel shame about an aspect of our appearance. This has the capacity to shape our futures because if we think we're not enough or we're ugly, we settle for less across every area of our life until that becomes what psychologists term our core belief, or our invisible psychological tagline, that is always lying in wait to trip us up.

Can you pinpoint the earliest moment you felt ugly or different as a child? Those seeds of discomfort are either watered and continue to grow (i.e. reinforced with similar experiences, cultural narratives and peer influence, for example) or they wilt and ideally some healthy self-confidence springs up in their place. My perceived difference was externally marked as shameful and undesirable before I had the chance to even acquaint myself with the idea of there being different body shapes and sizes. So often ugly is handed to us – and we can't refuse or return it.

According to psychologists, most of our core beliefs are formed by the time we're seven – yes, *seven*[6] – so it's unsurprising that when we're divided into 'pretty' and 'ugly' camps before then, we feel the success or failure associated with that label and it stays with us into adulthood. What we absorb as children – long before we're old enough to question what we're seeing and being told – influences the beauty standards we set for ourselves and that we hold others to. Even now, when I hear the word 'fat' – even if it's in a totally different context – I instinctively think somebody is talking about me. It activates childhood taunts and rejection, no matter how much body acceptance work I've done. So, an obvious question to ask as we try to unpick some of the lessons learned at a young age that were unhelpful or even damaging is how did we receive these messages and why did they penetrate so darn deeply?

Babies focus on what they see and any physical interactions with their immediate environment, like a carer playing with them. One of the earliest things they can identify is their own physical self, which at this stage is simply a source of wonder and joy – think of a baby's abject glee as they grab their own legs with a look that says: 'I HAVE FEETS!!' But as our brains continue to develop and we start to look at how we fit in to whatever immediate environment we find ourselves in, unsurprisingly, things get a bit more complicated.

According to the five stages of self-awareness identified by psychologist Philippe Rochat, the first level of 'identification' happens when toddlers can see themselves in the mirror and recognise it as their own reflection and not some other baby gazing back at them. This sense of self-awareness develops at around one to three years old.[7] This is when we begin to recognise ourselves in pictures or videos. At around 18 months, we also become self-conscious for the first time, looking for reactions when we do something naughty, for example – and we're particularly sensitive to criticism at this point in our development and comparisons to distinguish between 'us' and 'somebody else'. So, for example, if everyone around us is able-bodied or white and we're not, this could be the time that discomfort around difference of appearance to those around us, especially if they're a majority, may start to be experienced. This is particularly true if we receive messaging that our point(s) of difference are considered 'undesirable' or negative in some way.

Aged five, we're off to school, to be picked or passed over for teams, and praised or punished for our academic achievement. According to a study by Washington University, children develop a sense of self-esteem comparable in strength to that of adults by this age.[8] We understand that we're changing and growing, and we can also see ourselves from a third-person perspective. This means that, crucially, we can acknowledge how others see us. We're influenced by our peers' values and actions too, and language and communication also become crucial to our cognition at this stage, according to 1930s biologist and psychologist Jean Piaget[9], whose frameworks are still widely used. Arm in arm with this new self-awareness is an appreciation of the societal 'norms' and our place within them.

I saw this first-hand volunteering at a primary school in east London: we were drawing for the afternoon and a child of around six years old looked defeated as he told me he couldn't draw very well. Either he'd been told this or come to this conclusion himself through lack of praise or direct comparison. I could tell he'd taken it to heart, despite being so young. If we get negative messages about ourselves at this age, whether it's our ability, appearance or anything else, then that's a tough belief to change as adults.

Between the ages of 7 and 11, children start to think about things logically and consider other people's points of view, which is great news all round for humanity (and weary parents). But during this phase, children's thinking can become very rigid. We also become sociocentric, meaning that we can understand that others have their own thoughts, though we might not be able to guess what someone else is experiencing[10] which may explain any bullying around appearance, as a perpetrator around this age might not yet be equipped to understand the consequences of their actions or feel remorse. Psychologist Erik Erikson believed that comparison is a huge struggle at this stage, along with accompanying feelings of inferiority, often based on accomplishments like sporting prowess or academia.[11] Any disproval we experience hits us hard at this point too – unless it's counteracted by other ways to raise our self-esteem. Professor of Psychology and Human Development Gary Ladd writes that for children to have positive, open-minded relationships with their peers, they 'must be taught forgiveness and empathy and must learn to be accepting of individual differences'.[12]

Shockingly, a 2016 survey of childcare workers in the UK revealed that almost a quarter have heard children as young as three criticising their own appearance.[13] Jacqueline Harding, adviser to the Professional Association for Childcare and Early Years (PACEY), said of the study: 'The results are worrying. By the age of three or four, some children have already pretty much begun to make up their minds – and even hold strong views – about how bodies should look.'[14] The study revealed that almost half of childcare workers have heard negative body image statements from six-to ten-year-olds. Over a third reported having heard children say 'he/she is fat' or 'I am fat', 19 per cent have witnessed children avoid food because they fear it will make them 'fat' and a further 16 per cent have heard children say they wish they were as 'pretty' or as 'good' as another child. The same survey of childcare workers also examined what they believed was contributing to poor body image in children, with peers and parental influence as the top factors followed by media influence.[15]

If you're a parent or care for children, it may be uncomfortable to consider how the way we speak about our appearance or comment on that of others could be imprinting negatively on them. It's also hard to look at our own parents and caretakers critically, especially if we felt our childhoods were relatively idyllic (or we don't want to dive in and make them worse than they were). But it's worth sparing a thought for how our own worries about appearance can project onto those in our care. In the TV show *Mad Men*, set in the 1950s and 1960s, when Betty Draper crashes her car with her young daughter in the passenger seat, her biggest worry is: 'I keep thinking not that I could have killed the kids, but worse, Sally could have survived, and gone on living with this horrible scar on her face, and some long, lonely, miserable life.' Betty – prized primarily for her beauty – holds appearance as the definite marker of her daughter's chance at happiness, which does have an impact given the era the show is set but conveys how we can inherit a set of beliefs from our parents or those in charge of our care. A friend who has overcome years of disordered eating says that as far back as she can remember, her mother has commented on her weight as a barometer of how 'good' she looks, the moment she greets her. Although she knows her mother defines her own self-value according to the scales, her mother's weight obsession has driven a wedge between them.

The devastating and long-lasting damage of poor body image can, in Harding's words, lead to 'lower self-esteem, lower expectations about what you can become. It limits your vision of yourself. It also can lead to destructive behaviour.'[16] That's why we must ensure that our children are not taught to fixate on the way they – or others – look and that they are encouraged to embrace all difference as beautiful. Looking back, I feel heartbroken for that version of myself that believed I was ugly from such an innocent age.

We can police what we say and do, of course, but children also spend hours transfixed by magical animations and cartoons that are often the only things that give parents a modicum of respite from their wailing. We absorb a lot from them too, just at the age and developmental stage when we're starting to learn about the wider world. One glance at a toddler fixated by their favourite show, absorbing the colours, sights and sounds, tells you a lot about the power of TV. It makes sense that there's a link between cartoons and behaviour in children who watch them – we mimic what we see, right? The right cartoons are invaluable for childhood learning – TV can show us different family structures, homes and lives that might look wildly different from our own – but our little sponge brains are soaking up everything we see and it's not all positive.

At any age, when watching TV, we enter a zoned-out state of mind not dissimilar to hypnosis, as neurosurgeon Adam Lipson explains in an article for *Fast Company* about the effects of TV on our brains: 'There have been EEG studies that demonstrate that television watching converts the brain from beta wave activity to alpha waves, which are associated with a daydreaming state and a reduced use of critical thinking skills.'[17] So, even as adults, we're less likely to critically challenge what we are seeing on screen – from beauty ideals to political agendas. Handily, children also love hearing the same stories repeatedly, so the messages in what they're watching imprint deeply. This isn't a new revelation, and in the past, it's been taken advantage of for political gain. For example, during the Second World War, the US government requested the Walt Disney company to produce 32 anti-Nazi 'cartoons'. The two most famous examples were 'Education For Death: The Making of The Nazi' and 'Der Fuehrer's Face' (which even won an Oscar in 1943 for Best Short Subject, Cartoons).

Both were shown before playing movies at theatres and seeing Donald Duck in Nazi uniform quacking 'Heil, Hitler,' is quite surreal, not to mention offensive. Even before we had the studies to prove it, government and military agendas knew that children's minds are profoundly shaped by early influences and the cartoons they watch are the ideal means of indoctrination.

But even our more 'harmless' children's shows and films often tend to have a strong – and fairly straightforward – moral message. Good triumphs over evil and kind hearts and courage always win the day. Except, though this might seem innocuous, or like a positive thing, beauty ideals are often encoded in how this story is told, with bad frequently represented as 'ugly' and good as 'pretty'. They are pitted against one another and the dynamic is the same every time: pretty/good always wins.

Take Disney's *The Little Mermaid* (1989). Ariel is young, sweet and beautiful (she represents 'good') with long straight red hair and blue eyes. She'll trade in anything to be able to be with her prince, whom she obviously wins. Ursula, her wicked nemesis, is a sea witch and a kind of sickly bluey purple. Worst of all, she's old and fat – used by the film's creators to signify that she's ugly/bad. In the Disney version of *Snow White and The Seven Dwarfs* (1937), beauty and youth are conflated: Snowy's youthful pale skin is emblematic of her being 'good' while, conversely, the Evil Queen is constantly necking potions to prevent her reverting to being an 'old hag'. She's also got it in for our youthful and beautiful heroine. The list goes on. My point? When we're in this hypnotic state, and not long past the point of working out how the hell to grip our own feet, we are actively taught to fear and demonise ageing, difference in body size and diversity of appearance.

Disney is levelling up (see *Moana* (2016) and *Encanto* (2021) for examples) and Netflix has an assortment of cartoons with more diverse casts, but it's stories like this that generations of children grew up with and kids are still watching today; they're embedded in our narratives of the 'childhood experience'. It's telling that *Frozen* (2013) is seen as the modern-day *Cinderella* story and although hailed as empowering for little girls, protagonist Elsa is still white, slim and has long straight blonde hair. We're *still* being taught to prize beauty within extraordinarily narrow parameters and this uniformity is a disservice to all children, especially during these crucial self-esteem building years.

A study by psychologists at Turkey's Uludağ University asked girls aged four to six to choose what cartoon character they would most like to be. No surprises, Elsa from *Frozen* was the firm favourite. Researchers said: 'When we examined their interview answers, the reason they chose this character is due to her physical appearance and ability to make ice … Girls also want to be cartoon characters such as the girls from *Winx Club*, Rapunzel, Snow White and Cinderella. The reasons are their physical appearances and beauty.'

What these characters have in common is oversized eyes, flawless skin, flowing locks and tiny waists. It's tragic that these wildly unattainable attributes are already revered among young children as a beauty ideal but they're also eerily similar to the ideal beauty standards for adults too – the above qualities are the same desired look that most social media filters achieve. Beauty standards are smart, like that. When a beauty standard feels like it's an inner battle to overcome, that isn't a fact, it's conditioning. It's my belief that some of that inner turmoil that feels like it's a universal truth can be traced back to those early beauty ideals communicated to us through the brightly coloured, exciting cartoons we can't get enough of as children.

The same Turkish study drew other alarming conclusions from its research: 'One digital danger is how girls idolise characters in terms of their physical appearance and beauty. This may cause children to become perfectionists about their own physical appearance. They may even experience inadequacy because of their high standards. In addition, they may develop the habit of judging others according to physical appearance.'[18]

So, as well as suffering our own insecurities about our looks, which could then manifest through eating disorders, body dysmorphia, even an obsession with cosmetic procedures, we might also turn our inner malaise outwards. And hey, I wanted to be Snow White and Cinderella too as a kid, and having the power of ice like Elsa does sound pretty sweet. But at what cost to our happiness if we're unknowingly projecting it inwards and on those around us?

Aged around seven, I'd wake up super early and would – as many kids do – be glued to morning kids' TV. I was obsessed with a show called *Maxie's World*. Maxie had *everything*. Like Barbie come to cartoon life, she was the perfect teenage girl: a slim, blonde surfer who even sparkled as she rode a dolphin in the opening credits (I couldn't make that up). She even had a cool high-school boyfriend, which seemed impossibly grown-up. Each week, Maxie would be embroiled in high jinks but she would *always* come out on top. She was everything I wanted to be: beautiful, slim, admired, adored.

One episode that really stayed with me was called 'Fat Chance'. The plot is surprisingly adult for a child's cartoon (the 1980s were *so* rogue): Maxie's friend Ashley becomes paranoid that people think she's fat – which is obviously a huge problem. She becomes so worried that she stops eating and even passes out on the football fields. As cartoon narrative dictates, all ends well – but not because Maxie helps Ashley realise that she is a valuable, beautiful person at any size. Ashley simply realises she isn't fat at all. Hurrah for Ashley! Maxie is symbolic of the 'pretty girl' at school who never quite leaves you – she's always there waiting to show you how imperfect you are.

The pretty girl reappeared in many guises in the TV I watched. She manifested as Kelly Kapowski in *Saved by the Bell* (it always irked me, even as a kid, that the only person of colour on the show, Lisa, never had a serious love interest; what does that tell its teen audience?). Then there were the blonde twins in *Sweet Valley High*, who seemed to get away with everything (particularly the mean one, Jessica). And the list goes on.

As I entered my early teens, I would race home to watch Australian TV shows with their tanned heartthrobs, and British school dramas, where the boys lusted after the pretty, popular (always white) girls. I pulled out pictures of those hunky pin-ups from my beloved teen magazines and pored over them with friends at school. It was rare to see anybody of colour, save the occasional Black male model. And the pretty girls they featured in the beauty pages which I read religiously? They were mostly the living incarnations of Maxie or Ashley. When I look back at this messaging, it's obvious why it was stacking up like Jenga blocks of self-hatred that were subconsciously eating away at my self-esteem: the heroines who came out on top and got the guy were thin, conventionally pretty, white girls. And looked very different to me.

Have we done enough to ensure that our children and teens see themselves in the culture they consume? TV has become a little more inclusive with shows like *Pablo* (2017), about an autistic child, or *My World Kitchen*, a show narrated by celebrity chef Ainsley Harriott that started in 2018, which sees children cook recipes from their countries of ancestral origin. But it's just nowhere near enough. In 2019, just 6 out of 50 kids' shows had a BAME lead[19] and a study from Cardiff

University in collaboration with the British Film Institute (BFI) found that just 24 per cent of 4- to 18-year-olds said they saw people who look like them on TV. The same research found that disabled children, from ethnic minority backgrounds or the LGBTQ+ community felt completely invisible from TV.[20] Popular culture is a powerful force in the lives of most children and all deserve to see themselves represented and feel acceptance without doubling down on troubling values that can affect their entire futures.

Sadly, children's literature doesn't fare much better than TV shows and suffers the same pitfalls of the nostalgic gaze. A Centre for Literary and Primary Education (CLPE) report in 2020 confirmed that just 7 per cent of children's books published in the UK since 2017 feature characters from Black, Asian or minority ethnic backgrounds, despite the fact that 33.5 per cent of children in primary school in the UK are from these backgrounds. This doesn't even account for disabled children or other intersections.[21]

Many generations grew up reading Enid Blyton's children's books like I did, but it's now widely accepted that they contain damaging narratives. Often her stories were about Golliwogs, a rag doll-like character – with very dark skin and curly hair – based on blackface minstrel traditions from the 1800s[22] like *The Little Black Doll Story* (1937), *The Three Golliwogs* (1944) (with characters called Golly, Woggy and N*gger) and Blyton's popular Noddy books (1949) that became a TV show. In one book, Golliwogs even attack Noddy, steal his car and then leave him stranded.[23] How do you shake a stereotype like that when you hear it at such a young age? Perhaps you don't. When I was a baby, a young lad saw me and my mass of black curls and shouted 'wog' at me in my pram. This kid – aged about ten – probably didn't quite understand that this was a racist slur, my dad recalls. But it is likely that between Blyton's books, perhaps his family and peers, he knew what a Golliwogs looked like, enough to shout it at me. Golliwogs also featured on the back of Robertson's marmalades – a wholesome family favourite – until 2001 and you could even collect tokens to receive Golliwog toys – yet again, aimed at children.[24]

We do love our toys. We name them, refuse to be parted from them. We cherish them, even as adults. We create entire universes and spend many hours with them – in conversation, creating elaborate tea parties, fighting dramatic battles and – my personal favourite – directing doll photo shoots, an odd premonition into my future career directing beauty editorials for magazines. The star of my glamorous imaginary shoots and that of kids across the globe was of course Barbie, naturally. Each Christmas, I would circle the latest model in the Argos catalogue and leave it lying open around the house as a not-so-subtle hint for my parents. What I loved most about Barbie was combing through her glossy blonde hair (there were of course very few non-white Barbies to be found in the 1980s), which was the opposite of mine. Hers fell in a waterfall of golden silk, mine was a tangle of frizz that always misbehaved. There was even a girl at primary school who wore her long blonde hair in bunches down to her waist. I remember the teachers constantly cooing over it and saying how beautiful it was – she was like a real-life doll (I never heard anything positive about my curly hair, conversely).

Barbie, created in 1959, has of course come under fire repeatedly during her tenure and been forced to slowly modernise. Her unachievable hourglass proportions have been criticised (if she was real, she'd be five foot nine, weigh 110 pounds, and likely wouldn't have enough body fat to menstruate).[25] Back in the 1960s, for example, Mattel, Barbie's parent company, released 'Slumber Party Barbie', who came complete with hair rollers, a sleeping bag, a bathroom scale showing 110 pounds and a small book titled *How To Lose Weight*. Inside the book were the words 'DON'T EAT'. As recently as 2014, the Senior Vice President and Global Head of Design at Mattel, Kim Culmone, defended the Barbie's unrealistic shape, saying: 'Girls view the world completely differently than grown-ups do. They don't come at it with the same angles and baggage and all that stuff that we do. Clearly, the influences for girls on those types of issues, whether it's body image or anything else, it's proven – it's peers, moms, parents, it's their social circles.'[26]

Of course nobody's solely blaming Barbie for unrealistic, Eurocentric beauty ideals or the feelings of worthlessness they engender, but our dolls and their representations *do* make a difference; they provide one of our earliest beauty standards as children. In 2006, British researchers gave 162 British girls aged five to eight picture books that either didn't show bodies at all, or else featured Barbie or Emme, a more realistically proportioned doll. Once the girls had looked at the books, researchers asked them questions about their own body image: the younger girls who had been given the Barbie books were more dissatisfied with their bodies than those who read the Emme version or books with no pictures of bodies at all. For the oldest girls, aged seven and a half to eight and a half, the books they read didn't affect their body image overall at all. Why? Because it was too late. The older girls had been exposed to enough popular culture that they already suffered from high levels of body dissatisfaction, regardless of which books the researchers gave them.[27]

Back in the 1940s, American psychologists Kenneth and Mamie Clark carried out a series of experiments known as the 'doll tests', in which they found that when African-American children aged three to seven were given four dolls that only differed in skin colour to pick from, the majority chose the white dolls and they attributed positive characteristics to them. Clark reported that when he then asked the children which doll was most like them, some would become visibly upset when they pointed out the doll they had rejected.[28] This was during segregation in the United States, when the racist Jim Crow laws – state and local statutes legalising racial segregation – and other methods were used to discriminate against Black people. However, the experiment was repeated in 2020 with a gentler methodology by Assistant Professor of Curriculum and Instruction, Texas A&M University-Commerce Toni Sturdivant. Putting four dolls that were white, Latina, Black with lighter skin and Black with medium skin into a diverse classroom, they observed the behaviour of Black preschool girls for a term. Published in the *Early Childhood Education Journal*, the results were heartbreakingly similar to the original study over 60 years later. Writing for *The Conversation*, Sturdivant said: 'On the rare occasions that the girls chose the Black dolls, they mistreated them. One time a Black girl put the doll in a pot and pretended to cook the doll. That's not something the girls did with the dolls that weren't Black.' As the girls pretended to be hairstylists and played with the dolls, they showed preference for the straight Latina doll's hair and crimped hair of the white doll – but said that the Black doll's hair was too big or too curly – 'The children were more likely to step over or even step on the Black dolls to get to other toys. But that didn't happen with the other dolls,' Sturdivant added.[29]

The sad truth is that I don't think I would have chosen a dark-skinned doll at that age, painful as that is to reckon with. I already knew that my appearance wasn't beautiful and I too would have wanted a doll seen as prettier. Often, it's the case that children who are non-white are given dolls of their own ethnicity to be able to see themselves in toy form, which is important of course. However, dolls of colour are harder to locate and looking at toy shop aisles and online retailers, it's still challenging to find non-white dolls and soft toys; some LOL dolls come in varied skin tones, it's true, but they may also come with secret BDSM-esque lingerie that appears when the doll is submerged in water, so ... Mattel has launched more inclusive dolls in petite, tall and curvy sizes, and Barbie in a wheelchair, so there's a modicum of optimism for Barbie lovers hoping for a more inclusive future but that also relies on us ensuring *all* children play with these versions, not just a few.

Lindsey Filcik, mother of a child with Down's syndrome, said on Instagram: 'Imagine being a child with a disability and all you ever see are typical, able-bodied children. What message does that send you about yourself? That you are "abnormal". That you are not worthy of being shown to the world ... Lack of representation also hurts those children who are represented. They grow up with the incredibly skewed perception that everybody looks like them. And anybody who doesn't isn't "normal" and should be feared. That, my friends, is how racism and ableism can be perpetuated in our kids without us even realizing it.'[30] It can affect how we see ourselves and potential too, as model Ellie Goldstein, who has Down's syndrome and is the face of Gucci's recent Unconventional Beauty ad campaign, told *The Independent*: 'there needs to be more positivity out there and people should give us a chance and not be so ignorant ... let the world see that anyone can model and act with a disability.'

Toys are also responsible for a lot of the gender conditioning young children are subjected to. Research has shown that from the age of just two, girls gravitate towards pink and boys shy away from it[31] – the true power of cultural gender conditioning and marketing. If you've even glanced at the doll section of a toyshop or the girls' section of a clothing store, this will come as zero surprise. Psychologists have found that gender hierarchy starts to manifest young – and boys start to see femininity as a stigma, even in early childhood.'[32] While scientists seem to disagree on whether gendered behaviour is innate to us or not, what's true is that the construct of gender is handed to us before we can figure out our own identities.[33]

But it hasn't always been this way. Elizabeth Sweet, assistant professor in Sociology and Interdisciplinary Social Sciences at San Jose State University told the *New York Times* in 2014: 'In my research on historic toy advertisements, I found no period during the twentieth century when the gender-based marketing of toys was anything near what we see today. In the 1975 Sears catalogue, for example, toys came in many hues, and science kits and kitchen sets showed boys and girls working together. But with the growth of the consumer economy, toy companies worked to stimulate demand by honing their appeal to kids. Gender categorization provided a handy tool for toy companies to define target markets, and gender stereotypes drew the interest of young children forming their own sense of identity.'[34]

The point at which gendered toys became the norm also coincided with the backlash against progress made by the feminist movements of the 1960s and 1970s. 'Belief that males and females are fundamentally different, and stereotypes about women, grew in the 1980s and 1990s, despite broad support for gender equality,' Sweet said. This reminds me of the line I quoted from *The Beauty Myth* in the introduction – 'The more legal and material hindrances women have broken through, the more strictly and heavily and cruelly images of female beauty have come to weigh upon us.' Girls get given domestic toys or dolls that we are supposed to covet for their beauty and boys get more skill-based toys or 'action figures' (*not* called dolls) celebrated for their strength, like Wolverine or Action Man. This gender split helps cage girls into a narrative that they have nothing to offer aside from our looks and that their appearance is central to being female. And that limitation just keeps on being reinforced as we grow up – we can see where it starts, but where does it end?

My sincerest apologies if this chapter has ruined all your childhood TV shows for you or made you look askance at your favourite toys. But the truth is that these dolls, the cartoons, the Disney princesses, they're just not as innocent as we might assume. Like mini detectives, children are always looking to learn 'their place' from the world around them – and TV and toys undeniably help perpetuate social norms. When children have access to dolls that look like them but don't want to play with them, I think we can conclude there has been force exerted – often exclusion and racism – which has likely caused this to happen. *All* children should see themselves represented in the media they consume – and not as the friend or the sidekick, but as the hero too. But if we are to address the root of the messaging children receive – that *we* received in our formative years – that makes them say things like 'I am ugly', we have to go deeper than this.

Each time one of those standards was imparted to us as children, we add it to an imaginary backpack of 'self-loathing' that gets heavier and heavier as we grow up – before the burden of it becomes unbearable. We shouldn't live in a world where we experience normative discontent – a constant underlying unhappiness – each time we look in the mirror. And for that to become part of any child's life that they take with them into adulthood, influencing subsequent generations – it creates a never-ending cycle. Asking how this happened and when it began is the first step in releasing its claws from our self-esteem. In other words, once we have an awareness of how hierarchical standards in appearance are created, we can see how that played out for us as kids and is still playing out now.

In 2022, when the trailer for the live-action remake of Disney's *The Little Mermaid* was released there was clear divide on social media: videos of little Black girls gasping with delight at seeing a Black Ariel, and the opposite. A racist social media backlash against a children's film, by those clinging to the nostalgia of the original Disney version, online debate ranged from abject racism to some debating whether mermaids would need melanin-rich skin if they're underwater away from sunlight.[35] Although, perhaps the latter will be satisfied that, true to original form, blonde-haired, blue-eyed Margot Robbie will play Barbie in the 2023 movie.

I can't help but grieve and be furious that these beauty archetypes made me feel so ugly at such a young age. But at the same time, taking a more critical and challenging perspective on the limited and limiting beauty standards we've been force-fed has helped me close that loop of self-hatred. You know, the one that tells you you're not thin/pretty/straight-haired/light-skinned enough to be valuable. For so many of us – myself included – damage was done slowly and stealthily, without anyone realising or taking accountability. Uncovering it feels like an injustice and wake-up call all in one. Ugly isn't intrinsic – it was planted consistently during our childhoods. To say that realising this feels freeing is an understatement.

PS: Maxie, now I've watched her back on YouTube, was actually a bit of a twat.

A CULTURE OF UGLY

'No one can make you feel inferior without your consent.'

– Former First Lady Eleanor Roosevelt

OF ALL THE INGENIOUS ways that Western society has of sending us the message that we are falling short of its beauty standards, that we are failing too in the all-important quest to be considered pretty, and therefore acceptable, I think it's often the seemingly innocuous, run-of-the mill ones that are the most damaging. We are pretty good at noticing when a photo has been airbrushed to the point of absurdity. We can spot a crude bit of misogyny lurking in a comment about a woman's appearance. We know that behind the highlight reel of Instagram posts not everyone is #Livingmybestlife. There is a lot that is problematic and potentially damaging in these examples, true, but there are also many other, more subtle ways that we can be made to feel like we are failing at beauty and chip away at our self-esteem to make us feel ugly.

Let me introduce you to a staple of women's magazines worldwide: 'the (imaginary) celebrity beauty routine'. I've conducted hundreds of these interviews, delving into the grooming habits of the rich, famous and beautiful to glean any kind of insight into their real, non-edited lives. That's the stuff we want to know, right? The juicy detail that both answers our questions and fuels our eternal inferiority complex. 'How does she look *so* good?' is almost certainly followed by the almost accusatory 'But why don't I?' And then the final quandary: 'How can I replicate that?' Cue extensive googling for miracle potions and cosmetic surgery 'before and after' shots, ending with a mild sense of failure and defeat.

Invariably, bar a few gloriously unedited souls (musicians are usually the most unguarded, I've found), these sorts of interviews follow a tired formula. Rather than getting an honest snapshot of how they genuinely engage with beauty, you're faced with a perfection-peddling, borderline farcical 'beauty routine', all to perpetuate the myth that, essentially, said model/actor/singer just 'woke up like this'. *Sure*, it's coconut oil and good genes that keep you looking so young (rather than a legion of doctors and beauty specialists helping you get ready daily – the case for most top celebrities). Your mother bathed you in oak-smoked yak's milk while small bluebirds helped comb your hair? How *divine*! Your skin looks *so* good, what do you use? Oh, it's the cream you're currently peddling (how convenient!). Give. Me. A. Break.

Eventually, doing those interviews started to crush my soul (as did my editor's pleading: 'Did she not say *anything* interesting, at all?'). Beyond the snooze factor of dull copy, I disliked them because I knew they were selling self-loathing and fuelling comparison. One celebrity told me she barely brushed her thick, iconic hair – in fact, each morning, she simply 'shook it upside down'. Having waged a lifelong war with my fine strands, I felt a pang of jealousy when she told me this. Then, at the end of the interview, she swung around to speak to her agent and the real source of her Samson-esque mane was revealed: hair extension wefts. That's not to shame her or extensions in any way (I have them myself) but I'd fully fallen for the 'natural girl' vibes she'd made her career from and yet what she was selling wasn't real or the full story. She was just one of many I can recount: like the young actor who raved about body positivity on social media before asking for her 'back fat' to be airbrushed out of a shoot or the influencer who refused to be parted from her huge fake lashes and asked for so much retouching she looked like an avatar. I have the utmost sympathy for the celebrities caught in these webs of untruths too; after all, they are scrutinised endlessly and cruelly in a way that reveals the darkest sides of humanity. But celebrities' and influencers' insistence on showing us these fantasy 'real beauty routines' via magazines and social media is what propagates idealised, unattainable beauty standards that both unknowingly and knowingly sell us self-dissatisfaction.

Deep down, sure, we know it's all a charade – it's why the tabloids publish 'celebrities without make-up' stories and we click on them to see 'the truth' and glimpse reality for a moment. But it creates a confusing circle that keeps on looping until we're just not sure how we feel about our own appearance anymore. Even trends dressed as empowerment like #Nomakeupselfies are often in reality just a humblebrag, to show off having clear skin (and 'good genes') and invariably make people feel like rubbish. (There's a celebrity that does this routinely to flog their beauty line but never points to the copious amounts of filler, Botox, laser and regular facials they most likely have too. Nothing on social media is quite as it seems.)

In an attempt to get through these interviews, I'd try to push a celebrity to give me something, *anything* real, often by asking them, 'What was the first beauty product you owned?', reasoning that reminiscing about their childhoods might elicit a raw, genuine response. But all I ever heard was the same tired tale about a bottle of perfume inherited from some famous grandmother or an expensive red lipstick given to them as a rite of passage. I'm all in for a little fantasy – I love edgy shoots and whimsical editorials – but when someone is peddling a glittery version of adolescence that doesn't really exist, you have to question – why? It might have been occasionally true but, either way, it jarred so much against my first beauty experiences, I just didn't want to hear it anymore.

My first beauty product, since you're asking, was a crystal-coated, limited-edition Estée Lauder compact, delivered to me by carrier pigeon in a little Balenciaga backpack. I jest – obviously mine came from a grotty pound shop in my hometown. This shop was like a cosmetic purgatory, where crap make-up was sent to repent for its sins against beauty. It was overflowing with buckets of garish eye shadows and waxy lipsticks in cheap packaging. The scent of cloying, freeze-hold hairspray and designer perfume rip-offs (there were at least five kinds of 'CK One') filled the room. This shop was like Boots or Sephora but on the worst hangover of its *entire* existence, post 12 rounds of Jägerbombs and with a putrefying kebab stuck to its face the next morning. (Been there …) Naturally, 12-year-old me adored that shop. Importantly, it enabled my first beauty purchase: a green mascara.

If you're imagining a chic emerald shade, think again: this was a sickly pale metallic hue; like covering your eyelashes in mix of frost, snot and green slime simultaneously. For the sum of a whole pound – scavenged from the back of the sofa – it was mine, and my best friend bought an electric blue one too. Before long, we were experimenting with a mix of aquatic-coloured lashes – some days blue, sometimes green and often a mix of both – that made us look like, well, children who had been playing with make-up. Everyone told us we looked silly (a lesson for the future: bold sartorial choices often rattle the mainstream), from fellow classmates to our teachers, who told us to take it off, ad nauseum. We didn't care. We just liked the colours so we kept wearing it, eventually gravitating to glittery pound-shop lipsticks next. There was no thought beyond that; we didn't want to look pretty or natural like our other friends did with their pointless clear mascaras and tinted lip balms – fun and exploration were our only goal.

I remember that mascara and lipstick so fondly for a single pertinent reason: not only were they genuinely my first beauty products but also the first and probably last time my beauty choices *truly* belonged to me. It was – to refer to the queen of quotes, Eleanor Roosevelt – the last time I truly consented to what I was being sold. It's emotional to think about that mascara because, honestly, it was a gateway drug. I became increasingly attracted to cosmetics of every kind, particularly the transformative power of make-up. I adored it, collected it and sleuthed obsessively for information on how to apply it – although now it had become driven by a desire to fit in – beauty products sold me a way to escape feeling ugly.

I wasn't allowed to buy teen mags (the joys of strict Asian upbringings), so I'd scour charity shops and my friends' reject piles for second-hand copies with any beauty tips. Learning everything about products and their application became my second schooling: I'd ask for beauty books for birthdays and spend hours messily melting down lipsticks and mixing my own foundation shades because what I needed wasn't available in the shops. Sure, my now almost-perfect colour matching ability is a bonus, but what I was learning was teaching me more about beauty standards and the industry than I ever knew. I gleaned that my dark skin needed 'colour correcting' when I visited the beauty counters for advice or when hairdressers told me that my curly hair was 'tameable', but only when blow-dried straight.

A gradual vitriol had been creeping into my life, both undetectable and relentless in its quest for superiority. I'd feel its piercing criticism when I swiped on layers of concealer to cover my dark circles or when I blotted furiously at my oil-drenched skin with too-pale powder. Every brush stroke became a silent prayer, a plea for me to look like the girls around me held up as the beauty ideal. It may have started with the carefree joy of a bright green mascara, but I'd become hooked on the idea that beauty products could make me look more 'acceptable'. In that transition, I'd stopped wearing make-up for fun or for myself. It was a definitive moment – maybe you had one too?

For the rest of my teenage years, I'd get up an hour early to laboriously paint my face on and straighten my hair with these giant archaic straightening irons, all to make sure I looked 'done' as close to the standards I'd seen in teen magazines or on TV. Occasionally, I almost liked what I saw in the mirror, but if nobody commented or noticed me – and they rarely did – it would feel like failure or, worse, invisibility. I'd completely outsourced my self-esteem to anyone but myself and, despite the promise of help and advice, the beauty industry and beauty media that I loved just kept showing me I was ugly. I'd seen what 'pretty' looked like and no matter what products I bought, it wasn't me.

My elaborate routines remained but something shifted within me as I went to university. On my weekly trip to the local House of Fraser to get my beauty fix with these things called 'store cards' (who knew you had to pay interest? Not me!), I saw a new beauty counter. I approached it gingerly, the way that dogs creep up and silently sniff to see if you're a friend or a snack. My experiences with the other brands had been soul-crushing: often the counter girls would try to minimise or correct my features (everything on my face was a problem to fix, it seemed), before covering me in plum shades, which was obviously the training directive for dark skin back then. Although, at other times they'd just plain ignore me to serve somebody white. So, I was initially untrusting but this counter not only looked different – it was black and cool – it turned out to be staffed by a kindly man who explained what colours suited me, showed me how to apply them and even – shock, horror – complimented me on my skin tone, the first time anyone, aside from my family, had said anything nice about my face, actually.

From then onwards, dropping in to that NARS counter became my weekly pilgrimage. Everything I earned from my part-time job went on beauty products and saving up for Clarins facials. It was a double-edged sword. After feeling ugly for as long as I could remember, finding make-up I adored made me almost feel worth looking at and I realised beauty could make you feel incredible, rather than lacking. But on the flipside, it also fed my beauty addiction on a whole new level. Every time I felt down, I hit that NARS counter *hard* and, with zero exaggeration, at one point, I had almost everything they sold. Holidays abroad became entirely about my duty-free beauty shopping list and I'd save up for Crème de la Mer and MAC eyeshadows. So, from the age of 12, I'd put all my hope, self-esteem and self-worth into something external: magazines, other people's opinions, beauty products. As an astute therapist once pointed out, it's not just telling but perhaps also inevitable that my beauty obsession became an entire career.

Chances are this isn't your exact story, that would be weird as hell. But you might identify with that guttural ache of wanting to fit in, to be admired or to have the status of the 'pretty girls' at school so much so you'll do anything you can to achieve it. I thought beauty products might be what would get me an invite into that elite club and away from the ugliness I felt. And I still feel that familiar surge of hope each time a new cream lands on my desk promising to reinvent my face – it yanks me back to those teenage moments where I wanted, so badly, to feel beautiful. I entirely understand why the 'fix' of a must-have product can boost our mood – so much so that we're prepared to join overhyped waiting lists, get into debt or put our faith in unreliable sources. (A facialist told me that half of her clients had acid burns after taking skincare advice from random, non-expert influencers they followed online.) And, I became so obsessed with an eyeshadow palette I paid to have it shipped from the US (at huge cost) only to find that the shades were bland and every image they'd posted had been filtered. The quest for beauty can be incredibly unhealthy, not to mention costly. It's why we think 'solutions' like surgery or weight loss have the power to change our entire lives – that is, until we find another perceived flaw to obsess over.

We're not the impressionable children mainlining Disney princess tales nor status-concerned teens trying to fit in anymore, but we are, undeniably – as research supports – in the midst of a collective self-esteem and appearance crisis. While we may be seeing more diverse-ish ads, fashion brands using slightly larger mannequins and beauty companies extending their shade ranges to a performative 500 colours, we are still struggling with feeling ugly. What's tricky to grapple with – for me, personally and professionally – is that as we hit our low, our beauty culture is the biggest and most profitable it's ever been. The thing that tells us it can make us feel our best, isn't. Evidently, something has gone awry.

When did beauty culture begin?

There's plenty of evidence for beauty practices in the earliest beginnings of many cultures – it's a vast and subjective history that fills entire tomes. Prehistoric paintings show both men and women painted their bodies for rituals and archaeologists have found intact pigments (that's some *serious* staying power) dating back to the Mesolithic period, a casual 400,000 years ago.[1] Mineral pigments were mixed with animal fat to create extreme weather protection, like a prehistoric sunblock,[2] while mirrors, razors, tweezers and similar items have been found alongside the bodies of Bronze Age men (3300 to 1200 BC).[3] Susan Stewart, author of *Painted Faces – A Colourful History Of Cosmetics*, notes that a male mummy dating back to 3250 BC, from the ancient Chinchorro culture of Chile, had 60 tattoos and is 'early evidence of an inclination to adorn the body for the purposes of beautification as well as, perhaps, to signify belonging to a particular social group.'[4]

Often these beauty rituals had religious significance and ceremonial usage and in ancient times were a part of life for both men and women. Herbal remedies containing ingredients like moringa, castor oil and frankincense[5] were used in Ancient Egypt as moisturising agents (unrelated side note: they're also our modern-day skincare 'hero' ingredients too, which blows my tiny mind). Beeswax, resin and even fat-based hair gels[6] were even used to make mummies more irresistible in the afterlife (I'm really fighting the urge to make a 'dead sexy' joke here).

Ancient Greek philosophers spent a *lot* of time thinking about beauty. These men defined the ideal female beauty standard as having ginger or golden hair – chosen because gold was prized as a material, pale skin – as that represented nobility and not having to work outside, a slightly rounded figure – which symbolised fertility,[7] and a symmetrical face with dark brows. Sound familiar? What's genuinely shocking is that blonde, light skin, curvy in the 'right' places and a symmetrical face is – centuries later – the modern-day beauty standard many of us grew up being measured against. Be it *Playboy* bunnies, Marilyn Monroe, or even now, a platinum-haired Kim Kardashian.

Female beauty was also a competitive sport in Ancient Greece: 'Beauty contests or kallisteia were a regular fixture in the training grounds of the Olympics at Elis and on the islands of Tenedos and Lesbos, where women were judged as they walked to and fro,' says historian Bettany Hughes in a BBC news feature.[8] These sound a lot like ancient precursors to our modern-day beauty pageants like Miss World or, well, social media, where women are pitted against each other and their appearance scrutinised. But before you relegate this info to the part of your brain reserved for 'useless pub quiz facts', let's delve deeper into the beauty ideals of this time.

We have a *long* history of trying to quantify female beauty. A search through my inbox quickly yields a cosmetic surgery press release that helpfully explains what constitutes the perfect nose: apparently, it has a pointed tip and is of course, symmetrical. So let's take the obsession with symmetry for a moment: the 'golden ratio' theory was defined by Greek mathematician Euclid (365–300 BC) as a means to group and understand things of beauty, like art, music, architecture and, yes, humans. It involves using the complicated ratio to look at factors like symmetry and the distances between our features to define what is, mathematically, the most beautiful. That would be fine if we'd left it in 300 BC and our beauty measuring had evolved, ideally to the point where the measuring stick is forcibly torched.

Instead, every week I receive a press release using it to quantify female beauty, which most often lauds white, conventionally attractive celebrities like Angelina Jolie and Amber Heard, claiming that cosmetic surgeons have hailed them 'the most beautiful women in the world', due to their perfect face ratio, which should be two-thirds longer than it is wide. Those releases, masquerading as fact or, worse, as science, go on to become easy tabloid clickbait features designed to make us think there is some irrefutable, mathematical way of quantifying pretty. And all to sell us self-loathing, followed by a new nose if we fall short. But if we think about it for even just a moment, I think we can all agree that beauty – even as a philosophical notion – isn't quantifiable and is *entirely* subjective. Of course, Ancient Greece was home to many remarkable thinkers and early scientists, I just think it's also worth remembering that they were also charging around in chariots, drinking vomit to cure health woes[9] and believed that sneezing was an effective method of birth control.[10] They didn't know everything.

In medieval Europe, the most desirable female faces of the era had a 'plain, empty appearance' and, for modesty, the hair was covered by a veil, which also helped the face look larger. Higher foreheads gave faces more ... well, face, as well as being seen as an aristocratic feature and a sign of breeding and intelligence,[11] so many (mostly) upper-class women plucked their hairlines back or removed their lashes and brows entirely to meet the desired 'look' – though they were then met with ecclesiastical lectures about the sin of vanity. As Christianity continued to rise in Europe during the early medieval period, the rules around female beauty were committed to paper, (oh, great). 'Conduct books' acted like the magazines of yore and were written by men to instruct women on how to behave in both religious and domestic life. In one such tome published in 1371, called *Book of the Knight of the Tower* – basically a 'how to behave' for young medieval women – author Geoffroy de la Tour Landry condemns any women who uses cosmetics via a morality tale of a woman who paid too much attention to her looks: 'What, will this lady never be done combing herself! Staring at herself in the mirror? It proves however to be a mirror of evil omen and as it pleased God to make an example of her even as she stared into the mirror, she perceived the enemy who bared his behind so ugly and horrible that the woman lost her reason as if she were possessed by the devil.'[12] Fairly intense, yet still weirdly recognisable – 'Ladies, here is how we have decided you must look to be considered worthy. But if you attempt to make yourself look like that we will call you vain, vacuous and self-obsessed.' It's also another stop sign in our magical beauty history tour that should be screaming at you: 'our beauty standards were created by ancient dudes!'

During the Renaissance, caring about your looks became more acceptable and even aristocratic men wore make-up alongside their wigs. The invention of the printing press in the 15th century meant that beauty recipes could be shared more easily, alongside some early cosmetic product adverts, and a boom in trade meant that ingredients for these recipes were easier to source too. It wasn't all plain sailing though; the use of beauty products could still backfire for women – and it did. A letter written to *The Spectator* in 1711 describes the case of an 'injured gentleman' who had married one of the 'women who do not let their husbands see their faces till they are married'. He asked the paper for advice as to whether the man could 'be rid' of his wife (presumably she fell short of his expectations). *The Spectator* responds that this was a common trickery woman performed to torment men.[13] Three hundred years later, in 2012, a newspaper recounted an oddly similar tale of a man 'deceived by cosmetics'. Apparently, a husband divorced his wife just days after their wedding, having seen her without make-up for the first time: 'The groom said he no longer recognised his bride after her face got wet during a swim in the sea on honeymoon,' the paper reported.[14]

The link between beauty, sin and the supernatural too was a common trope rolled out against women throughout history. The word 'pretty' – very interestingly – originates from a number of sources such as Middle English *pratie* – which meant 'cunning, crafty, clever' while other definitions from Old Norse's *prettr* also suggest 'a trick' and old Dutch word *pret* referred to a 'trick, joke'. From its earliest origins it held a note of deception.[15] This speaks of much of the 'trickery' that being beautiful is often aligned with; from cosmetics historically being seen as duplicitous through to how beauty – then and now – is so often linked with the occult, with terms like 'magic', 'beguiling', 'astonish', 'bewitched', 'alchemy', 'illusion', 'wizardry' and 'allure' all being used widely within the industry to name products and describe their effects. Women still face the inconsistency of being scorned for obvious displays of vanity, while female beauty is still prized as our biggest currency. I guess impossibly high (double) standards for women's beauty are historically consistent, if nothing else.

Beautiful, or just plain rich?

Wealth and beauty signifiers have always gone hand in hand, with access to beauty products a marker of status – take the way an Aesop handwash signifies a posh bathroom, for example. Historically, beauty and fashion aspirations came from the ruling classes. In Ancient Egypt, perfumes made of beeswax and scented oils were worn only by the rich,[16] while in 600 BC members of the Chinese Zhou Dynasty wore gold and silver on their nails to denote their status, something that was forbidden to the lower classes.[17]

The public would see monarchs depicted in artworks like tapestries or paintings and often their appearance was emulated and elevated. The royal court set the fashions of the day. For example, during the 16th century, some women would bleed themselves with leeches to achieve the in-vogue ghostly pallor,[18] or paint fine blue vein-like lines on their skin to appear more translucent. The term 'blue blood' – which refers to having aristocratic heritage – is a translation from the Spanish *sangre azul* and originated from a name given to the oldest families of Castile in Spain, who reportedly never intermarried with other races. The blueness of their veins visible through their pale skin would have been compared favourably to those with darker skin at the time.[19]

The belief that pale equals wealthy goes back a long way (don't worry, we'll be looking a lot more at 'paleness' and beauty, and all that entails in a later chapter) and comes from a lack of a tan being a signifier of wealth privilege. Just like having more body fat/being fat used to be a sign that you had plenty of money and were well fed, originally, paler skin showed you could sit indoors all day and didn't have to work the land. The Romans used chalk, vinegar and orris root powder to lighten their faces in line with aristocratic beauty ideals,[20] while flour and harsh natural bleaches were used to get rid of freckles in the medieval period.[21] Clear skin has also – generally speaking – been seen throughout history as a marker of health, fertility and hygiene. Portraits of Queen Elizabeth I (1558–1603) depict her – particularly later in life – wearing what is most likely 'ceruse', 'a finely ground white lead powder, mixed with vinegar and applied over the entire face and neck'[22] to hide smallpox scars and whiten her skin. (Her red hair also became the fashionable shade of the era much as Princess Diana popularised a shorter haircut for women in the 1980s).

The white European obsession with pale first started to shift in the 19th century. As a result of the Industrial Revolution, the Victorian working classes were now working inside in factories rather than outside in the fields, meaning they were rarely exposed to the sun, which somewhat inverted the 'pale and wealthy' beauty ideal. In the early 20th century, as travel became easier and faster, leisure time and holidays – including abroad – became increasingly attractive to those who could afford them. In 1923, fashion designer and trendsetter Coco Chanel was accidentally sunburned on a cruise to Cannes, thereby making a 'tan' – on white skin, that is – a sought-after signifier of wealth, status and social aspiration. By the mid-century, advances in commercial air travel made going abroad more popular and aspirational – and, consequently, returning with a tan to show that you could afford to take an exotic vacation. When a long-held beauty ideal like this shifts so radically, it offers a veiled glimpse into who holds the power in society and controls the beauty standards. Let's pop an imaginary pin in this point, as it's something we will be seeing again …

It might not feel like looking wealthy is the driver for our own internal beauty standards but let's consider for a moment how many of our contemporary beauty ideals come from a desire to emulate the look and lifestyles of the rich. There's an intrinsic link between 'beauty' and 'luxury' and how that's sold to us. The bikini-clad models frolicking on far-flung beaches on magazine shoots, for example, or those dramatic perfume adverts on TV with film stars in couture who always seem to be running from something (who, what? Are you OK, hun?) often ending with some sort of dramatic water-based plunge. Beauty advertising sells us the dream of a luxurious lifestyle and what that might feel like. It's why fashion brands launch beauty lines, so everyone can have a little piece of their dream designer, even on a small budget. It is a way of democratising luxury and making it seem accessible.

The consistent message is that looking wealthy is what we should aspire to. Think of the enduring appeal of 'posh girl hair' or the 'Sloane' beauty trend – Catherine, Princess of Wales is the poster girl for this. The rich girl mandate has always been a 'barely there' look that appears to be natural, even if it isn't. The ideals associated with 'barely there' beauty are the 'superiority' of good breeding, clear skin that's tanned from a holiday (but not naturally dark) and long, thick, straight hair. I've worked on a number of luxury brand projects and it's been abundantly clear what aspirational and expensive looks like: straight bouncy, shiny hair – that is in no way 'ethnic'. The vernacular within the haircare industry often uses equestrian words like 'glossy', 'groomed', 'sleek', 'coat', 'mane' to describe hair that's seen as the most desirable and healthy. And who – pray tell – has been traditionally associated with equestrian culture throughout history and to this day? Rich, white people.

I'm not chastising the brands who market their products in this way. After all, they didn't invent the beauty standards that have elitism and Eurocentrism woven so meticulously into their core that it's hidden from plain view. But it does show how wealth and class are used consistently to sell covert beauty ideals to us. And now, it is a brand's responsibility –

in an age of inclusivity and awareness – to ensure that how they're selling us beauty products takes these factors into consideration, in the way they're marketed to us and who they choose to represent their brand. We need to be aware of it too, to know what we're *really* buying into.

Throughout history, fashion magazines have set the standards of appearance and defined what's ugly and what's beautiful for generations of women. As my career progressed and I began to work on huge titles, I couldn't quite grasp why change wasn't happening at a quicker pace – *and I had questions*. Why were women of colour or other intersections excluded from 'line up' features, where a group of women would be interviewed about their experiences and be photographed. Why did so many beauty shoots have an ultra-slim model, usually under 25? Why was everyone who worked on them behind the scenes predominantly white? Who made up this invisible force gatekeeping beauty and fashion standards at the big glossy magazines? Even though many of these titles embraced a certain amount of feminism to appear more relevant to changing times, it felt selective. An unaccounted presence, it sat on the edge of every meeting table as I pitched ideas that tried to push the boat out, but seemingly would go 'too far', further than they found comfortable, particularly when issues pertained to inclusivity – or the lack thereof. As author Mikki Kendall says in *Hood Feminism: Notes from the Women White Feminists Forgot*: 'The fundamental problem with white feminism has always been that it refuses to admit that the primary goal is shifting power to white women and no one else.'[23] This was what appeared to be happening here.

Women's media has always been a carefully designed way of reaching us with a set of rules or norms (like 'skinny jeans are out', 'a red lip is this season's look') or encouraging certain behaviour ('10 ways to get a summer body') – within its own agenda. The first women's magazine in the UK, started in 1693, was the *Ladies' Mercury*, which was published as an offshoot of the *Athenian Mercury*,[24] followed a little later by titles like *The Female Tatler*, *The Female Spectator* (offshoots of *The Tatler* and *The Spectator*, respectively) and *The Lady's Magazine*, which launched in 1770. Naturally, they were all modelled on the decorum of upper-class women who formed their readership and created their codes of conduct, and often, that code has remained.

American *Harper's Bazaar* launched in 1867 and had one of the earliest, and well-known, beauty advice columns, titled 'The Ugly-Girl Papers: Or, Hints for the Toilet'. Beauty expert of the era Mrs S. D. Powers, who was behind the column, was hugely popular for her 'tone of a wise aunt with endless advice on how to solve your beauty woes'.[25] She advised on everything from how to lose weight to getting that wasting, consumptive (tuberculosis) look, also a popular trend in Britain at the time.[26] (In case you're wondering, consumptive chic was a thing because the Victorians thought it only affected respectable, attractive women and that it was triggered by too much mental exertion and dancing.)[27] Here's an example of her extolling the virtues of TB: 'The fairest skins belong to people in the earliest stages of consumption, or those of a scrofulous nature. This miraculous clearness and brilliance is due to the constant purgation which wastes the consumptive, or to the issue which relieves the system of impurities by one outlet.'[28] Does this sound to you weirdly like a precursor to the juice cleanse? The Ugly-Girl Papers was so popular, it was published as a book[29] – such was the desire to look aristocratic.

Though digital platforms and social media have largely taken over the mantle of providing this content now, the signifiers of wealth and status can still be found in social media trends like the 'clean girl' aesthetic. The girl who looks like she's had nine hours' sleep, perfect skin without make-up, eats 'cleanly' and has everything, seemingly, sorted. She's the new digital incarnation of a magazine poster girl and she still sells beauty standards that existed back then: whiteness, fat phobia, classism and unattainable standards of beauty gatekeeping.

By the Victorian period, these early women's magazines were carrying advertisements for items like soaps, oils and smelling salts, but cosmetics still existed in something of a grey area. Rouge and powder began to be widely used but respectable women were expected to be subtle with them. As Sarah Jane Downing, author of *Beauty and Cosmetics 1550–1950*, explains: 'Because of the negative view of cosmetics they were generally sold via mail order and Victorian cosmetic manufacturers had no real idea of their effects once they had left the factory.'[30] Nor did they know much about their ingredients – which often included arsenic, lead, belladonna (deadly nightshade), opium and ammonia. The lead and vinegar mix – a skin whitener signifying youth and an elevated social class – that women used was called Venetian ceruse and could cause hair loss, rotten teeth and skin discolouration.

At a prestigious salon in London's New Bond Street, Mayfair, the infamous Madame Sarah Rachel Leverson promised to make anyone 'beautiful for ever' by selling them 'costly Arabian Preparations for the restoration and preservation of female loveliness'.[31] The potions she offered were expensive; her famous 'enamelling' process cost 20 guineas (around £1,400 now) and involved removing all the hairs on the face, covering it in an alkaline solution, coating it with lead and arsenic, which was then powdered over with rouge – talk about a facial from hell. She was eventually tried for malpractice and intimidation (she was said to blackmail women who couldn't pay upfront for her treatments) and sentenced in 1868 and 1878, but her story tells just how far women would go in the quest to look more beautiful.[32]

During the Edwardian period, cosmetics brands started to really flourish, particularly in the US. Silent movie stars widely influenced style trends across the globe and filled the pages of magazines. One of the best-known female entrepreneurs of the era was Elizabeth Arden (born Florence Nightingale Graham, 1884–1966), who opened her first salon in New York in 1910. Arden created marketing campaigns aimed at making cosmetics more socially acceptable and, of course, more profitable as a result.

The famous entrepreneur Helena Rubinstein (1870–1965) moved to Australia in 1896 from her native Poland and began to sell skin creams before opening salons across the globe. Rubinstein famously said: 'There are no ugly women, only lazy ones.'[33] Harsh? Sure. But in the context of the time, it gave women who were deemed unattractive more hope of marriage – if they put in the effort and bought her products, of course.

Another celebrated name who started a beauty business in this era was Estée Lauder. Born in New York in 1908 (and died there in 2004), as an industrious teenager, she began selling products at a local salon, marketing them as 'jars of hope',[34] which is indicative of the pressure women felt to be beautiful, the 'hope' they placed on cosmetics and the limitations of female status in society at the time. More than 100 years later, the hope that a product will change our lives still prevails as a backbone of the beauty industry: take sell-out wonder products and viral must-haves. I find it inspiring and interesting that the beauty industry has so many founding females, particularly in an age when women rarely started businesses.

Though men were also taking advantage of what was

becoming a seriously booming market. Charles Revson (1906–1975) created Revlon with his chemist brother Joseph and infamously launched the biggest range of nail polishes on the market, introducing the concept of matching lipsticks and nails. Russian-born Max Factor (Maksymilian Faktorowicz, beautifying Hollywood's elite and creating his own self-titled cosmetic line.[35]

The first Avon lady was also in actual fact a man. David Hall McConnell (1858–1937) launched 'Avon Calling' in 1928 (though it had existed since 1886 as The California Perfume Company) to sell women cosmetics discreetly in the privacy of their own homes.[36] American Harry Gordon Selfridge didn't get that discretion memo, though. The retail magnate opened London-based department store Selfridges in 1909,[37] with beauty counters that had items on display, rather than hidden away, so women could try them, removing that covert shame around buying products – and of course to sell more. The beauty industry had officially become mainstream and like all commodities, competition was fierce.

Yet, despite burgeoning sales and the scramble for customers, not *all* women were catered for by the mainstream beauty market. Despite their erasure from textbooks, there have been people of colour in the UK since the Roman era and by the 1920s, particularly in docking neighbourhoods like Tiger Bay in Cardiff, Limehouse in London and Toxteth in Liverpool, people of colour and interracial couples and families were more common than they had previously been. And yet they were largely ignored by these beauty counters and brands.[38] Finding records of where women of colour got their beauty products from in the UK is incredibly hard. The mainstream beauty industry certainly didn't sell items in darker shades, so many people made their own formulations with ground-up chalk and unregulated, unsafe ingredients.[39]

People of colour were made to feel unwelcome in many

mainstream shops. Any brands that did launch to cater for them were sold direct to the consumer. In the US, Anthony Overton, an African-American lawyer in Kansas, recognised that women of colour lacked cosmetics so he created the 'high-brown' face powder, which he sold via mail order and a network of salespeople who visited small, local stores. It was a hit and sales boomed so much that by the 1920s, even though Overton was born into slavery, he'd now become one of the wealthy elite.[40]

There are many other amazing stories of early beauty pioneers that we rarely hear about because the inventors and business owners weren't white. For example, Lyda D. Newman was an African-American suffragist and hairdresser from Ohio who patented and revolutionised hairbrush design in 1898. Her brush was easier to clean and better suited to afro-textured hair as it used synthetic rather than boar-bristles. Likewise, Ada Harris from Indianapolis is the forgotten genius who patented her design for hair straighteners in 1895. Another woman widely known as a pioneer in the afro-textured hair industry was Annie Malone. Born in Mississippi in 1869 to formerly enslaved parents and orphaned at a young age, Malone knew that style and appearance could indicate a woman's position in society.[41] She suffered with a scalp ailment resulting in hair loss and created her own home remedies. That gave her the impetus to start her homemade afro haircare line Poro, which was sold by women to other women, before eventually founding a beauty college that employed many Black women. She became one of the wealthiest African-American women in the US – until sadly the Great Depression hit and her fortunes declined. Sarah Breedlove, one of Malone's former employees, also created her own successful beauty line called Madam C.J. Walker; their rivalry is documented in the Netflix TV miniseries *Self Made: Inspired by the Life of Madam C.J. Walker* (2020).

We seldom hear enough about these inspiring pioneers and the mainstream beauty industry has only started to turn a corner and cater for people of colour in the last ten years in the UK at least (perhaps slightly earlier in the US). The changing times and the opportunity presented by social media for people of colour to vent their frustrations has had an impact and companies have now woken up to the chance to profit from the 'ethnic pound'. Despite there being a shift in what is available – in theory – for people of colour in the beauty aisles, The 2022 Black Pound Report examined the habits of BAME consumers and found that multi-ethnic consumers spend £230m a month on health and beauty purchases, which is 25 per cent more than any other consumer, but approximately four in ten Black female shoppers say they still struggle to find the right products for them.[42] It's common for women with afro-textured hair to pay more for haircuts in white salons – that is, if there's anyone trained to cut their hair at all, often it's not part of standard hairdressing training. Though the hair industry is taking steps to ensure that hairdressers are trained to cut, style and colour ethnic hair of all types, that change is happening frustratingly slowly, and this is still more likely to be the case in big cities, rather than the suburbs. Recently, I tried – and failed – to find my foundation shade at a drugstore in Kent and am routinely sent products that just don't show up on dark skin, without an alternative that does. So, how much has really changed if the right, exclusive kind consumer is *still* white? Perhaps not as much as we've been told.

The creation of 'beauty anxiety'

Brands sell at us almost *constantly*, from those ads that follow you about online to glossy marketing, to actual packaging, which is designed to catch our attention on the shelves. But in a fleeting moment when the feeling of ugly hits us – perhaps from a social media scroll and inevitable comparison – we often reach for an immediate fix or cure. Feeling lacking or unworthy because of our appearance can cause a very specific 'beauty anxiety' that feels fraught – it's one of the highest invisible taxes that female beauty has always paid. Though the beauty industry didn't create beauty standards – patriarchy and a colonial legacy have largely taken care of that – it has historically played a role in upholding these standards, without accounting for how it sells us the solutions to all our beauty woes.

Beauty marketing really came into its own in the early 19th century as companies looked for new ways to sell beauty products and thus new habits to the masses. Helena Rubinstein was reportedly the first to classify skin as 'dry', 'normal' and 'oily' in the early 1900s and used those classifications to sell her signature line face cream, Valaze. Now, women began to feel the normal functions of their skin (the formation of wrinkles and blemishes, the production of oil, the existence of dead skin cells) were somehow wrong, but, handily, they could buy Rubinstein's creams to put that right.

But Rubinstein wasn't the only one using this anxiety-creating tactic. Ever shaved your armpits? Thank Gillette for that. It launched its first anti-underarm hair campaign in 1915 and its first women's safety razor, to remedy an 'embarrassing personal problem' of female body hair, which hadn't been an issue before then.[43] Similarly, the concept of cellulite didn't really exist as an issue until the February 1933 edition of French magazine *Votre Beauté* magazine first mentioned it as a feminine problem. When Eugène Schueller, founder of L'Oréal, launched their first mass-market shampoo in 1938, he wanted to shift consumer habits to sell more product: this was considered unconventional in a time where people only washed their hair once a week.

According to Mark Tungate, author of *Branded Beauty – How Marketing Changed The Way We Look*, Schueller told his salespeople: 'There are 43 million people in France. Let's imagine that those 43 million people washed their hair once a week. We would sell 20 times the number of units that we sell at the moment.'[44]

Smart business, sure. That's undisputable. But the idea that marketing and manufactured maladies have changed the course of our personal habits and beauty routines ever since is unfathomable. These engineered issues and their convenient fixes are often still how we're sold beauty today – did we think we needed to highlight and contour our faces until Kim Kardashian's contour selfie in 2012 went viral, causing a slew of contouring products to fill the market? This is just another version of marketing cleverly perpetuating a 'trend' that sets up a perceived deficit, sneakily offering the solution. Whatever the beauty standard, the beauty industry will always help us achieve it to be 'acceptable'.

Alongside this principle, advertising and marketing have a whole raft of other smart tactics to sell us things and they're worth looking out for. One is 'priming' – which uses words that our brain automatically links with another idea; for example, seeing the word 'cat' means we'll find it easier to cognitively recognise 'mouse'. Or we'll link 'young' with 'beautiful'. 'Reciprocity' means that we feel a boost when we get something for free as we shop, like using points-based reward cards or the classic 'free gift with purchase'[45] that tempts many of us – this was actually invented by Estée Lauder in 1946.[46]

'Social proof' is where we see somebody 'elevated' do or use something first – influencers, in other words. Silent movie actor Lillie Langtry was one of the earliest brand ambassadors for Pears Soap in 1882, with her image and signature of approval appearing on the adverts,[47] while Max Factor used celebrities like American actor and singer Virginia Mayo to advertise their face powder in 1945, 'for a flawless lovely new complexion you have always wanted', selling patrons a sliver of her glamorous life. 'Scarcity' is used to create a sense of panic around something or the lack of it. That could be a limited-edition product that we're told will sell out or anything that has a waiting list.

During the Second World War, the beauty industry and society were able to use a whole new reason why women *should* wear make-up – to boost morale and support the military. Despite being a vital part of the war effort, women were required to be decorative too: a tired-looking woman was seen as having given up and admitted defeat – which was in turn seen as being bad for the troops and could signal 'weakness' internationally too. Compacts were shaped like war planes or military hats and you could even wear your hair in a patriotic way, as 'victory rolls'. The expectation of being beautiful and groomed as an expression of patriotism ensured a new urgency and anxiety to looking good at all costs to 'keep up appearances'.

In some countries, particularly Britain, women gained more freedom during the war years and entered workplaces that had previously been closed to them. Predictably then, when the conflict was over and there was a desire to return to the pre-war status quo, that came with various overt and insidious attempts to put the 'fairer sex' back in their place. In the UK, the 1950s was largely a time of austerity but in the US, there was a focus on excessive consumerism and an accompanying boom in advertising, much of it aimed at getting women to buy more things to make them attractive – and Britain soon started following.

However, by the end of the 1960s into the early 1970s, second-wave feminism was in flow. Magazines like US-based

Ms. (launched in 1972) started setting a new agenda that showed women a different life away from homemaking and talked openly about how advertising was being used to manipulate them into consumption.[48] Beauty trends favoured a more natural 'hippie' aesthetic and cosmetic sales declined while beauty brands knew they needed new marketing tactics to embrace this new emancipated woman. Revlon launched the androgynously named fragrance Charlie in 1973, with an ad campaign featuring celebrities captured in a more carefree, relaxed aesthetic.[49] Even Charlie's slogan sounds like a rousing feminist chant, being shouted in unison as they marched through the streets:[50] 'There's a fragrance that's here today, and they call it – Charlie! A different fragrance that thinks your way, and they call it – Charlie! Kinda young, kinda now, Charlie!'

Charlie's independence reflects the mood of second-wave feminism that was in flow at the time. But Charlie wasn't every woman. The first wave of feminism was largely led by educated, middle-class white women who sought, among other things, the right to work – something women of colour were often already doing through necessity, though often in lowlier roles. For white feminists, gender was the main obstacle; women of colour and other intersections were forced to navigate multi-layered levels of oppression. While the marketing of Charlie fragrance was selling one vision of emancipation, the work of the Civil Rights movement had just succeeded in bringing to an end segregation laws in 1964. The Johnson family, who were the founders of *Jet* and *Ebony* magazines, launched Fashion Fair Cosmetics in 1973, the first national make-up brand to cater for women of colour in the US. More traditionally white brands were starting to cater for women of colour too, due in part to the popularity of disco culture and Black female singers like Aretha Franklin and Natalie Cole.[51]

Model and businesswoman Beverly Johnson became the first African-American woman on the cover of a mainstream magazine when she featured on *American Vogue* in 1974 and the American supermodel Donyale Luna had been the first Black cover model on *British Vogue* in 1966. In west London, Black beauty pageants like Miss Black and Beautiful cropped up from the late 1960s, to celebrate Black beauty and establish their own beauty parameters outside of the exclusion of non-white beauty in the mainstream media. Black women could and did compete in mainstream beauty pageants in the UK but the winners, like Grenadian Jennifer Hosten, who was crowned Miss World in 1970, tended to have light skin and more typically Western features.[52] These wins were against a social backdrop containing plenty of racial tension and a culture that wanted to 'keep Britain white', amid mobilisation from the National Front. And in the UK, beauty products for people of colour were still hard to find in mainstream shops. Evidently, Charlie's image of carefree liberation wasn't felt by everyone.

By the 1980s, the UK and US had conservative governments, led by Margaret Thatcher and Ronald Reagan. A new social group, 'yuppies' – 'young urban professionals', – who were often college educated and well paid, became a target for beauty consumerism. The cult of celebrity seemed to be a way to sell anything and everything – from sports equipment to beauty products. But the biggest factor at play was that women had now entered the workforce in a significant way and beauty brands appeared to support the 'independent' woman – by offering them wares to spend their wages on and plenty of encouragement to do so.

Make-up boasted high-tech, long-wear formulas, designed to stay put 'day and night', presumably referring to post-work festivities, but the reality was the long hours many women in male-dominated industries were working to prove themselves, though that's less jovial as an ad strapline. Gone were the natural vibes of the 1970s and in their wake came airbrushed adverts selling a beauty standard that was impossible to achieve. Little wonder that tretinoin, an anti-ageing ingredient that had started to be used in skincare, led to a boom in the anti-ageing beauty market (oh, hi again, beauty anxiety) and haircare was now being designed to recreate the salon experience at home, with extended product ranges and the pressure to always look like the much-famed supermodels of the era. It's no surprise that notoriously male-run ad companies responded to female empowerment at work with objectification and pressuring women to focus more on their looks and body size – after all, women would never get those CEO jobs or run the world if they were too busy obsessing about how they look, would they? Talk about confusing times – work hard, look perfect, be thin, be tall, have huge breasts, but be 'free'.

We tend to look at the 1980s, with its huge, permed coifs and garish make-up, with a sense of amused nostalgia but there is a palpable undercurrent of panic to the beauty adverts of the time. In a 1989 Oil of Olay advert, Hollywood actor Kristine Sutherland is shown applying moisturiser, accompanied by the tagline: 'I don't intend to grow old gracefully… I'm fighting it every step of the way'. The battle to enter the workplace might have succeeded – but an increased pressure to resist visible ageing had opened up a new front on which they were told that had to *fight*. The Olay strapline might have read: *Ladies – you actually can't have it all, now you must really obsess about looking younger.* As described in *The Beauty Myth*, that came out in the 1990s in the wake of this era: 'Advertising aimed at women works by lowering our self-esteem. If it flatters our self-esteem it is not effective.'

Alongside delaying ageing, being thin was also mandatory. In this age of supposed empowerment, it was often presented to women through the lens of fitness culture, which had taken off in a big way. Statistically, eating disorders had been rising since the 1970s and there was at least now some public conversation following singer Karen Carpenter's anorexia and subsequent death from heart failure in 1983. The pressures women faced to look perfect in an increasingly looks-obsessed world were seriously mounting up – beauty anxiety was in full flow.

Who are we really beautifying ourselves for?

We are all subject to much of the same messaging about how and why we need to look attractive. It's a question without an answer, really, but one that is still important to ask if we are to unpack our own relationship with beauty culture and the status conferred on physical appearance. It can feel a little jarring to talk about patriarchy and the male gaze because we do now live in a society where we can discuss this openly, and broadly speaking, when something seems obviously sexist, it feels old-fashioned and receives complaints.

But it still exerts control over our beauty standards. I've seen that at some of the biggest publishing companies in the world who signs off covers and decides what is appealing to women is often a man. Like the male art editor I worked with, who always wanted our beauty shoots to be 'sexy' – whether we photographed a feminist activist or model – which never made sense to my experience of what women actually wanted in magazines. It's often the case that huge beauty brands and conglomerates have boardrooms full of men, running the show. That's not to say there's ill-intent here at all, but if we consider that historically, the application of beauty products has been primarily to improve one's appearance to be as pleasing to the male gaze as possible, how do we know who we're using it for? Can it ever be just ourselves?

An enduring message is that women must be beautiful in order to be loved – in our traditionally heteronormative culture. Take a Bourjois advert from 1939, featuring a woman sat at a dressing table holding a picture of her sweetheart, gazing at him longingly, waiting for his safe return from the war. The ad suggests that, while she waits, she could use her time instead to beautify herself in preparation for his return[53] – as if this will somehow bring him home faster, or more securely. This brings in the 'scarcity' technique again, which was particularly common in beauty advertising in the Second World War era, when anxiety about loved ones was at a height anyway. There was a physical lack of men creating a 'surplus' – that's the actual term used – of single women. As such, competition to marry was fiercer than ever and advertisers knew how to exploit this into beauty anxiety and profit. The ad comes from the male gaze, but from the female viewpoint, that is ultimately looking to please men – complicated, but oh so common.

Many beauty advertisements of the mid-century period from newspapers and popular magazines explicitly link high levels of grooming with the anxiety of keeping a man: as one Lux soap ad says: 'Husbands admire wives who keep their stockings perfect'. Another announces that 'Romance dies at the touch of dishpan hands'.[54] Meanwhile, Veto deodorant declared: 'Because you are the very air he breathes.' Although, to be fair to the creators of these ads, Roman poet Ovid had suggested almost 2,000 years earlier that a woman should take care of her exterior and interior traits to create a stable marital life so her husband would love her. So women have been blamed for 'letting themselves go' as the cause for marriage break-ups for a *very* long time …

We must be attractive – guided by whatever set of beauty

standards is on trend at the time – or no one will desire us. And if we are not desired (again, by a man), then, according to the patriarchy, what are we really *worth*? In the 1980s, women could work as hard as they liked, but the message was still very much that they were still there to be looked at. Adverts from the time explicitly reference keeping a man – just like the Bourjois ad from the war era – though this was more likely to be achieved by being sexy. A TV advert for the fragrance Jovan Musk Evening Edition from 1985 feels like watching softcore porn as actor Jayne Kennedy is shown spraying the scent suggestively across her body, finishing with her cleavage, implying you can spray it elsewhere too (don't, though, for that is a recipe for *thrush*). The tagline states: 'We help American women stay sexy'. Unlike Charlie a decade previously, which centred on independence and freedom, beauty marketing was selling 'sexy' to women from the perspective of male desire.

Popular scent Loulou's advert from the 1980s is voiced by a male narrator who seems to be following a woman as she walks around, then he creepily watches her through her window. It seems bizarre, but it mirrors the storylines of popular psychological thrillers of the era, like *Lady Beware* from 1987, in which the female protagonist is watched through the window of the shop where she works by a man who then stalks her. It seems to say that no matter what you do, the male gaze will always be dominant, and you are always being watched, ultimately letting women know who is really in control of them, their sexuality and their appearance.

Gender stereotypes were being enforced *everywhere* in the 1980s – so it's not a wild assumption to suggest that masculinity was being redefined in the wake of women entering the workplace but not in a progressive move towards equality, of course: men were starting to be sold toxic masculinity by the bucketload. Looking back, it's hard not to conclude that advertising was pushing hypermasculinity on men who felt – or were being suggested they feel – threatened by women's changing place in society. Beer ads from the time read like they're aimed at cavemen, the messaging essentially all coming down to: 'man up, look at some tits and drink this'. Music was doing the same: 'cock rock' bands like Mötley Crüe behaved exactly as you'd expect them to, using women as props in their videos. An Old Spice ad from the 1980s shows a 'rugged' man tugging a boat off the beach and into the sea, with a woman's voiceover talking breathily about his physical strength – it's hilarious, you should watch it.

What's less funny is that as leading feminists spoke out about the negative impact of pornography of the era, like the second wave of feminism, anyone who joined them was deemed as ugly or a man-hater. As Susan Faludi, author of the ground-breaking *Backlash: The Undeclared War Against American Women*, said in 1991: 'All that free-floating anxiety over declining wages, insecure employment, and over priced housing needs a place to light, and in the '80s, much of it fixed itself on women.'[55] If you were to ask a woman in the 1980s who she was 'looking good' for, she'd most likely say herself – just as we would now. You can't help but draw a parallel to today's high-glam beauty standards and trends and wonder: is it because we're in the midst of another feminist wave where we're re-evaluating so much – from racial inequality to definitions of gender and sexuality – maybe those dominant systems of oppression are feeling a little threatened again?

Re-reading the last 30 years …

Looking back now at the 1990s, the era I grew up in, some things have become very clear that were not to me then, as an impressionable teenager struggling with the beauty standards of the day. The 1996 advert for 'CK be' ordered 'be hot. be cool. just be', as thin models with jutting hipbones defined a new aesthetic that became known, appallingly, as 'heroin chic'. Meanwhile, chiselled CK under-wear models like actor Mark Wahlberg became the male body ideal. MTV played a huge part in sharing cultural norms across the Atlantic. Journalist Afua Hirsch wrote in a piece for the *Guardian* about how for her, as a mixed heritage woman, the era conveyed a split in body standards: 'It was the ultimate pornification of the female body in Black hip-hop culture, in which I was – by the middle of the decade – heavily immersed. White beauty norms became aligned with Kate Moss and other pale, bony models – some embodying profoundly emaciated, heroin chic – and the acceleration of unhealthy body images.'[56]

It was around this time that the beauty industry decided to go after a new market in earnest – enter teen beauty. Teenagers had been sold a heady diet of clothes and boybands since the 1950s but beauty was now less of a rite of passage into adulthood and more of a category of its own, with ever more entry-level products like tinted lip balms and body sprays sold as a stepping-stone – like a cosmetic training bra – between girlhood and womanhood. It's why they were inevitably sparky and pink, and so often looked like toys; Hard Candy's nail polishes even came with a fun plastic ring on. Teen magazines had long been the cool older sister you'd always wanted, ripe with boy advice and agony aunts to cure your woes, but now the main draw was the free beauty gifts that came with them, hooking girls into beauty at younger and younger ages. In the UK, *Sugar*, *Bliss*, *Mizz* and other titles aimed at and coveted by roughly 12–16-year-olds all mostly came with lip balm, eyeliner or other beguiling treats attached to the cover to persuade consumers to buy them.

Looking at wider pop culture, what women and girls were being sold still pandered heavily to male fantasy, rather than what women or teenagers might want. *Playboy* was now a lifestyle brand aimed at young girls and *More* magazine's 'Position of Fortnight' was routinely read by 14-year-olds across the UK. Sexualised videos for songs like Christina Aguilera's 'Genie in a Bottle' and Britney Spears' '... Baby One More Time' played on a loop on MTV, aimed at teenagers, but via the male gaze. The fragrance market had no end of scents to sell to teens, from those that promised to make you smell (feel?) like the two aforementioned pop stars who both created scents, as well as the preppy appeal of the Tommy Girl fragrance and more girlish perfume, Versace Pink Jeans. Despite the apparent strides women had made towards equality, there was a compliance to incredibly narrow beauty norms which – as I know too well – felt oppressive and non-negotiable. Anyone who didn't comply was seen as ugly or a bitch, says Allison Yarrow, author of *90s Bitch: Media, Culture, and the Failed Promise of Gender Equality*, who points to women like politician and diplomat Hillary Clinton as an example: 'The trailblazing women of the nineties were excoriated by a deeply sexist society. That's why we remember them as bitches, not victims of sexism.'[57] Even in pop culture, women like Jane in MTV's show *Daria*, Lisa Simpson, Nancy from *The Craft* and Miranda from *Sex and the City* – are seen as being difficult, dour or reckless for questioning patriarchal norms.

The rise of the internet brought us celebrity gossip and body-shaming websites. Thin was replaced by the even tinier size zero and celebrities like Lindsay Lohan, Mary-Kate Olsen and Nicole Richie (who all seemed to disappear a little more each week a new photo of them appeared in celebrity magazines) became the beauty ideals of the time. As is always the case with beauty standards especially in your impressionable teen years, fitting in, particularly being thin, meant everything. Thin was an achievement, like learning to drive or getting great grades – and was made to feel as important. Little wonder when even episodes of *Friends* – watched by the whole family – openly prized thinness as a beauty norm, from mentions of Rachel's 'chubby ankles' to how ridiculed 'Fat Monica' is. Other shows like *Fat Families* and even *The X Factor* openly demonised participants for not being thin.[58]

This was an era when glamour models were household names and featured everywhere you looked. The teen popstars that were marketed as youthful and wholesome suddenly appeared to 'grow up' fast: Britney dialled up the sex appeal and Christina's 'Dirrty' video signalled the end of her cutesy, merely suggestive pop days. Lip gloss got glossier (who didn't have a Lancôme Juicy Tube?) and boobs got bigger (thanks to Wonderbra, Victoria's Secret, chicken fillets and sizable breast implants). Courtesy of the internet, porn was now available for all to see online too.

Small cracks started to signal that the tide might be turning on limiting beauty standards. Dove's beauty campaign for 'real beauty', launched in 2004, felt truly shocking, simply for showing women in a campaign who didn't have abs (but who were fairly slim and attractive by conventional beauty standards) and the brand saw a 700 per cent uplift in sales. Plus-size (perhaps we'd term them 'mid-size'[59] now, which generally refers to anyone between a UK size 10-16, with anyone size 18 and over being referred to as plus size) models like Sophie Dahl had walked in major catwalk shows since the late 1990s and musician Beth Ditto performed and walked in Jean Paul Gaultier's SS2011 show to acclaim. Gok Wan's TV show *How to Look Good Naked* gave a platform to the women who had been ignored, criticised and forgotten about by fashion and beauty industries for decades (although the answer for every style crisis did seem to be a belted-in waist). It was the first time anyone had suggested that beauty could extend past the slim (literally) parameters that had been set for so long.

The demand for transparency and honesty grew in the 2010s. Protein World's infamous 'Are You Beach Body Ready?' ad created a backlash in 2015 and Nivea's 'White is Purity' deodorant campaign which ran in the Middle East prompted outrage in a way it might not have just ten years before. Social media platforms like Twitter (launched in 2006) gave people a 'visible' voice – prior to this, phone calls to complain could be ignored, emails deleted or letters thrown in the bin. Calls to make the beauty industry and beauty standards more inclusive were met with extended shade ranges: singer Rihanna launched Fenty Beauty – offering 40 shades of foundation – in 2017 and social media enabled conversations around cultural appropriation to be heard by the mainstream. But it raised big questions: namely, why hadn't it been done before?

All of this has helped lead us to the sometimes-confusing situation we find ourselves in today. On the one hand, you could say the power of YouTube, Instagram and TikTok and the opportunity they give people outside of the industry to showcase their creativity and influence the beauty conversation can only be a positive thing. Seeing people that might look like you online is a gamechanger for helping to normalise a wider spectrum of beauty standards – I've loved connecting with Indian goths across the globe. It's not just the big companies and media conglomerates dominating the culture and dictating how we should look and what we should buy. So much has changed: reality TV stars are as influential as models and Drag performers, once part of a subculture, have captured the imagination of the mainstream. On the other hand, the beauty industry is now absolutely huge, a global powerhouse – and everyone knows it. The rise in celebrities releasing beauty and wellness brands despite showing little interest in beauty previously makes it seem like launching a beauty brand is the new 'podcast' – everyone seems to have one.

Whoever and whatever inspires us from the new and more traditional voices active in beauty culture, we are still being encouraged to buy more than we perhaps need. And yet ... Despite the amount of influences we now have, a singular version of beauty has once more emerged, with sculpted faces, painted-on or even tattooed brows, very straight hair, pouting plumped lips and a certain oddly uniform look at the camera. It might be a passing trend, we can't assume everyone wanting this look feels 'lacking' in some way – I didn't feel burdened by my brows when I shaved them off in the noughties, after all. But it is interesting that as younger generations grow up with easy access to pornography, perhaps this leads to a pornification of beauty standards.

This whistle-stop tour of beauty history we have just been on has taken in plenty that seems mad, dangerous or just hopelessly out of date, even when it was mainstream just a few decades ago. So, the question is, what will we think when we look back on this period in time we are in now? The recent boom in the beauty industry might be compared to similar periods of growth, such as the 1980s and the post-war era. Those times also saw a large shift in gender roles that caused a patriarchal backlash. We have recently seen the growing influence of Black Lives Matter (BLM) and #Metoo and a challenge to long-held body standards, yet here we are, being pushed to obsess, fix and find dissatisfaction with every part our ourselves – just like women in the past. Looking back, our current cycle bears an uncanny resemblance to several historical points of female emancipation before patriarchy and capitalism swoop in to distract us from really levelling up.

The beauty industry and beauty products aren't *wrong*. We're not bad for liking them and getting pleasure from them – I'm almost rabid as soon as I get a sniff of anything from Sephora. As a form of self-expression, they're incredible tools for everyone. But all beauty is not created equally – and perhaps that's where the next chapter in this history lies, with ethical products, truly inclusive brands, the recognition of colonised beauty ideals within the industry and clocking where the male gaze, classism and Eurocentric values still dictate our appearance. Alongside this should be accountability for the part the beauty industry plays in upholding centuries of toxic beauty standards and commodifying women to the point where one in six women now feel dissatisfied with how they look.[60]

To go back to my original point – if we have so much beauty on offer, and more diversity, why do we loathe the way we look more than ever before? It's not inherently female to dislike our appearance or fixate on changing it at any cost to our happiness and self-esteem – that's not something that comes as a free gift stuck to the front of our first rattle. We aren't born with an internal 'self-destruct' appearance loathing button so something is *still* making us feel like we're lacking.

I think the beauty boom we're in presently has happened so fast and moved so quickly that we've barely had a moment to step back and consider what beauty ideals we are being sold and whether we agree with them. We use the phrase 'you do you' as a way of reclaiming our choices on everything from 'thirsty' social media pics to 'tweakments' or to justify spending money on beauty beyond our means like an addiction. But I'd like to pose this final, vital question: are we ever really just doing us, or are we enacting the current iteration of beauty ideals that we've been sold for centuries? Is that what's really at play when we feel like we *must* ward off a wrinkle with preventative Botox at 25, or we *have to* resize our noses so they look good on the 'gram? If we look back at how closely the beauty industry mirrored societal values and the views of the dominant gaze, chances are we just might decide that we are buying into something we don't agree with. We all deserve to reclaim the power over our appearance in a way that allows us to recapture the pure joy and lightness of my first encounter with that £1 green mascara. We just need that crucial brain space and context to step back and remember that everything we buy is being *sold* to us.

Take back the power

This is all well and good, I hear you say, but faced with the crushing power of the vast marketing budgets of the beauty industry, not to mention what sometimes feels like the whole internet, how exactly can I, one individual and busy person, climb out from under the weight of all this pressure? How do we resist attaching our hope and our self-esteem to anything from a sparkly whitening toothpaste to breast enlargement to an anti-ageing cream? I'm a big fan of slow beauty – the practice of using products to the end, thinking sustainably and regarding beauty as a pleasurable, sensory experience but when the lure of an impulse beauty buy, treatment or 'jar of hope' takes over, here's a little something I've started doing to work out if I really want it – or something else is at play. It's simple – just a series of questions to help me understand my thoughts and prevent all that clever marketing and societal pressure taking over completely. Let's take a face massaging device I was perusing as an example ...

Anita, why do you want it? I think it could help me look a bit younger.

Why? Because I'm starting to look older.

What was the catalyst? I saw a picture where I looked exhausted and it's freaking me the hell out.

Why? Because I don't feel old and I hate being categorised, but society treats women above 35 like they don't exist, and aren't attractive. Fertility being the cultural marker of female worth.

OK, but you know why that's the case though, right? (SIGH) Yes. Patriarchal views of women's appearance and the multiple industries that sell youth to women as the sole beauty ideal.

Go deeper – what's the real structural reason that's happening? Because the worse women feel about themselves, the less they'll achieve and stay out of the workforce/world/way. Instead of chasing their dreams, they'll spend their time worrying about their looks.

Who profits? Keeping women small, feeling old, unworthy and ugly also supports patriarchy and capitalism. Entire industries profit when we're sold stuff we don't need via the creation of beauty anxiety.

Who isn't feeling like this? Men – largely speaking. They don't have quite the same pressure to look under 30 their entire lives. Often they're said to look better as they age.

How does this make you feel? Furious that it's 2023 and this bullshit is still playing out. I'm fed up, angry and really done with it. Maybe this is why I'm tired …

BOOM! That's it. So, is there a non-product-related fix here? I could go to bed earlier and stop dicking about on TikTok until 1am and limit who I follow on social media to avoid comparison.

Anything else? I could use the retinol I've already spent £60 on first, try facial massage or use that facial voucher I have knocking about.

OK – so name three things you can do to change your mindset on this belief right now?

1) I'll add ten women my age or older who embrace their age to my social media feed and remove anyone I compare myself negatively to. (But I'll make sure I remind myself that anyone I follow could filter their pics or have had undisclosed cosmetic enhancements.)
2) I'll watch one TV show or film a week with women older than me, who I think are awesome. Or spend time with a friend or family member who fits that bill.
3) I'll make a moodboard of make-up, hair and fashion looks I want to try JUST because I love them and they represent me. And I'll try one new thing every week.

Great – still want the gadget? Not as much as before but maybe still a little bit.

Cool – can you wait a month, do all the above and then reassess it? Yes – absolutely.

WHITE AND UGLY

'Classically not beautiful is a fancy way of saying ugly, and denouncing you.'

– Actor Viola Davis

NOBODY IS BORN HATING their skin colour. We develop that belief because as we grow up, the reinforcement that dark skin is less desirable than white skin is *everywhere*.

I grew up being shown there was a hierarchy of skin colour. It was present in the cartoons and fairy tales I consumed and the dolls I played with. It was in the Bollywood movies I watched with my family that feature almost exclusively light-skinned actors and well-meaning aunties telling me to stay out of the sun for fear of me getting any darker. Maybe my clown efforts on the previous page might have been preferable (it's the closest I've been to white privilege, anyway).

As a teen in the 1990s, when first shopping for beauty, it was like we – women with dark skin – just didn't exist. The beauty aisles didn't cater for our needs, you rarely saw us on TV and we were seldom celebrated in magazines. On the rare occasions we were, it was alongside the implication that our skin tone was shameful or undesirable in some way. But I learned about the hierarchy of skin colour and race way before that, though.

Nursery was the most fun I've ever had. We made Welsh cakes every week, played games and sang nursery rhymes. It was almost sickeningly idyllic – like something out of another era. But primary school, especially the private one I was about to join, had an entirely different vibe. I wasn't a shy kid but I struggled to navigate this new community who all knew each other from nursery and already knew some of the basics of reading and writing. My notable skill? I could draw an excellent robin, which was essentially a circle with creepy-looking bird-arms – I was five, after all. Within a week of joining, my internal panic had taken over and I was swathed in itchy, furious stress-induced eczema (something I'm still prone to now). But amid this chaos, there was hope. And it came in the form of my new pal, let's call her Tara.

I met Tara in the playground one breaktime. She joined

a collective game of 'horses' – using a skipping rope slung around somebody's waist as reins – and we paired up, pretending to trot like ponies and giggling endlessly. After that, we instinctively sought each other out. She was in a different class but every break time, three times a day, we'd meet up and play together until the whistle called us back to our lessons. School felt a little less lonely now that I had Tara. Our friendship replaced the awkward 'I don't know anyone' shuffle I'd been doing and quelled that internal fear we all have of being left out or side-lined, especially as kids. Plus, she made *excellent* pony noises – always a bonus in a pal.

Two weeks into our friendship, as usual I went to find Tara at break time. I knew something was off immediately. Instead of her typical cheery approach, she was scuffing her patent shoes in the gravel and looking downwards sheepishly. I suggested we play with our skipping ropes, but without looking up, she said: 'Sorry. My mum said I can't play with you anymore because you're brown.' After an unbearably awkward silence, I muttered 'OK' and shuffled away. How are you supposed to launch into an eloquent diatribe on the inherent wrongs of racism when you're five – particularly when you don't understand them yourself? Her blue eyes looked up at me for a split second before I left; we never played together or even really spoke again. I never told anyone what had happened, not even my parents. I just buried it within. Shame has this manipulative way of making you believe its truth, as it swears you to secrecy. As I write this, I can still feel the sting of that moment so viscerally.

That feeling when I was told that I was 'different' and that this difference was considered negative was the first fall in a domino effect that began to generate a sense of inferiority within me. That incident wasn't the only one; they came in so many different forms. From consistently being overlooked to play an angel in the school nativity despite our tiny class sizes and my pleading – presumably a brown angel was too much of a stretch to imagine at least in those days – to being told my skin was the colour of poo as a retort, to a game of tag where instead of being 'it', you got 'paki disease'. Everything reinforced my feelings of otherness at an age when, as we all know, we're searching for safety, reassurance and to belong in our community. From five, it was made abundantly clear to me why I didn't: my skin colour and therefore my race. Even at this still-young age, I was tired of being treated as though I mattered less, but now, tragically, I almost expected it.

Another incident that wounded me at primary school was when another girl claimed that my beloved *The Little Mermaid* toy – from a McDonald's Happy Meal no less – was in fact hers. Our teacher took it from me and immediately gave it to her, unquestioningly taking her word for it. I felt the injustice and wrongdoing in every fibre of my being – but said nothing. The next day, she returned with a directive from her mother to apologise and give it back to me, but the damage had been done. It didn't feel like justice, it was yet another reinforcement and reminder of my place in an unspoken hierarchy based on my race. My skin colour meant that not only was I different, but I was also less believable and my feelings were less important than those of my white peers'. As an adult I can of course contextualise these incidents – thanks to therapy – they're microaggressions – but as a child, they just layered on top of each other, like Tetris bricks of shame, creating a quiet, omnipresent self-doubt. Conversely, Tara and this other little girl received some feedback too: that they'd always be believed, they'd always be accepted and they'd always come out on top (take a bow, 'white privilege').

Racism succeeds when you question your own intuition – effectively, you gaslight yourself. This never really goes away. Or at least, not yet, for me. I even asked a friend to check my examples above to see if they really were prejudice or if I was just being, y'know, 'oversensitive'. I needed somebody else to validate my experiences. Despite bucketloads of jarring experiences growing up, I know that I escaped from school very lightly. I have friends who were relentlessly taunted and even physically harmed by racist bullies during their formative years.

What's truly disappointing is that despite the decades between my schooling and now, we're still facing huge issues around racial difference. Figures from 2021 show that UK schools recorded more than 60,000 racist incidents in five years[1] and those are likely just the ones that can be proven. Mocking accents, features, appearance and name-calling are all too common – especially now bullying exists online too. In 2019, the chief executive of Race Council Cymru (RCC) in Wales, Uzo Iwobi, said that a three-and-a-half-year-old child at a Welsh school made an extremely offensive racist comment, which was part of a string of racist incidents at the school: 'Some of the language could not actually be attributed to a three-and-a-half-year-old, so they're hearing this from somebody,' Iwobi said, citing the lack of BAME history on the curriculum as one of the causes of the issue and highlighting the 'burning need to deal with this injustice'.[2]

Being othered for racial difference during childhood has the effect of ivy clambering up a wall – it's always reaching for the next foothold. The results can manifest as low self-esteem, anger, poor body image or an intense internalised self-loathing based on race and ethnicity, known as internalised racism. I felt this as a young teen when I told somebody I was Italian and not Indian, as it felt far more acceptable. It would be funny, if it wasn't so sad. Multiple studies have confirmed that racism directly affects childhood development too and when a child's stress response system stays activated at a high level for long periods of time it can have a 'wear and tear' effect on their developing brains, negatively impacting how they learn, their physical wellbeing and mental health. This fatigue from coping with racism in its plentiful stress-triggering forms could perhaps account for the reason for racial disparities in chronic illness and shorter lifespans (across all income levels).

Racism is a daily unwelcome companion from our earliest years, in which our only concern should be how to draw a robin that doesn't look *terrifying*. As a child of colour in Western society, you learn a lot of lessons. 1) You must work twice as hard to even be noticed, and often you're expected to. 2) You should keep yourself and your voice small to avoid repercussions, and 3) when something is unjust or unfair, raising it or causing a 'fuss' isn't an option – you will be labelled as argumentative. But I'm not a child anymore, none of us are, though we often still play by these limiting rules. Those limitations can affect our behaviour as adults – we might 'code-switch' in certain environments, for example, changing our behaviours, speech and appearance to blend into different situations where we might be the only person of colour. Being made to feel like we have to be small or try to fit in (often to co-exist safely) is also mirrored by the Eurocentric beauty standards we are held against and that are held against us, making us feel ugly.

In 2012, I wrote a feature about the (slow) changes the beauty industry was making to finally include people of colour; the hundreds of responses I received from readers saying how they felt they were finally being represented in the industry and that they'd experienced the exclusion I had growing up were overwhelming and incredible. In the piece, I framed the progress the beauty industry was making as a celebration, but I didn't feel quite as joyful about it deep down. Sure, there have been sizable changes to the beauty industry and mainstream media in how it considers racial diversity in the last ten years – that is great news. I'm often asked to enthuse about that and celebrate it, which I do – but never with an entirely full heart. Why? Because I hate the motive behind it: that after so many years of deliberate exclusion we must be seen to be grateful when white-owned brands create foundation ranges for us or when we're included in a luxury beauty campaign. It takes a global popstar like Rihanna to create a range like Fenty Beauty (launched in 2017), to centre people of colour in a way the beauty industry has failed to do for *centuries*. I'm grateful to her, of course – it was a seismic moment – but I'm not grateful that she *had* to create it in the first place.

The outward expression of an inner belief about racial stereotypes can manifest as horrific hate crimes but it operates in more subtle and covert ways too. Whiteness refers to a prevailing cultural norm, where having white skin – and the culture and system of privileges around it – is the implicit standard or norm to which all else is compared.[3] Everything that is not white is other, different or abnormal in some way and anything that sits outside of a Eurocentric beauty standard has been seen as ugly. Despite the multiculturalism we pride ourselves on in the UK, blonde hair and blue eyes are still the most aspirational attributes for women – one magazine I worked with would even see an uptick in sales if there was a blonde celebrity or model on the cover. Just recently, I overheard a group of white mums chatting; one was relaying her disappointment that her baby's hair wasn't blonde anymore, jokingly pondering if lemon juice might lighten it. Another agreed and offered that she was desperately hoping her unborn child would have blue eyes. The others nodded in solidarity – this was an agreed beauty norm. Sure, these comments might seem like a mere preference, perhaps they even mirror the parent's appearance, but they still tell of a hierarchy of attributes that are considered beautiful. And whenever we value one thing over another, we diminish the other.

Often, if the beauty of people of colour is celebrated, it's largely because they have a proximity to whiteness in some way. The 'curl ranges' of haircare brands are most often represented and promoted by models with light skin and ringlet curls, because this is more palatable and relatable to the white gaze than tightly coiled afro-textured hair. When a model with dark skin is celebrated, their features often fall within the remit of 'acceptable' ethnicity: their noses are small, their cheekbones are high, their hair is straight and they're slim. This allows them to still be aspirational to the white gaze, appearing as a 'white woman dipped in chocolate'.[4] Often those bodies that are allowed through by the beauty's largely white gatekeepers are hypersexualised, exoticised, seen as forbidden or exceptional.

Our concepts of beauty, ugliness and race have become so deeply conflated in a way that's created a lasting and devastating effect. Almost two decades ago, a US study called Denying Diversity compared the self-images of Latin, Black and white women who all agreed on what is thought to be 'perfect beauty' – white, slim, tall with a straight nose.[5] When I spoke to her for *Glamour* magazine, psychologist Dr Tina Mistry explained that, despite what we might see as some progress in representation, this beauty ideal still holds true: 'We carry this historical and intergenerational trauma from slavery and colonisation. We need to explore how that could have impacted the generations above us and how that's filtered down to the beauty standards of today,' she told me.

We live in a world with a strange dichotomy: where some often see a tan as the benchmark of a successful holiday or don't feel themselves without a layer of fake tan, while those with naturally dark skin are made to feel ugly, and othered. The 2011 documentary *Dark Girls*, which looks at colourism – a form of discrimination against dark-skinned people in favour of those with lighter skin from the same race – features a poignant scene in which a dark-skinned Black woman explains how the elevation of lighter skin over dark has deeply affected her.[6] She recalls as a child asking her mother to put bleach in the bathwater in the hope it would lighten her skin. Another woman revealed that she hoped her daughter wouldn't be as dark-skinned as she is. Actor Lupita Nyong'o told the BBC, 'I definitely grew up feeling uncomfortable with my skin colour because I felt like the world around me awarded lighter skin.' She added that her lighter-skinned younger sister was praised for her beauty: 'Self-consciously that translates into: "I'm not worthy".'[7]

When interviewing actor Charithra Chandran for *Allure* magazine, it struck me how, though over a decade younger than me, she faced a similar narrative on skin colour – 'I grew up with people telling me that I would be pretty if I was lighter-skinned. I remember [someone] said to my grandma, who is quite light-skinned, "Your granddaughter's cute. Shame she didn't take after you." She meant my skin colour.'[8]

We associate a term like 'white supremacy' with totalitarian regimes, dictators and the extreme and violent expressions of racism throughout our history and current events. But shocking events like the murder of George Floyd by Derek Chauvin, a white policeman, in 2020 have forced many to confront how white supremacy and systemic racism are still operating throughout our society today. But we are far less aware of how white beauty standards are the prevailing physical ideal and how this affects millions who do not have white privilege. White beauty standards are afforded their power in part because whiteness and proximity to whiteness has been the unquestioned norm for so long that their privileges are almost invisible to those who are elevated.

For centuries now, Eurocentric beauty ideals have been ascribed a higher value over all else and have been sold to all ethnicities as the beauty ideal – anything else has largely been considered ugly or in need of correction. The fundamental issue isn't just the representation of people of colour – that's a symptom of a much more deeply embedded problem. The bigger issue is the legacy of white supremacy that is gatekeeping our beauty standards. I wish my experiences as a child were a thing of the past, but they're not. That a friend's little girl recently asked why she wasn't white and pretty like her adopted mother is evidence for how the conversation hasn't moved on nearly enough – and how these beliefs about beauty are so easily transmitted. Over time, being made to feel ugly for your skin colour, racial characteristics or your heritage chips away at your self-esteem, self-worth and confidence, leaving you exhausted from the cumulative and unmerciful impact of feeling ugly.

So far, representation for people of colour in the beauty industry, the media, in fashion and the advertising and technology industries it's linked to has perpetuated racist beauty standards that kept people of colour from being represented on catwalks, in magazines and the beauty aisles, and have limited people's beauty choices. They have put the onus on us to push, lobby and create our own outlets. The issue is that none of this exclusion – which is often deeply nuanced and ingrained – can be wished away by token representation. Why? Because it has nothing to do with our skin colour, but everything to do with *whiteness*.

When did whiteness begin?

The skin of our primate ancestors was covered in protective fur and when we began to lose this, we gained pigment in our skin to protect it from the sun. As humans started to move beyond Africa, eventually there were mutations in the genes accounting for skin colour variants. Darker skin contains extra melanin, which limits harmful UV exposure in hotter climes, while lighter skin is better able to synthesise vitamin D – useful in areas with low UV exposure.[9] Research has shown that the light-skinned genes some of us have now are much more recent than science initially thought and it was between 12,000 to 6,000 years ago that skin colour differences became obvious.[10] So, our skin just adapted to protect us in our new environments – no hierarchy, no racism, no power to be wielded, literally just skin doing its job. That's simple and magical when you think about it, right?

Likewise, our features evolved to suit out environmental needs, as psychologist Nancy Etcoff explores in her book *Survival of the Prettiest: The Science of Beauty*, first published in 1999: 'Noses carry air into the lungs. They evolved into long narrow shapes in climates where the air was cold or dry and needed to be warmed and moistened before reaching the lungs. People of northern Europe of Middle Eastern ancestry often inherit long noses with narrow nostrils (perfect for restricting air flow). In humid environments, the short, wide nose common to many African and Asian people are more efficient.'

The long-standing preference for pale skin and its signifier of wealth or class can be traced far back into antiquity. Those who toiled outdoors would naturally see their skin tan and darken from sun exposure, while those who didn't have to do so remained lighter. In Ancient China, a preference for a 'milk white' complexion can be found in records from the Han Dynasty that ruled China from 206 BC to AD 220.[11] The Aztecs in central America also used cosmetics to achieve paler skin. In Korea, having 'jade white' skin is a beauty ideal that goes back as far back as the Gojoseon era, which lasted until 100 BC. In India, the now-abolished Hindu caste system (which has been abolished by the state but is still deeply embedded in the society) is often attributed to the arrival of prehistoric Indo-European Aryan settlers in India in around 1500 BC and has since been used to discriminate against people with darker skin, who were forced into lower castes with lower-paid work, while those with lighter skin tones had more social mobility and opportunities.

Interestingly, there also seems to be a correlation between paleness and perceived femininity: in paintings from Ancient Egypt, women are often depicted with lighter skin than men and in Ancient Japan, women sometimes whitened their faces with rice powder as a form of 'moral duty'. In her book Etcoff suggests there might be a biological factor: 'Women tend to be paler than men of the same race because women tend to have less hemoglobin in their blood and less melanin in their skin.'[12] Or it could also be attributed to women working indoors and men outdoors – it's likely that women depicted in art were privileged, so perhaps they didn't work or even go outside much at all. What we do know is that, thousands of years later, from Bollywood to the hip-hop videos that have shown repeated preference for light-skinned performers, the relationship between fair skin, privilege and femininity has become far more complex than just biological variants.

Research in 2008 by the University of Toronto also found that women tend to be attracted to darker features in men because they indicate 'sex and danger', while men gravitate towards lighter skin and its associations to 'purity and innocence'. Dr Shyon Baumann, a sociologist at the university, told the *Independent*: 'What the research shows is that our aesthetic preferences operate to reflect moral preferences. Within our cultures we have a set of ideals about how women should look and behave. Lightness and darkness have particular meanings attached to them and we subconsciously relate those moral preferences to women.'[13] Either way, both are social constructs that have become accepted as truths and beauty standards.

That subconscious association is everywhere in our society; just look at the phrase a 'black sheep'. It originally came from black wool being harder to dye but became synonymous with the mark of the devil from the 18th century. In our modern vernacular, it means a disfavoured or dishonest member of a group. Innocence in Christianity has traditionally been embodied by angels and virgin brides, almost always represented by the colour white. In East Asia, a light-skinned 'fair' heroine always showed virtue and goodness and in Western fairy tales like *Snow White and The Seven Dwarfs* and *Cinderella*, et al, it's the same case. Black was the colour of the underworld for both the ancient Romans and Greeks – becoming associated with mourning, death, evil, magic and folklore. According to Greek legend, Phaeton's chariot drew the sun too close to the Earth, resulting in the darkening of the faces of Ethiopians.[14]

During the Middle Ages, Europe entered a period of 'curiosity' about the wider world. Venetian explorer Marco Polo travelled the 'Silk Road' through Asia, reporting his findings and observing customs in the 13th and 14th centuries. The 'age of exploration' began in the 15th century, paving the way for the subjugation of peoples in the Americas, Africa, South East Asia and others by white Europeans. Christopher Columbus 'discovered' the Americas while looking for an alternative route to East Asia and returned there several times in the 15th and 16th centuries. In the letters he wrote about his travels, he made rudimentary observations of the people he found there with a chilling bias in mind: their suitability for work and their potential to convert to Christianity. He made notes on indigenous people's skin colour, rituals, habits and temperaments (including charming comments, such as 'like beasts' and 'excessively cowardly').[15] His accounts, rooted in otherness and a sense of European and Christian superiority, provided a basis for subsequent observations from other explorers, writers and academics of the time. These Europeans ignored anything they found that was contrary to their view of the people they encountered as savages and primitives, such as systems of government, international and regional trade links, skilled craftsmen and scientific knowledge.

Naturalists – the scientists of the era – were by the 1500s starting to collect and organise plants and animals into categories, a system known as taxonomy. They applied this system to humans too, looking at locations, skin colour, physical characteristics and habits, eventually leading to the word 'race' being coined in Europe in 1560, meaning 'people descended from a common ancestor, class of persons allied by common ancestry',[16] but also used to classify people into groups,[17] almost akin to a word like 'breed'. French physician and traveller François Bernier is considered by some to have created the first classification of humans into races in the 17th century. The categories he came up with were Europeans, Far Easterners, Negroes and Lapps.[18] The timing of this rather neatly (and ominously) matches up with the emergence of Europe's empires and the beginnings of the transatlantic slave trade.

The transatlantic slave trade route began to be established as merchants would export goods to Africa, trading them for gold, ivory, spices and enslaved African people. Those ships would then visit the American colonies, where the enslaved people were sold to plantation owners in exchange for commodities like sugar, cotton and tobacco, which were transported back to Europe and sold for huge profits. Between 1640 and 1807, when the slave trade (but not slavery) was made illegal in the British Empire, an estimated

3.1m African people (of whom 2.7m actually arrived) were taken to British colonies like the Caribbean and Americas.

Britain first began to establish control over the indigenous people of different regions in the 16th century. Colonisation often meant replacing indigenous culture, language, religions and traditions with British ones and almost always stripping indigenous people of their land, rights and freedoms. Other European countries with sizable colonies included Spain, who had a huge empire in the Americas. Portugal mostly focused its colonial attentions on the Indian Ocean and also Brazil, using the latter to produce sugarcane crops with forced labour from indigenous people and enslaved Africans. France's empire included parts of Africa and the Americas too, including chunks of what are now Canada and Louisiana – it was bigger than the Roman Empire at its height. The Dutch colonised many parts of the world, occupying African countries for many years. Such were the riches to be gained from crops, precious metals and the extensive commodity of non-European, non-white people for cheap and forced labour that these colonial powers often fought each other for control over a region.

Interestingly, before colonisation, there are accounts from European explorers that appear to marvel at elements of indigenous culture they encountered. Academic and author of *Don't Touch My Hair*, Emma Dabiri, quotes the writing of Alvise Cadamosto, a Venetian explorer who visited West Africa in 1455 and 1456. Describing the Jalofs of the south side of the Senegal river, in the oldest European reference we have to African hair, in *Voyages* (1455), he wrote that: 'Both sexes go bare-footed and uncovered, but weave their hair with *beautiful tresses*, which they tie in various knots, though it be short.'[19]

Dabiri explains, 'Once European objectives became characterized by the pursuit of enslavement and colonization, there was a dramatic shift in tone in descriptions of Africans.'[20] These previously observational accounts started to be replaced by more negative ones that revolved around a European obsession with African 'idleness', which introduced the idea that they weren't using their time productively – they were essentially lazy. Before being forced to pay high colonial taxes, African people had more time to look after their hair and self-care - but this, Dabiri says, was maddening to the British. As Cadamosto said: 'The idle husbands put [their wives] upon braiding and fettishing out their wooly hair (in which sort of ornament they are prodigious proud and curious), keeping them every day, for many hours together, at it. '[21]

These attitudes began to seep insidiously into every part of academia or thought. In the 18th century, Scottish philosopher David Hume proclaimed: 'I am apt to suspect the Negroes to be naturally inferior to the Whites. There scarcely ever was a civilised nation of that complexion, nor even any individual, eminent either in action or in speculation. No ingenious manufacture among them, no arts, no sciences.' (Hume's attitudes to race were conveniently skipped over as part of my philosophy degree, sadly – our current education system is absolutely part of the structure upholding racism.)

From here onwards, it was a short and inevitable step to a hierarchy of beauty with whiteness at the pinnacle and blackness equated to being little more than an animal. Colonisers justified their actions partly through appearance. Black people were seen as sub-human because they had wool-like hair and as such, were dehumanised and treated like livestock, which was also a method of rendering their suffering unimportant too.

Let's talk about words for a moment. In the late 17th century, the laws regulating slaves and servants, like the 1681 Servant

Act in Jamaica (copied for use in South Carolina), started to use 'whites' to describe the enslaving classes rather than 'Christians' as they had done before. One of the reasons given for this is because if Africans became Christians, then they – as fellow Christians – could no longer be enslaved according to church law.[22] By the 18th century, the term 'race' was being used for 'ranking' and sorting people in colonised nations to distinguish who was free or uncolonised (Europeans) from those who were owned and had been colonised (like the First Nations, Indians, indigenous people of South America, Africans and more). This was also when Christoph Meiners and Johann Blumenbach, naturalists of the era, were the first to use the term 'Caucasian'. The name came from the Caucasus mountain range, historically seen as being at the extreme eastern side of Europe, where the continent meets Asia. Caucasians, these men decided, were the most beautiful race.

During the Enlightenment period of the later 17th and 18th centuries, the focus on rationalism, away from religion and superstition, saw an increasing interest in science and a belief that it could be used to understand the world. Which sounds great, except that the new scientific disciplines were shot through with the biases of those developing them. With the result that racist categorisations and assumptions could now be backed up by 'scientific' rationale, setting a basis for the discourse on scientific racism we now have. White superiority became a scientific fact to many. After all – you can't question science, can you?

If you are going to enslave, demean, subjugate or otherwise treat whole groups of people as inferior to you, it helps if you can come up with a reason why it's OK for you to do so. This is, in crude terms, what the myth of white superiority, conveniently backed up with spurious science, did for colonialism.

The legacy of which we now have the task of dismantling. And part of that legacy is still found in our beauty standards, as I hope I have begun to show. Should we have learned the above in our history lessons as a part of a curriculum of ownership over Britain's colonising past, perhaps as a nation we'd be more adept at spotting the grip whiteness still has on our culture, society and beauty standards.

Colourism is one such beauty standard. It seems invisible to those who haven't experienced it, either benefiting from the privileges that lighter skin can give you, or the discrimination having darker skin can cause. Since its early years, Hollywood has used dark skin as a signifier of ugly, unsexy and unattractive. Dark-skinned Black female actors of the early Hollywood era, like Hattie McDaniel or Louise Beavers, were often typecast in matronly, desexualised 'mammies' roles, partly because their skin colour meant there was no chance of them being seen as attractive, or disturbing the segregated narrative that black and white couldn't – and shouldn't – mix romantically.

McDaniel won a Best Supporting Actor Oscar for 1939's epic *Gone with the Wind* – which she had to accept in a ceremony held in a segregated hotel. In doing so, she became the first African-American to win an Oscar. She went on to play a huge 74 roles in her career, mostly limited to playing a maid. In the US at the time, there was a fear of having traces of African heritage, which peaked during segregation in the US (which ended as recently as the 1960s). Under the racist Jim Crow laws in the American south, the 'one-drop rule' meant that anyone with a trace of African ancestry was labelled as Black, therefore subject to discrimination – adding to the 'fear' of dark skin and elevation of white skin and features as desirable.

You may think that we have come a long way from there, and in some ways that's true, but the idea of dark not being beautiful still persists. As recently as 2020, Viola Davis was said to be 'less classically beautiful than [Kerry] Washington', an actor who has lighter skin and features that are more in line with Eurocentric beauty standards, by the *New York Times*.[23] 'Less classically beautiful' cloaks what we all know to be true: whiteness is still controlling the beauty narrative. Lupita Nyong'o says she was once told she was 'too dark' for television at an audition and actor Zendaya Coleman has spoken about her privilege as a light-skinned Black woman, as the film industry's 'acceptable version of a Black girl'.[24] Do a quick poll yourself – the number of lighter-skinned actors of colour in Hollywood, particularly female, is stark compared to their darker-skinned counterparts. In 2018, Beyoncé and Solange Knowles' father, Mathew Knowles, admitted that in his youth, he only dated white or light-skinned Black women and that having light skin undeniably aided success: 'When it comes to Black females, who are the people who get their music played on pop radio?' Knowles said. 'Mariah Carey, Rihanna, the female rapper Nicki Minaj, my kids [Beyoncé and Solange], and what do they all have in common?'[25] That same trend continues across music, fashion and generally for many public figures.

In 2015, the Republican Party ran opposition videos featuring Democrat Barack Obama with significantly darkened skin.[26] In 1994, *TIME* magazine ran a cover image of O.J. Simpson's mugshot that seemed to some to have been darkened intentionally to make him appear more 'menacing', which suited their damning coverline 'An American Tragedy' – they later replaced the darkened picture with an unaltered one. This 'bad is black' effect was coined by Professor Adam Alter of New York University, who conducted studies that showed a link between skin tone and perceptions of criminality and general negativity.[27] Conversely, Kerry Washington, Eva Longoria, Beyoncé Knowles, Diana Ross,

Naomi Campbell and Lupita Nyong'o are just a few names in the list of mostly female celebrities whose images have been lightened for magazine covers or beauty campaigns in recent years to keep them in line with the beauty standards that *still* prize whiteness above all.

Examples of Hollywood starlets that eradicated visible traces of their heritage are plentiful: Rita Hayworth, aka Margarita Cansino, was actually Spanish and Irish-American and had extensive treatments to conform to Hollywood's white beauty standards, like painful electrolysis on her hairline to make it less low, dark and ethnic-looking. Merle Oberon was born in Mumbai, known then as Bombay, in 1911 and was Anglo-Indian – but obscured her origins by claiming to be from Tasmania. Even popular 1920s jazz singer Josephine Baker was known to use lemon juice as a skin lightener on her already light Black skin – and spoke of it openly. More recently, US news anchor Julie Chen Moonves (now in her 50s) revealed she had double eyelid surgery when she was 25 after a news director said that she'd never get anywhere because of her eyes: 'When you're interviewing someone you look disinterested and bored because your eyes are so heavy, they are so small.'[28]

The ways that whiteness has defined ugly and beautiful could fill an entire book of its own. Perhaps one of the reasons enough hasn't been done to dismantle colourism is because it's easier to look away than admit that practices like skin lightening still exist. As a kid, I'd often see my older cousins – all brilliant women in medical school – using complexion lightening creams; this attitude about skin tone was blatant, it was accepted, and it was *everywhere*. The skin-lightening industry is estimated to be worth billions globally. In Nigeria, 77 per cent of women use them and in India nearly two-thirds of skincare is for skin bleaching.[29] Though strong skin-lightening products aren't readily available or regulated for use in the UK, I've heard of strong lightening products being available under counters in parts of London from friends in the Bangladeshi community, for example, but because they're not regulated, these products might have side effects like scarring, burns and kidney issues.

Some of our most-loved beauty brands sell 'whitening' products in a variety of African and Asian countries, though they are usually euphemistically described – to ease consciences – as designed for exfoliation or to address hyperpigmentation. In this way, the beauty industry shirks its moral responsibilities for profit and Western media writes about it with an odd detachment, as if it's nothing to do with Western culture and a desire to gain some level of privilege associated with whiteness or to match up to Western beauty standards. But there's a more direct cause, as academic and colourism expert Dr Yaba Blay explains in a feature for *Byrdie*: 'At the time of so-called "independence", these European countries were flooding their colonial places with their products and using whiteness as a way to sell the products. People were attempting to gain some level of power and privilege that's associated with whiteness, and they started bleaching their skin in the '50s.'[30]

In South Africa in the 1970s, there was an epidemic of a severe skin issue called ochronosis because of excessive skin bleaching to achieve the privileges aligned with a lighter skin colour. In the same decade, Fair & Lovely, an Indian brand that has notoriously promoted skin-lightening creams and the ideal of fair being beautiful, was bought by Hindustan Unilever. The elevation of whiteness – and the creation of whitening and lightening beauty products – was a way to keep the legacy colonisation and beauty standards of white supremacy in charge.

Fair & Lovely often had controversial adverts featuring leading Bollywood actors until it changed tack after pressure in 2020, rebranding as Glow & Lovely. Bollywood actor Priyanka Chopra – who now also appears in TV and film in the West – was in some of those ads (though she has since apologised for it). In a Ponds advert from 2011, she's shown being dumped by her fair-skinned lover in favour of another fair-skinned woman. The advert claims the Ponds White Beauty Cream gives you a 'radiant pinkish white glow'. In a follow-up advert, Chopra is visibly lighter and wins back the admiration of her former lover. The dramatic format of the ad plays to the huge influence of Bollywood in India – but also to what skin-lightening creams sell: success, beauty, wealth and love. All through the guise of whiteness. Handing off the burden of colourism to those who experience it and accepting no responsibility for helping to eradicate it is to support it – to label colourism as a problem that just exists for another culture or race feels akin to dropping a match in a forest and saying, 'aw, poor trees' as they billow in flames.

Colourism can be just one of the traumas passed down the generations and often the way it permeates into our habits is subtle and can manifest in 'aesthetic trauma', a term coined by psychologist Dr Afiya Mbilishaka. She told *Allure*: 'This trauma surfaces when navigating romantic relationships, sexuality, sensuality, and attractiveness, and it also frequently affects how we act in the workplace.'[31] An Indian friend always wears a foundation that is a couple of shades too light, rather than one her own skin colour. The same applies to other forms of internalised racism – an Iranian friend recounted that her mother straightened her curly hair since she was a child, perhaps in order to look more European or 'acceptable' but now she still feels compelled to do the same. A Black friend moisturises her skin obsessively just as her mother did, so as to ensure she didn't look 'ashy', to avoid judgement from the white community she lived in. For people of colour, investigating these internal beliefs and where they come from is crucial. We could be carrying intergenerational trauma, from historical events and inequalities, that have affected the generations before us and often it can filter down into how we see beauty in ourselves and around us. That so many people must combat this every day as part of our mental load is truly *exhausting*.

Does tech have a whiteness bias?

Such is the nature of the human brain, as we go through life we collect bias from all sorts of places, mostly without realising and often while telling ourselves that we are being totally open and fair-minded. We absorb it from pop culture, the media, the views of our caretakers growing up, our peers and, increasingly, our tech. Science suggests that we are automatically biased towards our own ethnicities; studies have shown that infants of six to nine months show preference for their own ethnicity and bias against those who are different. The 'other-race effect' suggests that we are poor at distinguishing individuals from other races – hence that rhetoric often used for minority groups 'all looking the same'.[32] Bias towards our own race could even come down to our pack mentality, a legacy of cave-dwelling days – those who are in the pack are safe, those who seem different, other for whatever reason, could be a source of danger.

Unconscious (or implicit) bias refers to unconscious beliefs and assumptions that we don't recognise we have. This often comes into play when we have to make quick judgements and assessments. Whereas conscious bias is, obviously, when you are aware of your preference for or aversion to something, extreme conscious bias may manifest as physical or verbal harassment or exclusionary behaviour.

Conscious racial bias is generally easy to spot and call out. Like somebody on a dating app saying 'I only date white women' (which I saw just recently). But unconscious bias, by its nature, is harder to unpick. It comes in the form of not questioning why we hold certain beliefs, or not even recognising them as beliefs, rather 'facts'. For example, in the early days of my magazine career, people would openly say that make-up 'didn't shoot as well on dark skin tones' as the acceptable reason for excluding models of colour from beauty editorials.

This kind of bias is one more way of excluding non-white beauty from the mainstream, another excuse not to address lack of representation, sure. But – and bear with me here – there could be some truth in it, stemming from limitations within photographic technology itself. The medium itself was created by and for white people, and when photographic technology was commercialised, it catered to the more affluent and dominant white market. As colour film became more widespread in the 1950s, Kodak, which, at the time pretty much held a monopoly in the US, introduced something called a Shirley card. Your film was sent to a lab to be developed and a photo of a white woman with brown hair called Shirley – marked 'normal' – was used as the control for how colours should be adjusted. It took complaints from furniture and chocolate manufacturers in the 1970s, who were frustrated that you couldn't see their shades of brown properly in their adverts to force their hand to address the colour bias in the technology. Rather than, you know, considering people of colour.

Kodak and the other photographic companies did eventually try to redress this with 'multiracial' Shirley cards and Black, white and Asian Shirleys, though not everyone used them. As digital photography ended the need for lab-developed photography and Shirley cards in turn, some of this bias towards how people of colour appear in photography was carried over into digital technology. Nigel Atherton, photographer of over 30 years and editor of *Amateur Photographer*, told *Wired*: 'Exposure systems on cameras have always been weighted towards providing a pleasing exposure with lighter skin tones. Modern digital cameras and phones using AI are more sophisticated, but I find they still can't entirely be trusted when photographing darker-skinned subjects.'[33]

If you have dark skin and ever wondered why your face disappears into any background darkness, this might be why. And why magazine shoots of celebrities of colour are lightened or edited – though, often, far too much. What started as conscious bias – a belief that it wasn't important to cater to all ethnicities in photography – evolved to become a form of technology bias and literal 'white gaze' that we cannot even detect.

These examples illustrate something that is so important because it affects so many areas of everyone's lives and yet we hardly think about it, if at all. Our lives are now dictated by a small block of metal and plastic that is pretty much always in our hand or at least within reach. We might think that we are in control of the content we chose to look at on our smartphones but the reality is that so much of what we read, watch and see is curated by somebody – or something – else. Often we are tracked in order to serve us what our phones think we want to see from what we've been speaking about, watching and searching for. This wouldn't be so bad if the technology was a benevolent, fair dictator, free from the biases of the human society that created it – but, of course, it's not. And, because it's futuristic and forward-thinking, we so seldom stop to question its motives, like the buzz of a new friendship.

Many of tech's hidden preferences mirror some of the

most atrocious parts of society's treatment of non-white beauty. Back in 2016, Russia and Hong Kong-based Youth Laboratories, with support from Microsoft and NVIDIA, ran a beauty contest called 'Beauty.Ai', hailed as the world's first digital beauty contest. It had more than 600,000 entrants as contestants sent in selfies from around the world. Then, the founders let the algorithms pick the winners, like a 21st-century version of the judges in Miss World. You've probably guessed it – nearly all the 44 finalists were white, a few were Asian but only one had dark skin.[34] They had used 'deep learning', which is when the algorithm is trained via a set of categorised images (a bit like a modern Shirley Card), so when it sees something new, it can assess where it sits within that range. You can see how – depending on those initial images and labels – this could be deeply biased and, based on the results of Beauty.Ai (and plenty more examples like this), it undoubtedly is. We can tell that the images it's seen are essentially all 'Shirleys'. The bigger issue is that deep learning is widely used by giant companies like Facebook, Amazon, Microsoft and more, and it's often the case that the databases used for training the algorithms are shared between tech companies. This means that biases are often replicated across multiple tech global platforms, especially as the tech industry has always been a largely white male environment, in particular, the technical workers who build the software widely used across the industry.

There is always somebody gatekeeping what we see, whether that's in the fashion, beauty or entertainment industries, or the far less visible or accessible world of tech. In tech this manifests in multiple, often insidious ways that mirror the worst human attitudes. For example, Twitter's image-cropping algorithm was found to focus on white faces over black ones, while TikTok had a technical glitch that muted the Black Lives Matter hashtag in 2020.[35] And a bug in Google Photos was retrieving images of Black people when gorillas were searched for. Google responded by getting rid of image tags rather than fixing the racist AI.[36] This hidden bias is what MIT researcher Joy Buolamwini calls the 'coded gaze'. Her TED Talk shows how webcams can't detect dark skin, yet if she wore a white mask, the webcam picked up her face immediately with algorithmic bias in facial recognition. Buolamwini says 'There's an opportunity to create full spectrum training sets that reflect a richer portrait of humanity.'[37] But this requires a huge tech systems audit and training to increase awareness of the bias that tech actively upholds whiteness. And for a predominantly white male industry to dismantle its own privilege ... call me a cynic, but that seems an unlikely proposition.

In March 2020, American non-profit news organisation The Intercept reported that internal documents from TikTok instructed its moderators not to promote content from users with 'ugly facial looks' in order to retain new viewers. Which, in case you want a definition, includes but is not limited to: 'too many wrinkles', 'obvious facial scars', 'facial deformities' and 'chubby ... obese or too thin'. A representative from TikTok told The Intercept that these edicts were 'no longer in place and were already out of use when The Intercept obtained them', and that the aim was to prevent bullying.[38] Prevention, we might assume, by means of exclusion.

What this exposed wasn't shocking – when you look at who social media favours. The faces that tend to be in our 'discover' options and therefore who have the most followers often tend to be white or light-skinned. An Indian friend of mine showed me her phone and despite following mostly Indian content creators, her suggested follows were all white. Often, those who are most popular on social media have a similar 'beauty look' that is often the basis of the many face-changing filters that continue to be so popular on apps. These filters often westernise features and make them agreeable to the white beauty gaze with pale skin, light eyes and tiny noses.

More terrifying still is how this look has translated into the dominant beauty narrative and has influenced cosmetic surgery trends – with people now asking to look like they do when distorted with social media filters. What these digital altering apps and social media fail to address is the truth that underpins lightening somebody's skin tone or giving their face a more Eurocentric appearance or light eyes. It's that in celebrating these things as ideal beauty, and by using the filters that mimic this, it always invariably leaves out the role that colonialism and slavery have played in supporting whiteness as the ultimate physical ideal.

What's yours is mine, right?

Another way our digital boom has created an erasure of people of colour and elevation of white beauty standards is through cultural appropriation, which co-opts elements from another culture or identity without credit. But advances in tech – from filters to instant social media trends – has given the concept of whiteness access to whatever it wants – like a digital colonisation, known online as 'columbusing', when something is discovered that's existed forever. Beauty trends go viral so quickly online that before you know it an ancient cultural practice or feature is packaged as something new and exciting for Western audiences.

Take the recent 'fox eye' trend in make-up and cosmetic surgery mimicking the eye shape of those of some East Asian races. That feature is celebrated on a white person and yet it's one of the most common insults used against Asian people – celebrities and influencers are pulling their faces up at the sides for this look, while for many, that was the way they were mocked. As Kelly H. Chong, a sociology professor at the University of Kansas, told CNN: 'The cultural influencers from the dominant group legitimize it as a cool, style "trend" and, in the process, exoticize and eroticize it.'[39]

All of this makes my gripe with singer-songwriter Gwen Stefani wearing a bindi (and being seen as cool for it) in the 1990s seem really quite tame; nevertheless, it highlights how the beauty ideals of whiteness are now disguised within viral social media trends. Need more proof? Take one of the biggest make-up trends in the last ten years: contouring. When Kim Kardashian went viral after posting her contouring selfie back in 2012, it showed how our faces could be manipulated into looking entirely different with elaborate make-up techniques. Contouring as a make-up technique wasn't new – for example, actors like Vivien Leigh used it in the 1920s in an era of black-and-white movies. Max Factor popularised it in the 1940s at his make-up school and it came back into fashion in the 1980s and 1990s within Drag culture as a way to feminise and sculpt faces. Since then, trends in extreme bronzing, the mainstream popularity of Drag culture and, of course, Kim K, have ensured that contouring and highlighting has become a mainstream beauty practice. It's become one that has normalised minimising non-white features, such as slimming down noses using contouring techniques to fit in with the Eurocentric ideal of a slim, small nose. That trend for highlighting the ends of our noses to create a defined tip is, again, a beauty ideal that stems from whiteness.

MAC director of make-up artistry Terry Barber told me in a feature for *Glamour* that: 'Everyone is trying to look the same to fit into a social media and reality TV look. The danger is this is a Caucasian beauty ideal for all women. This new beauty ideal is also based on the idea of surgical correction – the highly sexualised kind you see on *Love Island* and *The*

Kardashians. When you put that look on women of colour, it's saying all racial features should be corrected to look like Caucasian ones. Like shading noses until they're razor-thin, it's become about correction and not enhancement. Worryingly, it translates as racial features need to be corrected.' I'd never tell anyone what to do or how to apply their make-up – it is self-expression after all – but it still breaks my heart seeing people of colour doing this as a 'trend' when the practice now represents something far more sinister.

The other issue is that some ethnic features are minimised to fit Eurocentric ideals, only seen as beautiful when accompanied by pale skin. In 2022, when the American model Hailey Bieber shared a tutorial for 'brownie glazed lips', a mix of brown lip liner and clear gloss, there was an outcry for Bieber failing to reference a look that Black and Latina women had been wearing since the 1990s in order to create a brown 'nude' lip colour that suited them, in a era when only pink existed as a nude lip colour.[40] That hits hard for those who felt mocked or ugly because of their lip colour: in my early twenties, a girl on a make-up counter actually covered my lips with pale concealer before applying a pink lipstick over them to 'even them out'.

Take the recent trend for more athletic-looking figures or a larger derrière (for which Black women and athletes have been scrutinised and derided). Jen Selter, an Instagram fitness influencer who landed shoots in *Vanity Fair* and *Vogue* in 2014, is generally credited with kicking off the trend for the latter. Butts became big news in popular culture, as seen in songs like Taylor Swift's 'Shake It Off' and Meghan Trainor's 'All About That Bass' and something that had been ridiculed and exploited, was now being appropriated by white culture, prompting journalists like Yomi Adegoke to write in the *Guardian*: 'Why does a black butt only look good in white skin?' She says: 'Class and skin are closely intertwined; for what makes a white girl with a chin piercing, brightly dyed hair and arm tattoo alternative and a black woman with the same modifications ghetto, bar the colour of her skin?'[41] Likewise, fuller lips have been celebrated on white celebrities like Angelina Jolie, Scarlett Johansson and Kim Kardashian as beautiful and aspirational features that some people now try to emulate with fillers and injectables, while many Black women were taunted for them.

Numerous celebrities and influencers have been accused of making themselves look like they're not of Caucasian descent or making their ethnicity seem ambiguous. In 2021 singer Jesy Nelson of the girl group Little Mix (who identifies as white British) appeared in her video for 'Boyz' with tanned skin, grills and braided hair, leading to accusations of 'blackfishing' which allows non-Black people to appropriate elements of being Black, without facing any of the discrimination that can come with it. The term first came to public attention in 2018 when a Twitter thread by Wanna Thompson, a Toronto-based writer, went viral. Talking in *Paper* magazine in the same year, she wrote: 'The thread exposed something that I've known all along – white women want access to Blackness but don't want the suffering that comes along with it.'[42] This leads to a cherry-picking of attributes. As Tina Fey wrote in her memoir, *Bossypants*, 'Now every girl is expected to have Caucasian blue eyes, full Spanish lips, a classic button nose, hairless Asian skin with a California tan, a Jamaican dance hall ass, long Swedish legs, small Japanese feet, the abs of a lesbian gym owner, the hips of a nine-year-old boy, the arms of Michelle Obama, and doll tits.'

When will it ever be OK – across all ethnicities – to be ourselves and to like ourselves, as we are? Increasingly, considering what we are up against in popular culture and the insidious machinations of technology, it feels like the truly radical and deeply necessary act we all deserve. History has some excellent inspiration for that: The Black Is Beautiful movement of the 1960s and 1970s (born from the Black Power movement) sought to re-affirm the elements of black beauty that Eurocentric beauty standards had tried to diminish. And the Indigenismo movement in Latin America looked to address a reclamation of its culture and beauty too: Mexican painter Frida Kahlo was seen as one of its icons, choosing to represent herself in self-portraits in traditional pre-Columbian attire and hairstyles, and with visible facial hair to reject Eurocentric beauty norms. More recently, I've loved seeing British-Asian tattoo artists reclaim this space and their tattooing heritage, in an industry that plays a heavy role in cultural appropriation, that has marginalised female tattoo artists and reduced women in the landscape to being 'decorative' – tattoo magazine culture so often had women with tattoos strewn sexily across motorbikes or cars as props. All while erasing tattooists of colour and pictures of tattoos on skin of colour on social media from our view (because, apparently, tattoos show up better on white skin – pass me the Shirley card!).

I have only scratched the surface of this topic here; there are many more traumas within the confines of race, heritage and beauty that deserve to be unpicked and addressed. But as I write this, whiteness is still a defining factor in appearance: in Texas, Treyvion Gray wasn't allowed to attend his graduation ceremony in 2022 because his locs were 'too long'- despite other children reportedly having longer hairstyles.[43] Things aren't any better for adults – in 2020 a federal appeals court in the US dismissed a case against a company who refused to hire Chastity Jones, unless she cut off her locs.[44] And in the UK, 41% of workers from BAME backgrounds have faced racism, including comments about appearance, at work in the last five years, according to the Trades Union Congress report in 2022.[45]

Due to my job, I get a specific view of how promoting whiteness in beauty standards remains completely acceptable. In the last few days, I've had four plastic surgery press releases with undertones of racial prejudice – from getting the 'perfect nose', which the emails tell me is slim, with a pointed upwards tip like actor/model Kaia Gerber and actor Blake Lively, through to procedures that lighten the areola around the nipple, as, presumably, dark areola are bad for some reason – perhaps because some women of colour might have them and that's enough? I've been sent hair oils – telling me it's a new TikTok trend but with no reference as to where that 'trend' has been taken from (it's most often associated with Indian cultural practices) – and have received three wellness 'gifts' that appropriated marginalised cultures without referencing or paying the originating cultures in any way. I couldn't believe what I was reading when a brand with a predominantly Black clientele sent me a release launching a collection that referenced ways to use their products to make 'noses slimmed, and jaws softened'. This week alone, I've been invited to three panel discussions that have been all white (how quickly we forget!).

Extrapolating how we feel about ourselves, about others and about our beauty routines away from the hold of centuries of conditioning, subjugation and habit is unfathomably hard. But I truly believe that everyone benefits when we examine how whiteness is still being sold to us as the beauty ideal. We aren't responsible for everything that's come before us – but we are responsible for what we do now – and the changes we can all make to shift archaic narratives. Considering where whiteness might be ruling your beauty standards and routines – no matter what your heritage – is a great starting point. Here's a few points to think about ...

Examine your beauty idols. Think about the five people you consider the most beautiful. Are they all of one ethnicity? Are their features 'perfect' by Western beauty standards? Is there a similarity at all? When we are fed a constant stream of similar face shapes and body types it's understandable that we might internalise this single view of beauty. If you start to seek out alternatives you will likely broaden your ideas of who is beautiful/desirable. Not only does this help our own self-esteem, making us feel more accepting of our own appearance, but there's a knock-on effect for anyone we happen to influence – from our children to our peers.

Hack the algorithms. No matter what your ethnicity, examine how many people of colour – across all ethnic backgrounds – are in your social media feed. I realised a few years ago that all the fashion and vintage influencers I followed online were white and straight-sized. Often that's because they are who we're 'suggested' to follow (hello, biased algorithms). Finding people in the areas you're interested in who aren't all white (or straight-sized, or able-bodied, or heterosexual, or cisgender, etc.) takes time, sure, but you'll get a much richer experience and help support others too.

Shop and support. A brilliant and relatively easy way to support women and people of colour (and those from other marginalised backgrounds) in beauty is to buy their products. It's as simple as that, and there's now many more to choose from, but they often don't get the attention they deserve, unless fronted by a celebrity.

THE WEIGHT OF UGLY

'When eating a salad feels terrifying, you know something is seriously wrong.'

I HAVE, LIKE SO MANY, been on and off diets throughout my life. I've fussed over points, carbs, calories and macros, and have measured out cereal so many times I can pour, by eye, precisely a recommended (tiny) 30g portion of Cheerios. I've dieted so incessantly that coming off them has felt like freefall; I've restricted my intake and conversely eaten everything in sight, so that it feels like a never-ending game of chess, using protein bars and chicken nuggets as pieces. Who might win today? Sure, I was trying to change my weight – a number on a scale I'd attached my entire self-worth to. But it's what we're told 'fat' means that really scares us – that we're unattractive and unlovable. (Would Fat Monica really have bagged Chandler in *Friends*? We're led to believe it's highly unlikely.)

Food became a comfort to me in my early teen years, but fat became an issue when I started going on regular shopping trips with friends. Whether we were in Topshop, Miss Selfridge or Kookaï, I was *always* sat on the sidelines watching as the others tried on tiny crop tops and shorts that even didn't even come in my size, even if I'd felt confident enough to wear them. By now I knew enough of pop culture's ultra-slim beauty standards to believe that nobody would ever love me because of my size and was stuck in a torrid dichotomy. Food was my security blanket in those moments when I felt huge, unfashionable and unlovable – but I also hated it too. It was, I believed, the source of all my pain. I coveted the ease with which my slim white friends inhabited their bodies: they didn't seem to worry about their size, what they ate or if their clothes would fit – although perhaps they just didn't say anything to me. I imagined that an entire part of their brain was freed up to enjoy life, while mine was consumed by constant anguish and self-loathing. Even when I did find something vaguely decent to wear, somebody would show up in something tinier (from Jane Norman, usually) and I'd just feel invisible.

That constant gnawing ache of feeling ugly and like my body was 'wrong' plagued my school life. I'd start the day restricting my food intake when my resolve was strong and then binge eat later, feeling exhausted and sad. I joined Weight Watchers at 16, counting complicated points from a book, but seeing only a bleak half-pound loss every week on the Scales of Doom. Coupled with the stress of academic averageness (that's 'failing' to Asian parents, by the way) and dire self-esteem, my binge eating started to dial up. Each time I'd take that book from my bag, out would come a flurry of chocolate wrappers, like confetti, and my portion sizes ramped up as a way of soothing my woes. Re-reading my diaries from that time feels so bleak: often they'd end with a plea to the powers above that this unending turmoil would be over and I just wouldn't wake up. I genuinely thought that it was better not to be alive than be here and be fat. When everything around you is implying or pretty much just telling you that you should hate yourself – TV shows, films and magazines; beauty standards and body ideals – eventually, you start to believe it. My diary entries often ended with: 'I hate being fat and ugly,' like the two were synonymous, which was what I believed then.

By the time I started university, I was a size 18, but a few more pounds weren't the only thing I took with me when I left home. I'd also started purging in secret, which I found relatively easily to do and conceal. Now, instead of my parents' freshly cooked Indian food, I could eat and drink whatever the hell I liked. To compensate and get to my 'goal' weight – the weight where I'd decided, aided by BMI charts, *everything* would be OK, I signed up for a fancy gym membership, hit it hard for a week, then tired of it (while berating myself for avoiding it and wasting money). I did the same with diet clubs and books. Uni was meant to be the best time of my life but often it felt like perpetual cycles of panic and misery. I avoided holidays, relationships and more because I felt like I was too fat to ever be truly lovable and accepted.

I started to create my own 'diet', which was fusing episodes of bulimia with extreme diets, like the Sacred Heart (a soup diet supposedly designed for patients before surgery, it's a bit of an urban myth as to whether it's true),[1] together as a mega-fix and even tried taking speed to lose weight too, adding it to my water bottle, like it was Ribena. As if things couldn't get worse, by my final year of uni, I'd developed a huge paranoia about attending lectures. I'd become convinced that everyone was looking at me because of my size and because I was ugly. It made the idea of walking into those giant lecture theatres unbearable (the speed probably didn't help). Now a size 14, I was at my lowest weight in years but I was too frightened to go to my classes. If it hadn't been for the incredible department secretary who helped me collect my lecture notes (for whom I will always be endlessly thankful), I would have absolutely failed my degree. I managed to catch up and pass – but obviously, sticking to this regime was too tough, I gained back all the weight I'd gone to great (physical) pains to lose.

It didn't occur to me that it was not really about my weight, even when the evidence was right in front of me, because I was smaller but just as unhappy, or perhaps even more so. I held an unshakable belief that everything in my life would magically fix itself if I was just thin – the 'before and after' shots on the TV shows at the time told me that was a given. They seemed to say: 'here's Trudy at 250lbs, now she's half her body weight she's finally found love/a job/happiness/et al.,' (which is something dating shows are still particularly fond of selling as a 'backstory', glorifying the thin = happy narrative). My desperation was at an all-time high as I then embarked on a milkshake diet totalling 400 calories a day. The weight came off *fast* and each week, my clothes started to become too big – it felt like the answer to all my prayers, despite the fact I couldn't concentrate during my MA lectures at all. I lost three stone in three months and was the smallest I'd ever been but, tellingly, I still *felt* fat. Friends told me that I was starting to look drawn, but that felt like a novelty to me so I took it as a compliment – thinness was the ultimate achievement, after all. This meant I was on the path to winning.

When my course (and wretched milkshake diet) ended, I went travelling around North America with friends. My first instinct wasn't 'hell yeah, let's party in the USA!' – it was 'would everyone we met think I was huge compared to my slim friends?' Followed by trying to figure out how to eat the smallest amounts possible while I was away. I knew nothing about nutrition – food and dieting were inseparable in my mind from years of misery and extreme dieting so I did what I knew how to do: restriction, bingeing and purging. That's when the picture at the beginning of the chapter was taken. Shortly afterwards, I threw up. By the end of the trip, my bulimia was back, I felt totally out of control, none of my clothes fitted and I'd put on a stone. The misery was indescribable; I felt like the weakest, most deplorable person alive. I'd just achieved a top journalism master's and had plenty of amazing internships lined up but to me at that time, nothing mattered like being thin did – I felt like an all-round failure, entirely based on a number on a scale.

Looking back on that period of my life, from a child to a young adult, I feel a tidal wave of regret for the time snatched by the thin-obsessed culture and the fat-shaming diet industry that I grew up with. The toxic culture around body size and weight has made so many of us feel like our worth rests almost entirely on the number on a scale. So many generations of women have damaged eating patterns that become an invisible hidden generational trauma, all from the pressure to be thin, and everything we are told thinness brings us or represents – like acceptance, self-control and beauty.

If this tale was a film or a Halloween episode of a teen sitcom, a foreboding soundtrack would cue up right about now. That's because the protagonist (that's me, friends) is about to make a pivotal life choice. Where is the worst place you could imagine that a fragile, broken human obsessed with being thin and beautiful and never quite measuring up could find themselves in? You guessed it: women's fashion magazines.

A career in magazines was all I'd ever wanted. I'd worked tirelessly since I was 15 to prove to myself – and my family – that I could divert from the familial path of medicine to do something different. And now here I was, in the midst of the glamour and creativity I'd always wanted to be part of. But it was as though the gods of chaos were rubbing their hands with glee, saying: 'Let's make this situation *even* worse.' I loved fashion as an artform and my style often expressed what I couldn't say for myself. I'd always dreamed of working in an office where racks of beautiful clothes were filling corridors. I started my internships in pursuit of landing a dream assistant job, but quite unaware of how elitist and un-diverse this environment would be across the board – from ethnicity and background to, of course, body size.

Some of my placements went well but even when the editors praised my hard work or writing, it barely registered. I just couldn't take in anything good about myself. Other experiences, however, were scarring. At one prestigious women's title, I spent my long days doing repetitive 'returns' of clothes borrowed for shoots to fashion houses and lugging heavy suitcases upstairs, with barely a word from anyone. On top of the disappointment of not learning anything about fashion journalism as promised, I felt unseen and taken for granted. The office atmosphere was cold and fraught; it felt like insecurity was piped in through the air conditioning. I did learn something, actually: that thinness was an obsession, even for the already thin. Each morning, various team members asked me to get them a small cup of porridge made with water for breakfast from a nearby café – a whole bowl of gruel was presumably too many carbs. They talked constantly about diets. Two were doing the 'Master Cleanse', a famous 1940s diet of cayenne pepper, lemon juice, maple syrup and water that Beyoncé helped resurrect around the time. When I'd get their lunch, it was often the smallest portion of sushi available, gone in four small bites.

I'd been quiet, but polite and as helpful as possible, often staying late to get it all done. I was happy not to attract much notice, until I did – or rather, my choice of attire did. 'Who would wear cowboy boots, they're *awful*,' one editor sniggered to her sinewy colleagues. They all turned, looked directly at me and laughed. My stomach lurched as a familiar sense of melancholy washed over me, I knew this feeling well. (The irony of cowboy boots being covetable right now is *not* lost on me, let me tell you.) A couple of weeks into that placement, it finally dawned that even with my above-average journalism experience, what mattered most here was how you conformed to the beauty standard – white, thin, 'expensive'-looking.

By the end of that stint, there was nothing left of me. No spark, no enthusiasm, no hope. Any confidence in my ability was gone and each day, I slunk in, wanting to go unnoticed. I spent my lunchbreaks in the nearby park silently crying (being able to be miserable inaudibly was a key skill for working on women's magazines, I realise in hindsight) and couldn't wait for it to be over. In my final week of packing up fashion returns, I heard somebody squawk about needing a coat to be returned to a designer urgently. It was life or death – as everything here seemed to be. 'Send *her*, she can walk it over,' one of the many sinewy blonde editors said, gesturing towards me like I was a pot plant. Another slightly nicer one interjected: 'Let's send a courier, it'll be quicker and saves the trip.' But the mean blonde couldn't let it – or me – go: 'No, send *her*. She needs the exercise anyway.' Stunned, I said nothing to being fat-shamed so audibly. I took said package and walked it 20 minutes away to another building in the rain – I didn't have enough energy left for silent crying that day.

There was nothing I liked about myself by now. I'd retreated even further inwards, so much so that during my 'exit interview' the editor told me: 'You need to be louder and have more presence. I *give* you the permission to be confident.' Like it was *that* easy. Like turning on a button that pepped me up, as if I was a plug-in Stepford wife. To this day, her privilege and arrogance still enrages me, as do the words of that fashion editor who fat-shamed me. I often wonder why. Was it a result of feeling inadequate herself and her lack of skill? (Even at my level, I could tell she wasn't a standout stylist.) Or perhaps by making me feel fat, she made herself feel thinner and more superior? I could fill a book with deeply problematic incidents from my time interning and working on women's magazines, but at least now I do know this: the wounded wound others. The biggest culprit here isn't the vile people we encounter, it's a bigger systemic issue that makes one person believe they're better than another, based on appearance and the industries that support this beauty hierarchy. Since that time, I've questioned whether my desire to be part of this industry was a form of self-torture, or almost akin to Stockholm syndrome – but my captor was tiny designer clothes that would never fit and thinness I'd never achieve.

That placement thwarted my fashion journalism ambitions but it didn't stop me wanting to be thin, or to work in magazines. I'd noticed that the features departments seemed much nicer, so I eventually got my first job on – drumroll, please – a health magazine. Now I had a *legitimate* reason to obsess about calories and diet trends all day long. I'd managed to cut down, and then finally stop the bulimia, partly thanks to a kindly psychologist who gave me some understanding of the turmoil in my mind, but also because my teeth would ache incessantly as a result, often waking me up at night. But the diet-binge cycle remained. I'd buy diet pills off the internet (I've had diet pills analysed for a magazine feature since and they're often full of caffeine, filler, vitamins and sometimes even antidepressants) and try every new health fad. My weight anguish was my one constant companion in the big city, if I ever felt homesick. The two things that occupied my mind were my job and my weight.

It was then that I made one of the poorest decisions of my life. I know what you're thinking – how can it go downhill from here? Is there anything worse than being so broken you let a sub-par editor treat you like a dog turd or take headache-inducing speed to lose weight and nearly fail your degree? Yes. Yes, there is. My parents invited me on a family trip to India as I hadn't been in a few years. I struggled with India: the food there was so hard to resist, everything was a carb and the force-feeding aunties who showed their love through pakoras and samosas were unrelenting. So I said no. But if I had gone with them, I'd have seen my grandmother one last time, before she died later that year. I chose my obsession with being thin over her. It was my worst move yet – and I hated myself even more for it. I was trapped between hating my obsession with being thin and still, above everything else, wanting to be thin.

Thinking about the missed time, missed experiences and missed memories is searingly painful. I genuinely believed that being thin equated to happiness, success, acceptance – it mattered more than anything and anyone. I feel devastated for my former self and for anyone who still feels trapped in this cycle of self-hatred that I've gradually – through self-acceptance and rejecting traditional beauty norms – started to escape. But if you've ever struggled with body acceptance, chances are the list of what you've given up, when you really think about it, is as huge as it is heartbreaking. Perhaps like me, that extends to what you put up with in terms of awful treatment at work to bad partners, because you internalised the toxic message that being fat means you are worthless. When you hate the way you look, it's impossible to compartmentalise; lack of self-esteem leaves no area of your life untouched, from your work to your relationships.

There is rarely one clear-cut reason for some people gaining weight while others don't. It encompasses a wide range of reasons from genetics, hormones and individual brain-wiring, through to economic and environmental factors. If it really were as simple as 'just eat less, move more', the diet industry would not exist. The (hugely profitable) diet industry would also not exist if we simply accepted all bodies the way they are and came to realise that beauty and health comes in all shapes – something I wish I'd realised far sooner. Money is at the heart of so many of the ways we are made to feel ugly.

'Fat', 'obese' or 'overweight' (or their playful cousins 'plump' or 'chubby') have been loaded up with so much shame and hate, ruining and affecting so many lives. Just as the view that fat people are fair game for bullying, health-shaming is archaic and deeply damaging, as is the rhetoric around thinness equating to being attractive, healthy, disciplined and even morally superior. Being thin just means you're thin, but that's not how we're sold it. Even when my eating disorder was acute, deep down, I always had a feeling that the weight loss I was trying to achieve was not the thing I really wanted. So why was I so obsessed? Why did thinness have such a hold over me – and so many of us?

If you've seen one of the many 'ideal body types through history' videos online (if not, take a look), you'll know how significantly society's standards and expectations of women's bodies have changed over time. And how arbitrary those changes seem when looked at side by side. It seems an obsession with the female form and how it 'should' look (read: how the patriarchy would like it to look) goes back almost to our earliest beginnings. For exhibit A, meet The Venus of Willendorf. Found in Austria in 1908, she dates back to 28,000–25,000 BCE. She is just one of many figurines in a group known as 'the Venus statues' of prehistoric and ancient women and goddesses. They all show a similar aesthetic – a rounded, faceless woman, who looks almost hypersexualised; the body parts related to fertility are exaggerated in size. Experts mostly agree that the statues were carved by men and often they represent erotic and idealised forms of beauty and sexuality[2] – sort of like prehistoric porn, you might say, or erotic images at the very least.

The beauty-obsessed ancient Greeks suggested that the ideal man would have had long limbs, broad shoulders and a muscular, defined body, depicted in statues of the time, that weirdly almost mirror the physiques of a *Men's Health* magazine cover model or chiselled *Love Island* contestants. Women's beauty standards were even higher, says classicist and writer Natalie Haynes in the *Guardian*. Ancient Greek painter Zeuxis was tasked with painting the mythical figure of celebrated beauty Helen of Troy, but couldn't find a single woman to model for him who he considered beautiful enough so he copied the features he found most pleasing from five different women, 'It's hard to avoid the conclusion that human women have fallen short of idealised women since their earliest portrayals,' Haynes observes.[3]

The ideal female body in the view of the ancient Greeks was smaller and thinner, with narrower shoulders and smaller breasts than the Venus figurines depicted, but retaining the wide hips and thighs – the pear shape, it would probably be called today (there are so many crass terms to label women's body shapes, generally fruit related, while a 'dad bod' is almost a badge of honour). The new ideal was still robust – rather than very thin or frail-looking – and she parallels today's Western desired female body type as lean and strong – but not *too* strong, naturally.

As we approach the Middle Ages, for the nobility, food was abundant and being a larger male was a sign of wealth. William the Conqueror was apparently quite fat – his size is mentioned often in contemporary sources and he is praised for going to war 'despite' this encumbrance. The depictions of clergymen – also in the higher echelons of society – often showed similarly large physiques. He might be mostly mythical, but think Friar Tuck in *Robin Hood*. Henry VIII, who very much exists in the popular imagination as a man who liked a banquet, was, from the dimensions of his armour, estimated to weigh 400 pounds (more than 28 stone).[4] So from here we can see the association between power and a man's size.

Being rounded or plump wasn't entirely negative for women either at this point. Nude paintings of medieval females often show rounded stomachs. As the poorer classes didn't have enough food to eat, naturally being fat was aspirational and carried connotations of elevated status. In fact, if a woman was slim, or extremely thin in medieval times, it might suggest she wasn't interested in pleasures of the flesh, like food and sex. Control over food and extreme fasting was also a part of religious life – we often see saints depicted as tall and thin. At the time, what a woman could do was incredibly limited and becoming a nun was the only other life choice offered to those who didn't wish to marry and have children.

So, when did thin start to become beautiful and fat switch to ugly? The answer isn't linear, but it is alarming – and something that is conveniently hidden from plain view. Puritan influence during the 1500s and later 1600s meant that a lot (anything fun, basically) was condemned and 'intemperance' or excess consumption of alcohol and food was high on the list. Puritan reformers like English entomologist and naturalist Thomas Muffet were leading this charge; Muffet penned a 400-page manual on food and how to, essentially, not eat it.[5] Muffet's goal was to change how the English ate and Scottish physician George Cheyne, who rose to notoriety in the 1700s, felt the same. He was 476 pounds, then gained attention for prophesising his 'milk and seed diet' that had helped him lose weight. What spurred him to lose it?, you ask. He felt that his sensual pleasures went against God's will. Cheyne's approach to diet attracted flocks of upper-class English women to his clinic and alongside the diet, he also recommended fasting, even purging. Influential writer Lady Mary Wortley Montagu was said to have followed his diet regime (she often wrote about body size in her famous 'letters', which described her travels to the Ottoman Empire).

Popular media, like *The Spectator*, often featured 'men railing against corpulent women as low and improper'.[6] As it was rich women who were increasingly trying and aspiring to be thin, this distinction meant that fat was also linked to being a lower class. It's a curious coincidence that those same women are the ones that have historically controlled the narratives of body standards in fashion magazines, right? Food for thought.

Why did these women want to lose weight, in a way they hadn't before? During the Enlightenment, there was growing thought that beauty should reflect the nation's moral compass. That compass was driven by religious influence, of course, but it wasn't just because of this. Brace yourself. As Europeans established their colonies from the 1400s, othering the different body types of the people they were subjugating was another handy technique to legitimise what they were doing. Some Western writers of the 19th century insisted that people in African countries saw fatness as the ultimate ideal. This was connected to their supposed laziness – a reported disinterest in hard graft was seen as 'obesity of mind'. If you were fat, you weren't working hard enough for your oppressor. Another writer was horrified by 'uncivilised' men desiring fat women: 'The Greeks praised the slender and graceful figure – the Moors prize fatness to obesity; and their women are fatted for marriage as our turkeys are for Thanksgiving or Christmas.' In India, a British observer accredited the 'rotundity' of the Brahmins to 'ghee and indolence', also citing the belly of the Hindu god Ganesha as being representative of the desired body standard.[7]

Sabrina Strings, sociologist and author of *Fearing the Black Body*, wrote that establishing superiority through body types was a prevalent narrative in European writing and thought that 'placed black people at the bottom of the hierarchy, claiming their gluttonous nature to be one of their more base characteristics'.[8] This was in contrast to Europeans, who had self-control and willpower. Fat became a way to classify people into who was the most superior, it seemed.[9]

There was a distinction to be made – to put it crudely, those who were colonised, were uncivilised and prized being fat. Those who were in power, and civilised, were thin. In 1752, a work called *Crito: or, A Dialogue on Beauty* was released by historian and anecdotist Joseph Spence, who revealed that the English model of beauty is superior and distinct from all others.[10] He believed that Flemish artist Peter Rubens' famous portraits of voluptuous women were lower in value compared to those of thinner English women. Naturally, this comparison of body shape was aimed primarily at women and he even created a hierarchy and scale by which he scored English women, with skin colour and shape being the two top distinctions.

To be thin and light-skinned was the top achievement, as celebrated portraits from the 18th century onwards depicting women showed. Painter Thomas Gainsborough, for example, often detailed thin female bodies, with long necks and tiny waists. There was one distinction though – you could be *too* thin. In his 1870 book, *Personal Beauty: How to Cultivate and Preserve it in Accordance with the Laws of Health*, author Daniel Brinton said that for women, a 'scrawny bony figure' is 'intolerable to gods and men'.[11] (It's worth noting that, of course, this is history body-shaming thin women too.)

The imperialist lens on body size is undeniable and it's telling that by the late 19th century, the Victorians had adopted these hugely biased attitudes and started to see 'excess' weight as a sign of being stupid, lazy and even promiscuous, even though much-loved monarch Queen Victoria was described as 'very large, ruddy and fat' during the latter part of her reign.[12] One of the voices leading this anti-fat morality charge was Cesare Lombroso, an Italian physician and criminologist who wrote *The Female Offender* in 1895, in which he used graphs and tables to compare the weights of slimmer, 'moral' women with overweight sex workers: 'This greater weight among prostitutes is confirmed by the notorious fact of the obesity of those who grow old in their vile trade, and who gradually become positive monsters of adipose tissue'. He also makes assumptions about women in prison and insane asylums being heavier. Lombroso argued that criminals are 'primitive savages who are evolutionarily backward compared to normal citizens'. [13]

In *Woman Beautiful* of 1899, author Ella Adelia Fletcher says that: 'wherever the fat woman finds herself in a crowd – and where can she avoid it in the metropolis? – she is in effect an intruder. For, she occupies twice the space to which she is entitled, and inflicts upon her companions, through every one of her excessive pounds, just so much additional fatigue and discomfort [...] She is the innately selfish woman who makes her very existence an offence.'[14] Charming. In this, we see the beginning of how, as women have gained more freedoms in the Western world, we've simultaneously been exhorted to take up as little space as possible – by being othered for not being thin enough. The *Dietetic and Hygenic Gazette* from the 1900s even suggested a 'link' between obesity and 'mental weakness'[15] – something we still see echoes of today, as those who don't have enough 'willpower' are berated by trainers on TV shows like *The Biggest Loser*.

There has been a long link between views of morality and body shape. Self-control, self-discipline and willpower might be the motto of our modern-day fitspo posts, but they have long been celebrated as virtues and linked to food. Though this was primarily aimed at women historically, in the Victorian period, thin became a diktat for men too. Muscular Christianity started as an attempt to reclaim the Church from the mostly female attendees – who some believed were weakening it – by forging a link between Christianity and sport. Organisations like the YMCA and the Boy Scouts promoted the idea that a man should physically discipline himself to be healthy and have influence 'in the same way, a country must assert control over socially disruptive forces in order to become a great and holy nation'. That sounds pretty ominous but the premise was that participating in sport ensured you had 'morality, physical fitness and manly' character. The movement was another factor helping to forge the notion that fat people, across all genders now, were undisciplined, lazy, and immoral.[16]

Prior to the Victorian Industrial Revolution, clothes were handmade to fit the bodies that were to wear them. Whether made at home or by tailors and seamstresses if you were rich, clothing was generally much more bespoke – even if it was a hand-me-down that was adjusted. But in the 19th century, the invention of mass-produced clothing meant that garments could be made faster and more cheaply in factories. By the start of the 20th century, much of the clothing in the UK was sold in department stores rather than being bespoke. This led to the creation of more standardised dress sizes – so now bodies had to fit the clothes that would be put on them, rather than the other way around. If you've ever felt a sense of achievement 'getting into' a smaller size or conversely, having to go up a size, you will know this can affect how we feel about ourselves, even though we know logically sizes aren't standardised and vary hugely – not even across just the entire fashion industry, but from batch to batch and according to brand/designer – depending on where they are made. But spare a thought for the Victorians, who were now buying 'off the rack' for the first time amid a period of huge societal changes and obsession with health in academia and pop culture of the era.

The Victorian period saw much social reform, such as legislation protecting workers (both children and adults), the abolition of the transatlantic slave trade and public health initiatives. While society was still largely hierarchical in terms of class, people started to move around much more, entrepreneurs took the opportunity to make money in new and developing industries and the middle classes grew.

As the old boundaries that had largely maintained the status quo between rich and poor started to shift and become more porous, it follows that the 'large and wealthy' began to lose their 'fat cat' status as food and wealth was distributed (comparatively) more evenly. What now governed everyone was how 'respectable' you were seen to be and, in an era known for its sexual prudishness at times, women who might previously have been seen as being plump, fertile and sexually desirable weren't anymore. This is also when the term 'anorexia' was coined in 1873 by Queen Victoria's physician, Sir William Gull, although cases of 'nervous consumption' had been reported since the late 1600s.[17]

During the early 20th century – a period that saw strides forward in medicine – the rates of infectious disease dropped, life expectancy rose and there was a cultural focus on health and outdoor exercise. The life insurance industry boomed and as a consequence being able to quantify health in some way in order to set premiums was seen as crucial. Insurance companies turned to 'weight tables' marking a move of body size away from connotations of wealth, or a colonial and moral distinction to a scientific and medical problem. We know weight tables like this as BMI (body mass index) charts now; they're often used by fitness and health professionals to work out if your weight is 'healthy'. The height-weight index our BMI system is based on was first described by Belgian mathematician (so, not a doctor) Adolphe Quetelet in the 1830s as a way to diagnose obesity (which wasn't seen as a problem yet) and to work out what the *'l'homme moyen'* or the 'average man' was. All of the participants in his study were white European men. The data didn't look at their health – it just wanted averages.

In the 1970s American physiologist and dietician Ancel Keys suggested that Quetelet's unsophisticated formula was a smart way to screen for obesity. Keys, like Quetelet, measured 7,000 'healthy' men from a mixture of ethnic backgrounds (a small win, though still no women or a mixture of body types). We know now that BMI falls short because it puts athletes in the overweight or obese categories due to stature and muscular composition. And it also fails to account for women and the body compositions of different ethnicities.

Jessica Rabbit, Marilyn Monroe, Kim Kardashian ... they all pay homage to the Gibson Girl. She was created in the US by advertising illustrator Charles Dana Gibson, an American artist in the 1890s, as a character who became popular in titles such as *Life*, *Collier's* and *Harper's Weekly*. She combined two stereotypes of womanhood: the 'fragile lady' and the 'voluptuous woman' rolled into one. She had an hourglass figure with an unnaturally tiny, corseted waist and a large bust, hips and buttocks. Much like Helen of Troy's image was assembled by the painter Zeuxis from multiple women, she was totally made up, like our modern-day photoshopped images or super-filtered social media posts – since the days of yore, we really have been made to chase unattainable standards of beauty.

The Gibson Girl was an early 'pin-up' and was both a widely distributed and widely assumed model of an ideal beauty of the time. She was described as a 'new woman' – independent, well educated and taking more of an active role in society than previous generations. Undeniably influential, despite not actually being a real woman at all, she was still 'fragile' – too much vigour might challenge the ruling gender and stereotypes of femininity at the time (and that still exist ...) after all. Inadvertently or not, Gibson had defined what an American beauty looked like with his idealised woman.

The Gibson Girl's tightly corseted figure was almost impossible to emulate and though she might have been seen to embody a modern woman, she was entirely the result of male creation and fantasy – and she was still controlled by the male gaze: tellingly she was even against suffrage.

Let's talk corsets for a moment. Worn since the 16th century, they were originally known as 'stays', to shape the torso and flatten the bust into an elongated shape that was fashionable at the time rather than as a means of reducing the waist. They were designed to be supportive rather than restrictive – although bending over likely wasn't an option. The term 'corset' came into use at the start of the 19th century and by around 1830, they were shorter than their predecessors, being used to define the waist and support the bust – but were soft and less rigid as steel replaced bone and wood as the main support structure. During the mid-Victorian fat-shaming period, corsets started to be used to reshape the waist rather than support it and tight lacing became a norm for many women. By the Edwardian period, the S-bend corset was the most extreme form seen so far – it forced the torso out at the front while making the hips jut out at the back – all while creating that tiny Gibson-esque waist. By the 1920s, they'd become less restrictive, as curves were now unfashionable and had morphed into shapewear – which was worn by many women until the late 1960s before being revived in a modern guise as Spanx during the noughties obsession with thinness and again more recently with Kim Kardashian's shapewear brand Skims, launched in 2019.

That extreme figure of the S-shape and the Gibson Girl isn't too dissimilar to the body ideal today: an exaggerated hourglass – the kind that women are now getting injections, implants or fat transfers to achieve. Though the Gibson Girl was meant to represent a 'modern' woman of her era, her unrealistic shape created by the restrictive corset is indicative of the correlation between beauty standards becoming more extreme and impossible to achieve, just as women become more emancipated. This extreme man-made body ideal, designed for women to aspire to and to make them feel lacking about their bodies, had a primary function: to distract them from the matter at hand – y'know like freedom, being able to vote, not being male property and all those little details.

Health warnings about tightly laced corsets from doctors started to shift the ideal a little as the 20th century progressed. The First World War saw shortages in materials and rationing was introduced in the UK, which meant that women had to get creative and make rations stretch as far as possible, both for food and repurposed clothing as life and style became more functional. Women took over jobs and roles that men had always occupied during the war and even began wearing trousers if they could source them from men. After the war, there were welcome changes in the rules governing women's freedom. In 1918, in the UK, the Representation of the People Act allowed women over 30 who met a 'property qualification' to vote and most men aged over 21 could by now vote.

Notably, all of this change coincides with the rise of Hollywood and the beginning of the commercial beauty industry as we know it now. It also created what writer Naomi Wolf terms 'beauty work': 'Inexhaustible but ephemeral beauty work took over from inexhaustible but ephemeral housework. As the economy, law, religion, sexual mores, education and culture were forcibly opened up to include women more fairly, a private reality colonized female consciousness.' Totting up the many hours we've toiled in pursuit of achieving a beauty norm is beyond impossible for many of us (if only we were able to bill somebody for time spent removing body hair alone!), but it's now seen as a part or expectation of the female experience. But one thing does correlate: the more freedoms women achieve, the more we are encouraged to take on extra 'beauty work'.

Why? To remain pleasing to the male gaze and to remain preoccupied and distracted by moulding our appearance to suit patriarchy's whims. In a way, the housework we 'left behind' has been replaced with the upkeep of 'beauty work' in whatever form it takes as an extra, invisible job.

During the 1920s, body standards and fashion benchmarks shifted again for women. The ultra-slim flapper became the fashionable body type, embracing a more 'boyish' figure. Corsets had morphed to de-emphasise curves in accordance with these new fashion trends and a variety of styles became available, such as the 'sports corset' and 'hip confiners'.[18] The culture of flappers was exciting: they smoked and drank in public, danced at jazz clubs and their sexual freedom was shocking to the Victorian morality of the previous generation. They were also very thin. On the surface, it does look like a certain type of emancipation, but for body shapes, it was more like a pinball machine, pinging from one unachievable body extreme to another. The 1920s simply presented women with a *different* body aesthetic to chase after and aspire to – one that, for most, required dietary restriction.

But the 1920s was when Western women, collectively, started to diet. Historian Joshua Zeitz wrote in his book *Flapper: A Madcap Story of Sex, Style, Celebrity, and the Women Who Made America Modern*: 'The expectation that they starve themselves in pursuit of flapperdom [was] a very real dilemma for many young women in the 1920s.'[19] Thin was now seen as the way to be youthful and curves were almost deemed old-fashioned, a rhetoric we still carry around being 'young and thin' and 'old and fat'. Slimmer figures had become associated with youth culture – music, dancing and more relaxed attitudes to sex included – and beauty standards like 'thin' were being used as a marketing strategy. Tobacco brands in particular saw a way to capitalise on this and linked weight loss with smoking to sell cigarettes directly to women for that means. A Lucky Strike ad from the era declared: 'To keep a slender figure, No one can deny, reach for a Lucky instead of a sweet'.[20]

Extreme and unscientific diets are not a later 20th-century invention, though. In 1558, Luigi Cornaro restricted his diet to 12oz (just under 340g) food and 14oz (roughly 400ml) wine a day and in the 1800s Lord Byron restricted his diet and used water and vinegar in an attempt to aid weight loss – an approach copied by his female admirers, making him an early celebrity influencer of sorts. Famously, in the early 1900s, beef tapeworm eggs were swallowed as a pill. This could result in weight loss, but also vomiting, meningitis and epilepsy – truly a bitter pill to swallow.[21]

Hollywood's influence on beauty standards can't be understated. Since its early days in the 1910s, directors believed that the camera added weight to people so they favoured slimmer actors, creating pressure on female actors to be thin. Madame Sylvia was the movie industry diet coach and was even hired by film production company Pathé towards the end of the silent era. She believed fat came out of the pores and that there had to be some suffering to get results (a perennial fave in the diet/fitness industry – see also Jane Fonda's 1980s motto 'No Pain, No Gain'). Sylvia promised to 'slenderize, refine, reduce, and squeeze' her clients, like actor Gloria Swanson, into shape.[22]

While male actors had to keep up with gruelling stunts and physically demanding scenes, there was less pressure on them to conform to an extreme body type – it's interesting to compare the men of the golden age of Hollywood (Marlon Brando, for example) with their gym-honed counterparts today. It was their female co-stars who faced the most pressure to be thin – some film contracts even had weight clauses in them. In the late 1920s, Molly O'Day was told the studio would cancel her contract if she couldn't fit into a specific dress size.[23] O'Day's story is a tragic one: while still in her teens she felt such pressure about her weight that she underwent an early prototype of weight-loss surgery. It was a dangerous procedure and for O'Day it ended in pain and scarring: she was forced to retire at just 26. [24]

As we have seen in many areas, Hollywood was setting the mood and the bar for body ideals for women throughout America and internationally. Ann F. La Berge, author of the paper 'How the ideology of low-fat conquered America', said of the time: 'Women's magazines regularly featured diet columns, diets, and recipes. Counting calories was the preferred approach.'[25] Hollywood and fashion had attached a monetary status and glamour to the ideal of thinness, and there were many who were ready to cash in on women's bids to lose weight to look like their successful and lauded Hollywood idols. As one tobacco brand put it: 'Cigarettes are like women. The best ones are thin and rich.' That association still prevails, of course – particularly in high fashion, where brands still rarely stock over a UK size 14. Thin is still mostly seen as a prerequisite to being truly glamourous, fashionable and wealthy – but maybe now with a vape, rather than a Lucky Strike.

After the stock market crash of 1929 and the Great Depression that followed there was a semi-return to conservatism and focus on self-improvement in the US. The styles of the time kept the slim hips from the 1920s but combined with the large breasts and a tiny waist of the Gibson Girl, embodied by actor Mae West. 'The perfect 1938 figure must have curves but it differs from the perfect figure of past decades in relationship of curves to straight lines. Now, though, the ideal figure must have a round, high bosom, a slim but not wasp-like waist, and gently rounded hips,' an article from *Life* instructed.[26] Talk about prescriptive, and controlling.

And yet this was also the era in which the food industry ramped up its innovation and we started to see things like pre-sliced bread, more canned food, frozen food – and the 1930s was also the period in which a lot of the classic chocolate bars that we still know today were invented, like the Mars Bar, Smarties and KitKats. The British were one of the biggest sugar consumers in the world and now we were being sold products that were not particularly nutritionally sound, that make the consumer more likely to put on weight if eaten in quantity.[27] Enter diets like the Grapefruit Diet, aka the Hollywood Diet, which involved an 18-day, 500 calories restriction, existing on grapefruit, orange, toast, vegetables and eggs.

In the years of the Second World War, rationing has actually been shown to have improved the overall health of the British public – a result of increased fruit and veg in most people's diets to bulk up meals, home cooking, limitations on meat, cheese and butter. Luxuries like chocolate were also rationed.

Women again had access to jobs previously closed to them, to fill wartime labour shortages – though they received on average 50 per cent less pay for doing them.[28] As a small consolation, their clothes became less form-fitting and far more utilitarian. There was a real shift from trousers being seen as subversive to functional. But just in case we got too comfortable, another body ideal entered the forum – it was the era of the pin-up. Whether photographed, painted or caricatured, risqué images of young (pretty much always white) women had been popular with men since the early 1900s as a rebellion against traditional Victorian prudishness – the Gibson Girl with her unfeasible hourglass shape was their original big sister. During the war, they boomed and acquired their name, as young soldiers, sailors and airmen used them to decorate the military accommodation they found themselves in. Actor Dolores del Río was said to have the 'best figure in Hollywood' – with *Photoplay* magazine noting her 'warmly curved' and 'roundly turned' body.[29]

Women were still being exhorted to diet – with products like Bile Beans (first launched in the 1890s) being sold to them more and more. These pills were dressed as a slimming supplements but were laxatives – another parallel with modern times and the rise of social-media peddled slimming teas and drinks. Meanwhile, doctors had started using those early insurers' weight tables (inspired by Quetelet, page 134) to evaluate health and weight – lucky us.

In that post-war boom of the 1950s in the US, the hourglass was officially back as the fashion media seemed to prize exaggerated femininity with hip-skimming circle skirts, lower necklines and pointed 'sweater girl' bras and jumpers, popularised by Hollywood's glamorous film stars and a little reminiscent of the Gibson Girl, or even the Venus figurines. But there were mixed messages – ads of the time advised thin women (who were the height of fashion just a couple of decades ago) to fill out their curves using products like Wate-On, while magazines such as *Woman's Own* published articles on how to lose weight, in what had become a narrow remit for a beautiful body. Housewives were exhorted to retain their figures and burn calories however possible – from dusting to calisthenics and hula hooping. Slimming had become a cultural obsession and the first radio broadcast of an exercise class in the UK started with Eileen Fowler on BBC Radio in 1954 – who was the original Rosemary Conley.

You might well ask did men face any pressures to change their bodies during this time? They did, though they're not nearly as extreme. Being fit had been prized for men since the Victorian period, but Hollywood's obsession with slim physiques and the camera adding weight saw stars like Laurence Olivier and Cary Grant, with their lean and athletic-looking frames, become the male body ideal. In his heyday of the 1930s and 1940s, Charles Atlas became an inspirational figure for many men in the US, going from 97 pounds to a bodybuilder's physique, after he grew tired of being bullied by larger men and wanted to revenge on the lifeguard who 'stole' his girlfriend. He eventually became a pop culture icon and people were inspired by his transformation. Atlas's success started to sell the message that for men, physical size could give you confidence. But as always, the pressures on male appearance – though tangible – weren't nearly as bad as they were for women. From the turn of the 20th century, what was deemed the desirable body shape for women changed drastically in almost every decade. And of course, everyone was expected to measure up.

This was dramatised wonderfully in the TV series *Mad Men*. One moment, Joan is the office siren, all curves and wiggle dresses and Marilyn energy. She's seen as sexy and at times promiscuous. Then, as the fashions change as America heads into the 1960s, Joan seems almost matronly and old-fashioned alongside the younger characters, with their more gamine body shapes and loose shift dresses. It's a fascinating depiction of how women can be made to feel obsolete by swift changes in fashion and body ideals and the political, social and economic structures that influence them.

The fashions of the 1960s were again orientated around youth, reverting back to favouring more 'boyish' cuts, like those of the 1920s, with de-emphasised hips and shorter hemlines – young women rebelled against restrictive shapes and uncomfortable underwear needed to create them in a similar way to how the flappers had rejected the Gibson Girl figure.

Looking at the politics of an era alongside its fashion and beauty ideals is always revealing. The 1960s and 1970s certainly saw a rebellious sense of style, while being an intense period of female emancipation. In the UK, for example, the contraceptive pill launched in 1961 (only available to married women until that changed in 1967). The 1967 Abortion Act legalised abortion up to 28 weeks, requiring two doctors to agree that continuing the pregnancy would be harmful to the mother or child's physical or mental health, while women went on strike for equal pay in Dagenham in 1968 and protested against Miss World in 1970 outside London's Royal Albert Hall.[30] Labour MP Barbara Castle became the first female secretary of state; the first Women's Liberation Movement conference was held at Ruskin College, Oxford, in 1970, while in 1973, the Brixton Black Women's Group had formed, aiming to raise consciousness of the specific issues affecting Black women. By 1975, the Sex Discrimination Act passed to 'render unlawful certain kinds of sex discrimination and discrimination on the ground of marriage and establish a Commission with the function of working towards the elimination of such discrimination and promoting equality of opportunity between men and women generally; and for related purposes'.[31]

Yet while women appeared to be defeating patriarchal oppression on a number of fronts – take the Grandassa Models, a group co-founded by photojournalist and activist Kwame Brathwaite to celebrate Black beauty[32] – there was still that ever-present pressure on women to look flat-stomached and slim-hipped to fit into the fashions of the time. This era saw diets like the Cabbage Soup Diet (tried it, gross), low-carb diets (see ya, bread) and the egg and wine diet of the seventies (unimaginable, really) that all promised to drastically change (mostly) women's body shapes. During the 1970s, the diet industry and diet culture ramped up exponentially as diet shakes, books and gadgets started to enter the market significantly. Weight-loss pills like Biphetamine in the US and Dexamyl in the UK, which were amphetamine based also became more readily available. (Did I mention the time in the 2000s when I took some now-banned diet pills, double-dosed, and ended up walking and talking at double speed and couldn't sleep for a week? It was like permanently being on fast forward, and pretty scary. I didn't know when it would end.) By now, the amount of industries invested in thinness and making a profit from it was huge: Tobacco, fashion, health, food and drink, pharmaceuticals, advertising ... Thin was being 'sold' directly or indirectly by all of them.

Some pushed back against the body-shaming fashion, advertising and diet agenda that was being thrust so heavily on them. In the US, the fat acceptance movement was founded as a way to celebrate fat bodies and remove the shame and stigma that had grown since the Victorian period – around bigger bodies. The National Association to Advance Fat Acceptance (NAAFA) was founded by Bill Fabrey and Llewelyn Louderback in 1969 because both men were tired of their wives being ridiculed because of their weight. Their activism took the form of 'sit ins' or 'fat ins' in Central Park, which protested fatphobia as attendees burned pictures of Twiggy and ate ice cream. And they tried to address fat phobia in schools and the media. The Fat Underground formed in California too, calling for Fat Liberation, with a Fat manifesto in 1973 calling for 'equal rights for fat people in all areas of life' and making 'reducing' industries – as dieting was then often called – accountable. By the 1980s, the movements in the US had inspired others globally. The London Fat Women's Group formed in the mid-eighties, remaining active for years.

In 1978, British psychotherapist Susie Orbach published the ground-breaking *Fat Is A Feminist Issue*. She wrote of the era: 'As women are encouraged to become smaller and smaller and the Western Obsession with health=slimness=happiness=diet intensifies, more and more books are rushed into the marketplace offering new, permanent weight reduction schemes or advice on how to dress slim, minimise "bad points" and project the perfect body. Slimness, first marketed as a way to emulate the jet set, has developed a life of its own. Success, beauty, wealth, love, sexuality and happiness are promoted as attached to and depending on slimness.'[33] Orbach's book still resonates today, unfortunately. In particular, her discussion of the way in which the culture of thin and aversion to fat was not only selling a false beauty ideal but also promoting poor eating habits that ultimately helped the diet industry flourish.

While all women are affected by pressure to measure up to constantly changing ideal body shapes and led to believe that their worth is intrinsically bound up with their size, this hits women in the public eye especially hard. When Cass Elliot, singer in The Mamas & The Papas, first wanted to join the band, a male band member was reluctant to allow her to perform for audiences despite her great voice because she was overweight. After numerous hits, when the band split she tried relentlessly to lose weight with diets of the time and as she embarked on a run of shows in Las Vegas, she underwent a six-month crash diet, losing over 100 pounds. It ended up hospitalising her and damaging her stomach and throat; she died of a heart attack in her sleep, aged 32, in 1974. Perhaps the years of crash dieting, intense fasting, poor nutrition and stress had taken their toll, but the press reported that she'd choked to death on a ham sandwich, which wasn't the case. Her daughter, Owen, said, 'It's been hard for my family with the sandwich rumour. One last slap against the fat lady. People seem to think it's funny. What's so darn funny?' It's a similar case for Elvis, who died in 1977. Though the official report says his death aged 42 was due to cardiac arrest (perhaps from the amount of prescription meds he took), other theories suggest it was constipation and his well-documented love of 'unhealthy' foods leading to him 'dying on the toilet'. Even the king of rock 'n' roll is not exempt from being jibed at for being fat.

News of Monica Lewinsky's affair with then-president, Bill Clinton, broke in 1998 when the former White House intern was just 24. Among the misogynistic attacks she received in the press, Lewinsky was mocked for her weight and talk-show hosts made jibes about having her jaw wired shut – and all the slut-shaming that implies. As she later told *Vanity Fair*: 'I became a social representation, a social canvas on which anybody could project their confusion about women, sex, infidelity, politics, and body issues.'[34]

Meanwhile, celebrities who visibly lost a lot of weight, like talk-show host Oprah Winfrey in 1988, who lost 67 pounds on a liquid diet called OPTIFAST, were celebrated for their success, as though it were an achievement on par with winning a prestigious award. Oprah has since spoken about how her metabolism was affected by the diet and how it felt when she gained the weight back. Weight loss started to make the headlines as 'news', as did reports of people being fired or seen as not the right fit because of their size.

When a celebrity who was previously fat then loses weight – take Adele or Rebel Wilson for example – there's an even more intense scrutiny on their new body, alongside media obsession over 'how they did it'. There's often intense speculation and words like 'sexy' are attributed to them in a way never previously. All of it is confirmation of what we have been sold repeatedly: fat means you're unhappy, and unsexy. It echoes sentiments that multiple books from the 1990s reference, which is that 'there's a thin person inside you' and they're better than the existing you in every way.

While riot grrrl and counter culture were embracing feminism and self-expression through the arts, that was translated into mainstream pop culture in a highly commercialised form with all-girl groups like the Spice Girls. On the one hand, they offered a new 'bolshy' narrative for women in pop music of the era and discussed everything from safe sex to 'girl power'. But the group's members were hand-picked by male record execs and given one-dimensional identities that young girls could pick from to emulate, though they all were, of course, slim. To many, they were symbolic of female rebellion, though others associated them with the questionable 'ladette culture' of the era. Mel B admitted years later that eating disorders were so normal in the group she only noticed when band members shrank dramatically. And Mel C has recently spoken about her bulimia and the shame she experienced on being fat-shamed by the media and men in the industry.

Everything – even the pop culture that was progressive, and 'first of its kind', often harboured fat-shaming views. *Sex and the City* (first broadcast in 1998) was empowering women to explore and talk about sex more, it also body-shamed people in a way that was seen as totally normal at the time. In Season Three, when Carrie turns up at her ex-boyfriend's new wife Natasha's event, Samantha brings over a friend of Natasha's to tell Carrie that Natasha used to be 'fat in college'. Naturally, Carrie seems to revel in it – she's got one up on her rival, as fat had, over the decades, become a way to establish rank over another, from its colonial start. Miranda joins Weight Watchers (which, FYI, was founded in 1963 by Jean Nidetch, self-described as an 'overweight housewife obsessed with cookies') to lose her baby weight because the scales read 152 pounds (roughly 10.8 stone), attaching shame and paranoia to that specific weight. When Samantha visits friends unexpectedly they're shocked about her *enormous* 5lb weight gain as a result of comfort eating. Her weight is spoken about like it's a huge, pressing issue.

It's telling how far British women took *Bridget Jones's Diary* (2001) to their hearts, as weight and diet obsession was something we all related to and Bridget's hang-up with weight was central to her identity and character. At least she got a happy ending, as there was a handsome man (Mark Darcy, played by Colin Firth) on hand to reassure her that she was, in fact, acceptable, even at roughly a UK dress size 12 or 14, telling her he liked her 'just as you are'.

As if there weren't enough outlets adding to body anxieties, helpfully, Hollywood stepped in to make what amounts to a comedy sub-genre dedicated to mercilessly mocking fat people, something I remember all too well. In *Shallow Hal* (2002), Gwyneth Paltrow – in a fat suit – plays a character who eats everything in sight and is treated with disdain by her family. She's not seen as lovable until Jack Black's character (himself, not a slim chap) is hypnotised to like her. Talk about ever-present double standards. In 1996, Eddie Murphy also donned a fat suit to play both lead roles in *The Nutty Professor*, one of whom is in pursuit of the love that eludes him as a fat person. Disney movie *Heavyweights* (1995) saw kids sent to a fat camp – run by a fitness-crazed director played by Ben Stiller – as they go to extremes to lose weight. It seemed there was no end of comic mileage in fat bodies.

Dr Katariina Kyrölä, lecturer in media studies at the University of Turku, Finland, and author of *The Weight of Images: Affect, Body Image and Fat in the Media*, says there's often a disconnect in how fat characters – particularly women – in mainstream TV and film comedies since the mid-1990s have had a 'continuous incongruence and tension between the fat character's body image, the way they see themselves and the way others or a particular other see them'. She points to the stereotype of the 'deluded fat woman', like the character of Rasputia in *Norbit* (2007) – Eddie Murphy in a fat suit *again* – as a 500-pound woman who wears a bikini, or Martin Lawrence as an overweight FBI agent in *Big Momma's House* (2000). They're portrayed as confident women, but in a hyper-comedic way, because Eurocentric beauty standards dictate they should feel ashamed of their size. As Kyrölä notes, in these cases it is men playing the character of a fat woman and a mammy stereotype, which create a pantomime-like caricature of fat Black women and their desirability – something Hollywood has created and policed since its earliest days.[35] You cannot be fat, happy and confident, it's *incomprehensible*.

Growing up amid this sort of fat-shaming had a lasting effect on me that meant my size was a source of embarrassment and had the potential to be mocked at any point. These views come at us from every angle and industry – even our entertainment. Cumulatively, it has the effect of indoctrination and propaganda. That's why it's so vital to look back and consider what harm has been done from the media we were consuming as younger people. It doesn't mean we have to reject all of the TV from the 1990s and 2000s, but if we can re-evaluate this stuff from fat-suit Monica in *Friends* to the Disney princesses we adored, when we watch them, they should feel archaic and we should notice. If we don't, and they don't jar even a little, perhaps we do need to gain a greater awareness of what we might have tolerated and internalised as a beauty norm.

Being fat meant you were lazy, bad, weak and fair game for public harassment too, endorsed by TV 'nutritionists' like Gillian McKeith (*You Are What You Eat*, 2004–06) and fashion makeover shows like *What Not to Wear* (started in 2001), which saw presenters Trinny Woodall and Susannah Constantine 'help' somebody nominated as being style-challenged – at its peak, the show drew in over 7 million viewers. They would review the footage, comment freely on the person's style and dress sense and parts of their bodies, with tummies and boobs being a frequent 'issue'. Meanwhile, *Supersize Vs Superskinny* (2008–14) compared the diets of a very slim person the team thought needed to gain weight because of their picky eating habits and somebody fat, who was shown as being gluttonous. They were forced to stand side by side in their underwear as their weekly food consumption was poured into a shoot/tube to show how much or how little they ate – and why it was the wrong kind of thing to be eating. The heavier person invariably took the brunt of body-shaming on the programme that ultimately prized thinness. Clips from the triggering show are awash on YouTube, where it now seems to have found a new audience of people suffering from eating disorders.[36]

All of this is connected – like a montage throughout the decades that links everything together in a body-shaming constellation. The normalisation of disordered eating and narrow body standards meant that as a teenager growing up in the shadow of the eighties diet obsession and in the heart of the nineties thin obsession, it was almost *expected* that women had a difficult relationship with food. When I meet somebody who didn't, they seem like a curious case study – I'm fascinated by how they managed to escape it.

Diets started to feel like an identity – what were you on this week, what would you pick? By the late-20th century, decades of extreme body ideals and pressure to diet had created a maelstrom of conflicted beauty standards that were seriously affecting the mental health of many women. 'Nothing tastes as good as skinny feels,' declared supermodel Kate Moss, while Elizabeth Hurley declared that she would kill herself if she were as 'fat' as fellow actor and beauty icon Marilyn Monroe.

Though anorexia rates in Europe and North America had been rising sharply over time (they appeared to briefly stabilise in the 1970s), rates of bulimia now continued to increase in the 1980s and 1990s.[37] Despite this, a *New York Times* article from 1985 by Carol Lawson reported that the obsession with weight and size was ever-present: a poll released at the time stated that 47 per cent of teenage girls and 39 per cent of teenage boys in the poll said they personally knew someone they thought had anorexia nervosa. Lawson wrote: 'The current increase in anorexia nervosa is believed to be linked, in part, to the public's obsession with exercise and fitness and the pressure to look thin,' as celebrities also spoke up about their eating issues.[38] However, it's important to note that such a complex condition is often more than just about seeing thin women lauded in the media. At times my eating disorder felt like it gave me control in a world that I had so little control over, though any relief was momentary – and my anxiety continued.

The 1980s also saw men beginning to be sold a dramatically different body ideal in such a powerful way that women have for decades. There was a slimmer look during the 1970s for men, but that changed in the 1980s, as pumped-up bodies – led by the bodybuilding trend – became the ideal body shape, with zero ounce of fat on view. Actors like Arnold Schwarzenegger, Sylvester Stallone and Jean-Claude Van Damme became heavy-lifting icons and high protein and low-carb diets began to take hold. As we saw earlier in A Culture of Ugly (*see also* page 49), changes in the meaning of 'femininity' and women becoming more powerful in society have a knock-on effect on the perception of masculinity. That hyper-masculine body ideal permeated every aspect of culture – take popular films of the era like *Rocky* (1976) and *Top Gun* (1986), and songs, like 'So Macho' by Sinitta (1987). The chorus of Bonnie Tyler's 1984 classic 'Holding Out for a Hero' contains the lyrics, 'He's gotta be strong, and he's gotta be fast, and he's gotta be fresh from the fight.' Why were men being exhorted to be as big and muscular as possible? Industries like fitness and diet spotted the money-making opportunities, but we were in a period where women were entering the workplace in greater numbers than before. Did men feel like they had to be physically much larger than women to reclaim their space and gender roles? Perhaps.

But fitness was being weaponised against women too. The beauty standard of thin was starting to morph into a new guise: toned. Toned was slim, but with some definition; it required more than just eating very little, it also required working out. Amazonian supermodels became the new body goals in the 1980s like Naomi Campbell, Linda Evangelista and Cindy Crawford – super tall and sculpted, with large breasts and small hips, without being visibly ripped, which might have presumably been a threat to men and disrupted the narrative of what femininity looked like. As such, the fitness industry that had been so focused on men aimed its target at women.

Celebrity workouts by everyone from Elizabeth Taylor to Cher had encouraged people to do aerobics alongside their calorie counting and had even influenced fashion trends for leg warmers and leotards across both sides of the pond. By the late 1990s workouts became much more intense: from step aerobics, indoor cycling classes to Tae-bo, a mix of martial arts, aerobics and boxing – all promising to maximise calorie burn, torch fat and give you toned arms like Madonna or Jennifer Aniston. No 'bingo wings' were allowed.

By the 2000s it felt like there was no middle ground and body standards seemed to become more and more extreme: either you were very thin, or you were fat and unsatisfactory. This was the era when the deeply damaging trend for size zero was coined by American designer Nicole Miller and fashion stylist Rachel Zoe, herself incredibly thin, was the *stylist du jour* for young female celebrities like Mischa Barton, Nicole Richie and Lindsay Lohan – who were under heavy scrutiny from the press and public. Jutting-out hipbones and ultra-flat midriffs declared a war on 'love handles' and 'muffin tops' as workouts became even more intense, like 'Insanity' which launched in 2009 as a supercharged home workout. If you didn't do these things or at least be seen to be trying to lose weight, you were regarded as lazy, even though it was hard to find anything to wear to the gym. That's because the fashion fitness industry still showed you who was desirable enough to wear its garments. It wasn't until 2017 that Nike launched a plus-size range, followed by Adidas in 2019.

In the late 2000s, the tide seemed to be turning very slowly towards a more inclusive approach to bodies. After over a century of fat-shaming, fat phobia and rising obesity rates, research concluded that negativity around weight wasn't a motivator to lose pounds, but the opposite of this. Shock horror! But why hadn't anyone seen it before? Because they'd looked away: kindness and acceptance doesn't sell quite so many diet books or fitness gadgets. Around this time, a semi-kindness entered consciousness, but it wasn't that all humans – irrespective of body shape or size – deserve equal treatment. It was that weight loss required kindness; thin was still the goal, but now you could be nicer to yourself as you willed yourself to lose the love handles.

A new wave of fat acceptance had started in the late 2000s as a community of mostly plus-size women of colour were seeking a space that appreciated their bodies, using hashtags like #Fatacceptance and #Bodypositivity on blogging platforms like Tumblr and LiveJournal. When blogger Gabi Gregg went viral in 2010, it was a signal to brands that there could be money in the plus-size fashion sector and increased body inclusivity. They eventually started to realise that, far from being berated at every turn, women of all sizes wanted to feel represented. More size-inclusive beauty campaigns like Dove's Real Beauty in 2004 and plus-size models like Sophie Dahl, Crystal Renn and Ashley Graham became famous. In 2014 Victoria's Secret released the 'Perfect Body', their body-positivity campaign, though the line-up mostly featured white models who granted were bigger than their regular models, but still sat within the mid-size range. There was a pattern here – of picking fat women selectively: often they were white or light-skinned, with slim faces and hourglass proportions. You could now be fat-ish – but to be celebrated for it still came with caveats.

We're now in an era that's embracing the body-positivity movement (it even entered the Oxford English Dictionary in 2021) and it provides inspiration and community for those who feel the pressure to conform to narrow body standards or want to see their bodies celebrated when the mainstream still fails to do so. But this does feel like it's been co-opted and commodified. Everyone deserves to feel great about themselves at every size, but the faces of the movement who feature prominently in ad campaigns (and are likely also favoured more by beauty-biased algorithms) are so often under a size 16, white, pretty and hourglass – perhaps with a little cellulite and a jiggly stomach. Or even very slim white women, like Louise Thompson – who appeared on *Made in Chelsea* – and published a book called *Body Positive* with diet and fitness advice – the opposite of what the movement stood for.

Though everyone might feel the force of the pressure to look a certain way to meet beauty standards, ultimately, not everyone has experienced fat phobia or fat-shaming in quite the same way. The hardships of not being able to shop on the high street, asking for seat belt extenders, or nobody wanting to sit by you on the bus or being verbally abused for your size, can be deeply othering experiences. Stephanie Yeboah, author of *Fattily Ever After*, told the *Guardian*: 'The only time I've been admitted to hospital because of my weight was because I was beaten up for being fat. We're not promoting obesity, or telling people to be fat, we're just saying, if you're fat you don't have to hate yourself.'[39]

It's telling that 'body acceptance for all' has come at the price of the erasure of women of colour who started the modern body-positivity movement. It's a hard truth to swallow when you consider that colonisation was part of the reason fat bodies were demonised in the first place. But the liberation of marginalised bodies is so necessary: according to the Women and Equalities Committee report in 2021, 12 per cent of cisgender participants reported feeling very negative about their bodies, compared to 23 per cent of transgender participants who reported feeling 'very negative' – the report said that 'not a single transgender respondent felt "very positive" about their body image.' Likewise, 71 per cent of disabled respondents feel poorly about their body most of the time and 40 per cent of LGBT adults experience shame due to their body image. It's just another way that the people who need it most are pushed out of the conversation.[40]

As to Yeboah's point, we're surprised when we see fat women with confidence, because it goes against the narrative that they have to loathe themselves and feel undesirable. Despite being hugely inspirational, plus-size influencers and body-positivity activists are still subject to online abuse. It triggers some people to see everything they've been told about beauty standards dismantled; it disrupts the status quo that means 'everything makes sense'. In 2016, plus-size influencer Callie Thorpe's wedding picture went viral as people's minds were blown seeing a beautiful, happy, plus-size bride in a tight dress, with no hint of self-loathing or body shame – the opposite of the expected bridal slim-down that women are expected to follow, with months of self-deprivation leading up to the big day.

There's still shock when anyone above a size 16 is shown as being happy with their bodies, with a conventionally slim partner, like Jenna Kutcher, who wrote about having 'Mr 6-pack' as her husband and the trolls who told her she didn't deserve him because she was apparently too fat to be with somebody who looked like him. It doesn't tally with what we've been told is attractive, or how we've been told we should look to be attractive and desirable – which is slim. In 2015 actor Gabourey Sidibe's sex scene in *Empire* caused a #Myfatsexstory hashtag to trend but conversely, a backlash too, presumably by those outraged her character Becky – a fat, dark-skinned Black woman – was paired with and desired by a successful, straight-sized rapper. And in 2016, a Weight Watchers advert aired in Australia and New Zealand that received backlash for trying to appeal to women who felt self-conscious during sex because of their size.[41]

As 2000's fashion trends and beauty trends come back into fashion (with modern-day caveats – I haven't seen the shaved-off eyebrows I had, yet), will hipster jeans bring with them the obsession with hip bones again or ultra-flat stomachs for midriff-baring tops? The desire to be thin above all and the obsession with thinness is what made that era a nightmare growing up for so many women (and the men forced to show ripped, waxed torsos at every given opportunity). But if patterns in history are a predictor, following the rise of empowering and necessary movements like #Metoo and Black Lives Matter then it could be the case that as women and people of colour take up more space and airtime, there is a societal backlash that shows up as colonised beauty ideals. That feels like the perfect opportunity for patriarchy – via fashion and beauty brands – to support trends that, just as in the 2000s, champion a limited range of body shapes. And signal a return to elevating thinness as a beauty standard once more.

In January 2022, Beat, the eating disorder charity, administered the highest number of eating disorder support sessions in a month in its entire history – a 7 per cent increase from the year before, perhaps also due to high CAMHS (children and adolescent mental health services) waiting lists and a result of the surge in eating disorders during lockdown too. YouTube and TikTok are awash with #WhatIEatInADay videos that feel like a combination of 1990s/2000s surge in pro-ana (promoting anorexia) websites, and magazine features that often ran celebrity diet diaries detailing what said celeb ate in a day – but now are under the guise of 'health'. In 2020 research from UCL found that Gen Z are more worried about weight gain than other generations: 'It is generally now widely accepted that the media, and social media in particular, can precipitate or feed into poor mental health and disordered eating,' Dr Heather Naylor, Clinical Director at The London Centre for Eating Disorders and Body Image, told *Dazed Digital*.[42]

The truth is that it feels like we are being played again and again when the bottom line is that it shouldn't feel like this much of a challenge to accept ourselves as we are. But there is so much going against us. What would the diet industry do if we stopped trying to lose weight? (Maybe it would rebrand as 'wellness'. Oh, wait, it did – more about that in The Ugly Side of Wellness chapter.) The fashion, fitness and food industries also all have a stake in how we feel about ourselves and our bodies. They are making money out of making us feel lacking and ugly.

Whatever size you are, if this is something that still controls your life – whether that comes in the form of calorie counting, coveting thinness in others or restricting what you do or wear because you think you are 'too big' – do you really want it? Or is it a cultural habit, formed, as we have seen in this chapter, from layer upon layer of bullshit, telling us over centuries how our bodies 'should' look?

If there was a moment in the past where you felt fat-shamed, close your eyes and re-imagine it for a moment. In my mind, I revisit those Topshop changing rooms as a kid and instead of sizes 6–14, I see a wider selection that meant I could wear what my friends did. I then pick up a teen magazine and see styles modelled on a variety of body shapes, types and ethnicities. And on the teen shows I watched religiously, the love interests touch across a whole spectrum of 'beautiful'. It feels calming and limitless. That's the world we should have had. You deserved more and I did too.

In a time when we're collectively levelling up about our responsibility to see other viewpoints, and our own privilege, tackling fat discrimination has been the sole responsibility of those who it shames. But people of all sizes can and should message the fashion brands who still cater for selective sizes to tell them it's not good enough and what their selectivity is really saying (as a reminder: that they just want thin, white people to buy their clothes). Dismantling this might also entail challenging our own internalised fat phobia by being mindful of what we say to each other about weight and body size, particularly in the presence of younger people (a friend's 6-year-old daughter asked if she might get fat if she ate a biscuit ...) who might take their cues and be influenced by us.

It's not my place to wave a wand and say 'be happy as you are' – because with an enduring history of fat-shaming and fat phobia that is still active, being body positive isn't that easy. (Like that magazine editor said to me, 'I *give* you the permission to be confident!' Er, no. That's not how that happens.) It might mean replacing body positivity with body neutrality – a middle-of-the-road approach which means you neither hate, nor love your body, you just accept it – and doing whatever it takes to reframe our link between body size and self-worth. Following women on social media, my size or larger, made a huge difference to my self-perception. It normalised my body in a way that made me realise that everything around me I'd absorbed and been shown about body size was deeply limited and limiting. But we can also make the decision as to whether we want to keep actively supporting the industries that profit from toxic body standards and if we choose to buy into upholding thinness as a finite beauty standard.

If you take anything from this chapter, it should be that fat was created by patriarchy to maintain power over white women, to enforce the class system and to establish colonised standards of beauty actively designed to make women of colour feel like they don't measure up. It was created to control all of us: now is the time we have to *collectively* start dismantling it and what it really stands for.

FIXING UGLY

'You can't fix ugly'

– Tom Jackson, Season One,

Queer Eye

QUESTION: HOW MANY TIMES have you 'fixed yourself in a single day? By 'fix', I mean changed or concealed something on your body to match a beauty ideal. Take a standard day: we wake up, perhaps shave a variety of body parts in the shower, then do something to our altered/coloured/extended hair. We apply make-up to hide our natural dark circles or give ourselves 'contour' and carefully dress to mask our perceived flaws. We apply deodorants and perfumes to hide odours, we paint our nails to appear groomed.

We fix a lot about ourselves, often on autopilot – these are just 'things' women are expected to do as an invisible part of our daily to-do lists. Sometimes it's our preference or something we *think* is a preference, it can be tricky to truly know if we want to or feel like we should. But more often there's a sense of societal obligation and fear of judgement if we don't meet those standards – like wearing make-up for work to look professional or ensuring our hair is coloured so we don't look 'old'. Sometimes, if we stop for a moment, as I did just today, applying foundation on my face to 'even out my skin tone', we might realise that as we fix ourselves, we tell ourselves we *need* fixing. It's like painting on a gentle coat of self-loathing as we colour correct our faces. My point? Each time we hide or mask a part of us, we risk telling ourselves a story in our heads about how we don't measure up or we're ugly. Like the opposite of a pep talk, every single day. Over time, those micro-feelings grind us down until something becomes unbearable. Then, we might continue playing that self-loathing soundtrack, or we might 'fix' it temporarily – or permanently, with cosmetic surgery.

Pretty much everyone these days has given cosmetic intervention at least a passing thought. How can we not? It's fired at us from every conceivable direction. Reality TV hocks it, social media sells it to us as a route to looking 'flawless', celebrities talk about their 'good genes' while we strongly suspect they've had something done. It is *everywhere.* Which has given us the mindset that 'everyone has done it' and 'it's no big deal' – in fact, most of us probably know several people who have had some 'work' done. But it is just that – work.

As we've seen, fixing ourselves has been part of our invisible workload for centuries. Cosmetic procedures are now another, increasingly accessible option with payment plans and cosmetic surgery tourism offering lower prices (though sometimes, also complications). The UK is the fastest-growing market for facial filler[1] and British plastic surgeons reported a 70 per cent rise in requests for consultations in 2020,[2] and yet our levels of body confidence are decreasing in the UK.[3] The NHS defines body dysmorphia as 'a mental health condition where a person spends a lot of time worrying about flaws in their appearance'.[4] This psychologically complicated condition can result from genetics, chemical imbalances in the brain or trauma – like being bullied for your appearance. But there's no word to describe the knowledge that as we hate our appearance more and more, there are industries profiting from that. It's hard to pinpoint where this started – did the boom in cosmetic surgery cause us to feel worse about ourselves, or did it offer us a solution? Of course, cunningly, it positions itself as the latter, while never taking accountability for the former. Why would it?

Everywhere we turn, a fix like a one-day recovery boob job[5] or injectable 'tweakments' such as filler or Botox are being sold to us as being as easy to access as popping to a Pret for an artisan cheese and pickle baguette over our lunchbreaks. Even the word 'tweak' suggests it is little more than buying a lipstick or a new way to do a smoky eye. Treatments are being offered to us at an increasingly young age too; before we've even decided how we truly feel about ourselves, or been given a chance to grow into our bodies, we're offered something to fix us. Worse still, the procedures marketed at us are often to address an 'issue' that we didn't see as a problem in the first place, giving us an insecurity we didn't have before.

Increasingly, social media is gamifying dissatisfaction in our appearance. Take a recent TikTok trend for covering noses with a finger to see what they would look like smaller, dressed up as a 'challenge'. How many teenagers who had previously given no thought to their nose are now questioning its size or shape? *Huffington Post* wrote about the case of a girl called Zoe (whose name was changed) who, after being teased at school about a bump in her nose, aged 16, had a consultation with a cosmetic surgeon who agreed to the procedure, and then drew her attention to 'imperfections' she hadn't previously been aware of: 'I distinctly remember him using the words "bulbous tip",' she said.[6] Supermodel Bella Hadid admitted regretting a nose job she had at the wincingly young age of 14.[7]

The 2008 documentary *My Perfect Vagina* has always stuck with me because it summed up how we're sold insecurity and it's incredibly graphic viewing too. It featured a 21-year-old woman desperately seeking a labiaplasty (surgery to reduce the size of the labia minora), who says: 'It might seem extreme to other people but I don't think of it as like, you know, "dangerous" [or] anything like that because I want it so much.' She'd been picked on about it by her sister, who commented on the way it looked and told partners about it, even causing a break-up – talk about a rogue sibling. She details male friends making fun of her about it and said: 'I just thought I was so different to everyone else that I wanted that to be changed.' She became so self-conscious about it that she eventually underwent surgery and the 'excruciating' recovery but said, 'It looks so much better than it did before, doesn't it?' Her body anxiety came at a period that was incredibly critical about women's appearance, likely set against the digitalisation of pornography in this time, which influenced the rise of bikini waxing trends, laser hair removal and 'designer vaginas'. The lengths we'll go to in order to feel 'normal' are often extreme and though previous chapters explore how and why beauty standards exist in the first place, often the beliefs about what's 'normal' or what's 'acceptable' feel like they're just a fact, something we must adhere to at all costs – and that's without a harsh sister.

I found it telling that this young woman didn't see any danger in the surgery, because fixing this perceived issue outweighed any potential negative outcomes. That's often the true cost of being made to feel ugly – how far you'll go and what you'll risk to fix it. The cosmetic surgeon who performed the labiaplasty said he'd received criticism for doing so... 'Really I'm not going to talk about whether it's right or wrong [...] no one can force anyone to go for surgery. The way we treat patients, if it affects them psychologically and it can help them, why not? So if the excess skin is there and you want to trim it, you trim it.' The real question should be: 'If [insert force damaging our self-esteem and controlling our beauty standards] wasn't quite so powerful, would we feel so bad about ourselves, leading to us literally having bits of our bodies sliced off?' But of course that's never a conversation anyone making money in these industries wants to have. It's fine to cut into us, but why cut into their profit margins?

Over the years I've interviewed a number of cosmetic surgeons and received similar comments around the ethics, batting back the responsibility for making these huge life-changing choices to the patient. That would be fine if patients were making them from a truly unbiased, informed perspective – but when what's 'ugly' is defined everywhere we turn, as is the 'fix', that's not always the case. We're so entrenched in a society that wants to fix women in particular, from a very young age, that we seldom see what we are being sold – and who in the room benefits from it.

Third and our current fourth waves of feminism have advocated for freedom of choice around beauty, arguing that it can be empowering rather than oppressive, as it was often viewed in the second wave when razors were ceremoniously flung away. But I think we've left something behind: and that's ourselves and how we feel and deserve to feel. We can of course be feminists and adore beauty and have cosmetic surgery – but that doesn't always mean it's empowering, even though that is how it's now being sold to us – just as cosmetics were in the 1970s. A spritz of 'Charlie' didn't actually give women any freedom after all.

That's not to say all cosmetic procedures are bad – at all. They are a feat of medical advancement and a lifeline for many who have reconstructive surgery following cancer, pursue gender-affirming surgery or have hailed breast reductions as a huge ease of discomfort, allowing them to live more physically comfortable lives to name only three examples. These are just a handful of many ways that in particular plastic surgery – 'to restore the function and appearance of tissue and skin so it's as close to normal as possible' – and cosmetic surgery – 'carried out solely to change a person's appearance to achieve what they feel is a more desirable look' (NHS definitions) – has helped change people's lives for the better. It's just that we now *expect* people to fix anything that falls below the current and ever-shifting standard of perfection, such is the ease of access to cosmetic procedures. Hate your ears? Fix them. Your teeth? Whiten them. Your laughter lines? Fill them. And our surprise, confusion and/or envy when people don't submit to those standards is often thinly veiled. Phrases like, 'It's great that you embrace your curves' or 'Your nose gives you character' come across as compliments with a hint of 'good on you for trying to love yourself as you are'. Elizabeth Haiken, author of *Venus Envy: A History of Cosmetic Surgery*, notes in relation to our attitude to 'fixing' ourselves: 'In 1923 Americans clamoured for an explanation of why Fanny Brice, beloved vaudeville actor, successful comedienne, and star of Florenz Ziegfeld's new Follies, had bobbed her nose. Forty years later, in similar circumstances, Americans asked a very different question. When Barbra Streisand emerged on the natural scene – ironically, her first significant role was as Brice in the musical *Funny Girl* – Americans wanted to know why she had not.'[8] The difference was the rise of the cosmetic surgery industry.

We think – and are encouraged to believe – fix the problem and the issue, and the bad feelings we have about it will go away. On the surface, they might but the wider problem still exists and still lurks, waiting for its next chance to make us feel ugly. If we can acknowledge that we are trying to fit into criteria dictated to us by a few lingering overlords – patriarchy, white supremacy and industries built with a capitalist agenda – who profit from us hating our looks and paying to change them, then that is at least a step away from their power. It gives us a moment to pause and to remember that feeling ugly isn't an intrinsic part of womanhood, it's been put there by those who reap the rewards of it, and by beauty standards that hold up a perfected unattainable version of beauty as the standard, or ideal to aspire to. I think it's significant that Marilyn Monroe is still widely considered to be an iconic beauty of all time, despite having reportedly had cosmetic surgery to her nose and chin. This isn't to shame her in any way – more to illustrate that we're not being held against fair standards.

If you're interested in surgery or 'tweakments', I hope this chapter will help you to make a more informed decision. The choices we make, how we fit a beauty ideal – or don't – and the fix we're offered to make sure we do, are the result of external forces that are almost impossible to detect and escape. I've felt the weight of failing to meet beauty standards so that cosmetic procedures are something I've considered too but I just think we all deserve to have a contextual basis to make the right decision that's truly empowered and that is right for us. And that we have a measure of the industry if we do decide to go ahead. But it's so often the case that 'fixing' ourselves isn't the cure-all because the lens we see ourselves through is what's broken.

Why does cosmetic surgery exist?

In 1907 general surgeon Dr Charles Miller wrote the first text about cosmetic surgery called '*The Correction of Featural Imperfections*'[9] but in those days the medical community viewed cosmetic surgeons as 'quacks', so it wasn't well regarded universally. The term 'plastic surgeon' started to be used by a group of practitioners who wanted to distinguish themselves from 'beauty doctors', who carried out work they variously called 'featural', 'beauty', 'cosmetic' or 'aesthetic surgery'.[10] It's an interesting split in surgical history and shows how the medical community saw cosmetic surgery performed by 'beauty doctors' and plastic surgery vary in terms of hierarchy pretty much from the beginning.

A 1908 court case report revealed how rudimentary the early procedures were – we're talking rhinoplasties involving paraffin wax being injected into the nose and moulded into the right shape, which could cause cancer and migrate to other body areas too.[11] The Derma Featural Company started advertising 'treatments' for those plagued by 'humped, depressed, or… ill-shaped noses' and who loathed their wrinkles, in British magazines like the *World of Dress* in 1901. Though rare at the time, they signalled that the possibility of being able to change one's physical characteristics was starting to enter public perception.

But what to fix first? One of the first issues 20th-century plastic surgeons sought to operate on was 'saddle nose', characterised by the loss of the bridge, which could be caused by syphilis, trauma or infection.[12] Chicago surgeon Dr James T. Campbell recognised the stigma around saddle nose and said in 1904: 'By shaping their features like those of normal men, we will earn lasting gratitude.'[13] That was likely true but his words were indicative of the power of a beauty standard and how a cosmetic surgeon can uphold them by correcting for aesthetic purposes to 'normalise' faces in accordance with societal and ableist beauty norms. And secondly, he's establishing that these procedures were morally sound – after all, if people are grateful, then that's a job done well, right? Elective plastic surgery for appearance over function (although often these cross over) had arrived.

During and after the First World War, military surgeons and doctors worked alongside plastic surgeons and dentists to tackle those horrifying never-seen-before injuries caused by weapons of modern warfare. Lots of procedures were experimental and results were mixed but the soldiers were naturally grateful for the work the surgeons had done. Those wounds were seen as both a surgical issue to fix and a social problem too – how would the men cope in an appearance-driven society, when they looked so different? Returning function to patients' faces was the primary goal but restoring appearance was considered almost as important. Some of the most renowned European surgeons of the time were now dedicating their focus to helping soldiers rebuild their bodies post-war, which helped elevate reconstructive surgery within the surgery field and wider medical community, as well as continuing an ableist agenda.[14]

After the war, however, in Europe the practice wasn't highly sought. In France, for example, there was reportedly only one surgeon practising plastic surgery after the conflict had ended. Meanwhile, in the US, plastic surgery was far more embraced and now surgeons were eager to train in it. Why the difference? There is a 'new self-consciousness' about appearance, suggested in the plastic surgery literature of the post-war period that wasn't apparent before, which also correlates with the timeline of rising celebrity influence through Hollywood, mass media and early beauty culture. A rise in the focus on capitalism, advertising and therefore consumerism of all kinds, essentially. And a change in the social structures driven by The Great Migration, where large numbers of African-Americans moved to northern cities from the Southern states.[15] Beauty standards always shift when a status quo of some kind is threatened – in this case much was in flux.

Rather than a reputable institution, plastic surgery was now starting to look like the Wild West of medicine: lawsuits were brought against surgeons like J. Eastman Sheehan, reported in the *New York Times* in 1926 to have been sued by an unhappy patient for $100,000 after they were left 'disfigured' by a facelift.[16] In 1935, notorious US criminal on the run, John Dillinger, paid $5,000 to 'underworld surgeons' Wilhelm Loeser and Harold Bernard Cassidy to change his appearance. He had a rudimentary facelift, removed several moles and scars, filled in his famous cleft chin and used chemicals to burn off his fingerprints. The procedure proved excruciating and Dillinger was decidedly unsatisfied with the results. Upon looking in the mirror, he supposedly exclaimed, "Hell, I don't look any different than I did!"'[17] Incidents like this led to a board forming, to legitimatise and regulate plastic surgery – but also added notoriety and public awareness of the field.

Plastic surgeons' skills were needed once more as

the world went to war again in 1939, to treat servicemen who had suffered disfiguring injuries, which led to further advancements in techniques. You've heard of the phrase 'the devil makes work for idle hands', right? After the war ended in 1945, once all the casualties were fixed, there was a surplus of plastic surgeons with not a lot to do. So, they turned their attentions to creating new advancements, with the aim of progressing the field of cosmetic surgery.

These pioneering techniques could be translated into what was turning out to be the highly lucrative field. As Michelle Smith, research fellow at Deakin University, Melbourne, points out in a feature for the *Independent* called 'The Ugly History of Cosmetic Surgery': 'The surgical fraternity – and it is a brotherhood, as more than 90 per cent of cosmetic surgeons are male – conveniently places itself in a history that begins with reconstructing the faces and work prospects of the war wounded. In reality, cosmetic surgeons are instruments of shifting whims about what is attractive. They have helped people to conceal or transform features that might make them stand out as once diseased; ethnically different; 'primitive'; too feminine; or too masculine.' What had started out as reconstruction became about fitting in, as cosmetic surgery to adhere to beauty standards began to be more commonplace – and there were now plenty of cosmetic surgeons endorsing it, from the good to the unscrupulous and capital-driven.

There was – and still exists – a huge part of this story that feels like it's been conveniently buried. Academic works detailing the inferiority of ethnic features and superiority of European ones were consistent during colonisation and slavery, alongside widespread examples of scientific racism. They collided in the 1920s when psychologist Knight Dunlap wrote 'Personal Beauty and Racial Betterment', in which he detailed the ideal beauty 'condition' as having no identifiable signs of race. In particular, no visible 'negroid characters', no signs of disease, weakness or deformity and appearing as close to European-looking as possible.[18] If you didn't meet that standard, then cosmetic surgery was waiting to offer you the fix.

Thus, being able to help people 'pass' more easily in a racist society was seen as a beneficial thing – or so the industry largely told itself. According to her biographer, the aforementioned Fanny Brice was likely to have had a rhinoplasty to fix her 'Jewish nose' in the 1920s.[19] In fact, in the US many of the first people to have cosmetic surgery were Jewish, as Haiken explains: 'Surgeons and in America who by the 1930s had defined the Semitic or Mediterranean nose as undesirable had probably become acquainted with the scientific theories that had influenced American ideas about beauty in the previous decades, as well as new disciplines of psychology and psychiatry.'[20] They reasoned, if somebody with these features was judged, mocked or seen as ugly, it could affect their job prospects or quality of life, which would be: 'just as likely to cause an inferiority complex as a congenital abnormality or a traumatically induced defect,' Haiken explains.[21]

But likening the burden of racial features to trauma or disability isn't just troubling as a deeply racist narrative, it's also worrying, because cosmetic surgery in general is still considered a fix to ease the distress of those who don't fit into society's beauty norms.

When magazines talked about cosmetic surgery, fixing 'humped' or 'large' noses was their ruse, rather than alluding directly to race. Though blepharoplasty – which is eyelid surgery – had been practised for aesthetic purposes in Japan in 1896,[22] it wasn't until WWII that the surgery to Westernise eyes became more popular in Asia and then the US. The US occupation in Japan, conflict in Korea and the widescale selling of American culture through Hollywood films, magazines, pin-up magazines like *Playboy* and American soldiers meant that Western models of beauty prevailed, as did those who could profit from correcting the 'oriental eye'.[23] The surgery took off across Asia and remains popular to this day: a young woman I met in Seoul told me it's often given as a graduation gift – she'd received hers from a male relative.

Cosmetic surgery for African-Americans gained popularity in the 1960s, the delay in this becoming sought after was potentially due to dark skin being more likely to develop keloid scars[24] and slower rates of facial ageing due to higher levels of melanin. But during the Jim Crow era (1877–1950) that enforced racial segregation in the southern American states, there was an evident disdain of Black facial characteristics by white Americans. Wide noses and large lips were exaggerated in political propaganda and cartoons which further perpetuated racist caricatures and labelled Black features as undesirable. By the 1970s, surgeons had reported a rise in the number of nasal surgery requests from African-Americans, one surgeon even suggesting this was their attempt to deny their heritage – though more likely they were being forced to measure up to white beauty standards and to compete for work in a society still inherently sexist and racist.

During the 1980s there was an increase in demand for the kind of nasal surgery 'King of Pop' Michael Jackson had (involving slimming down the width and creating a pointed nasal tip), though many cosmetic surgeons believed it was more about 'refining' rather than 'Caucasianising' the nose.[25] Perhaps it helped them sleep better at night. Refining the nasal tip is commonplace in rhinoplasty and noses that have a pointed tip are often the 'norm' or an ideal, but they are still based on Caucasian standards of beauty and cosmetic surgery is one of the industries gatekeeping those ideals.

Boobs became a post-war obsession ...

Boobs, bosoms, breasts ... whatever word you use, they've been through *a lot*. Women mostly wore modest clothes reflective of chastity until the Middle Ages and in the 15th century, King Henry VI even complained when dresses started to become more revealing as 'baring the breasts' became fashionable in court. Breasts had largely been seen as pretty functional until the 17th century when smaller breasts became the more desirable size. Why the sudden preference? Larger ones were seen as being lower class or undesirable due to being explicitly linked to non-white races. English explorer Richard Ligon reported of the women he saw in Cape Verde in 1647, that their breasts would 'hang down below their Navels, so that when they stoop at their common work of weeding, they hang almost to the ground, that at a distance you would think they had six legs.' As Marilyn Yalom, author of *A History of the Breast*, notes in the *Guardian*, in certain points in political and economic history, 'a specific conception of the breast took hold of the Western imagination and changed the way it was seen and represented.'[26] Colonisation was undeniably one of them.

By the 1920s, when smaller breasts and androgynous clothes without cleavage were all the rage, surgeons started to perform breast reductions to fit in with fashion. It may not shock you to know that by the 1930s men were still controlling what women should do with their boobs and how they should look. Surgeons came to agree that huge breasts were a mental and physical handicap to their bearers. As for breast enlargements, although some earlier attempts using paraffin injections were made in the 1800s and with fatty tissue taken from the abdomen and buttocks during the 1920s and 1930s,[27] breast augmentation wasn't a very well-known procedure – nor a safe one.

In the 1940s, small breasts, previously desirable, had now officially become a 'problem' to be solved and a new insecurity to worry about. Fixing this new issue meant that lingerie brands like Frederick's of Hollywood invented the first push-up bra with padding in 1947. In the US, Ern and Bud Westmore's *Beauty, Glamour and Personality* book from 1947 showed how to increase bust size with exercise – even stating that the female bosom had always been a symbol of 'health and beauty'. All this combined to create a mild hysteria around having a larger breast: seriously, women never get left alone. It followed the tired pattern of patriarchy exerting its control via beauty standards, when it can no longer through legislation or physical force. The big boob boom happened when women were enjoying more freedom and had been given more control over their reproductive rights with the contraceptive pill in the 1950s. Coincidence?

The busty look that Hollywood actors like Marilyn Monroe and Jane Russell embodied and the fashions of the time, like Dior's New Look (1947), celebrated a smaller waist and large breasts. Now, everywhere you turned, big boobs were presented as the ideal, or a goal. *Playboy* launched in 1953 with previously unpublished nude images of Marilyn Monroe (used without her consent or profit)[28] and celebrated mostly large breasts. Ruth Handler and her husband co-founded Mattel, Inc. in 1945 after she saw that her young daughter Barbara made paper dolls of adult women. She realised there was a niche in the market to let little girls 'imagine' the future.[29] But the doll's look was modelled on a German comic strip character named Lilli, originally a racy character for adult men used in tobacco shops – and you guessed it – Lilli had a rack on her, just as Barbie – the epitome of American beauty – did. Imagine what this imprinting could do to a young child, in terms of how they see beauty and femininity and a lack of cleavage being a 'problem' to fix.

So boobs had already been through a fair bit already without routinely going under the scalpel: over the course of 30 years, they'd gone from being totally out of fashion to centre stage (as long as they were perky, not too big and looked good under a tight sweater, of course). But augmentation surgery was still largely trial and error. Implants using different materials like Ivalon sponge, which cosmetic surgeons thought performed better than the fat grafts previously used that tended to liquify, were causing bigger issues.[30] The dangers started circulating, including hardening and shrinkage – alongside a cancer risk of the sponge.[31] In 1953, LA plastic surgeon Robert Alan Franklyn was featured in *Pageant*, a newspaper supplement, with the headline 'The Operation that Remoulds Flat-Chested Women'. The piece revealed that Franklyn had invented a way to help women – who he believed suffered from 'micromastia' – or smaller breasts – with a new type of implant – the perfect combination of shaming something entirely normal, creating insecurity and claiming to be able to solve it.[32]

In his 1960 book *Beauty Surgeon*, Franklyn details the plight of a woman called 'Linda Lee' with a photo story: 'She was a lonely girl. She rarely had a date… the fact that she was under-endowed as a woman had already left a strong impact on her personality.' Later, Linda appears with 'surgifoam' implants (a type of imitation foam rubber) and Franklyn says her life was completely changed by the surgery – now, she had a beau, she went to the beach. It was self-promotion taken to a whole new level (something still prevalent in cosmetic surgery); Franklyn's behaviour troubled colleagues, as did his lack of plastic surgical training records.[33]

An unlikely influence on the rise of breast augmentation was the manufacturing world, which speaks volumes to how other industries that you might not think would have a direct impact on beauty standards can have a vested interest in pushing beauty anxiety. Post-war, there was a new fascination with artificial substances and silicone had become a hot new material used for a wide variety of industrial purposes, as well as the cult US 1950s toy 'silly putty'. But it interested cosmetic surgeons as it also mimicked the feel of natural breast tissue. During the US occupation of Japan (1945–52), to make themselves more attractive to occupying American soldiers (which speaks to those Western beauty standards again), sex workers were known to inject silicone directly into their breasts, which could lead to gangrene. For a while, silicone was being directly injected into American women's breasts too, before it was realised there were side effects.[34]

Plastic surgeons realised these issues – which were now becoming litigious – could potentially be remedied with a 'sack' to hold the silicone. In 1962, when the American housewife Timmie Jean Lindsey went to have a tattoo removed in Houston, Texas, she was asked by her surgeons, Drs Frank Gerow and Thomas Cronin, if she'd like to volunteer to try a new procedure and so the first breast implant surgery took place. Lindsey went from a B to a C cup with silicone implants and made plastic surgery history: 'I don't think I got the full results of them until I went out in public and men on the street would whistle at me,' she told the BBC.[35] Thomas Biggs, who was working with Gerow and Cronin in 1962 as a junior resident in plastic surgery told the BBC: 'The plastic surgery world was absolutely set on fire with enthusiasm.'[36]

The industry has become masterful at selling cosmetic surgery procedures as feats of medical marvel, necessary and as easy to achieve as picking up some eggs at the supermarket. Often, emphasis is placed on the 'ease' of a procedure, accompanied by 'before' and 'after' pictures that erase the backstory and coupled with social proof – or, in other words, the line 'everyone does it'. The message that women could 'fix' themselves to match the beauty standard was, by the 1970s, becoming firmly established but this was also the era when Page 3 started printing pictures of topless models in *The Sun*, normalising what 'attractive' breasts looked like, which was most often large and usually white – there were just five non-white women in its 44-year tenure. Men were being told that they were supposed to like big boobs as a norm of heterosexual male sexuality but now British women were now being held to this standard too.

By the 1980s, the US Food and Drug Administration (FDA) had issued warnings due to 'reports of adverse events in the medical literature' as safety concerns began to emerge about silicone. That didn't stop surgeons creating brochures detailing their surgeries, including silicone implants that looked like an Argos catalogue of 'before' and 'after' pictures. The economy was booming, women had really entered the workplace, and breast implants, like the flashy new car or home, were sold as a form of status symbol – *Cosmopolitan* US even claimed that they 'had a better contour than the real thing!' – and were a way to 'get ahead' in a man's world. Ruth Holliday, Professor of Gender and Culture at Leeds University's School of Sociology and Social Policy, puts the 1980s boob boom down to 'post-feminist thinking' which emerged at this time. She told CNN it 'was all about showing how empowered you were. It was about women reclaiming their sexuality, both from the patriarchy and the feminist movement itself. Within the realm of plastic surgery that translated into emphasising all the parts of their bodies that were already widely eroticised by society – thighs, curves, breasts – to own and show off their femininity.'

So much female representation at the time was controlled by men and catered to the male gaze (film, porn and music, you name it …) and it favoured women with larger breasts. So, were implants sold as empowerment to line the pockets of the cosmetic surgery industry or were they an empowered choice? The evidence seems to point towards the former. All of which bears an uncanny similarity to current cosmetic surgery trends, but now perhaps rather than the promise of equality in a man's world, it's of fame on social media or reality TV. Men – tellingly – still aren't subject to anywhere near as much pressure to 'fix' themselves.

In the 1990s, silicone implants were banned in the US (and approved again in 2006) due to safety concerns and the industry switched to saline implants. But despite the negative experiences reported by a number of women and covered by the media, the surgery itself remained popular. Women could make money by courting the heterosexual male gaze, which in turn fuelled a sense of getting one over on the patriarchy. You only have to watch the slow-mo shot of nineties' icon Pamela Anderson jogging along the beach in the TV series *Baywatch* (1989–2001) to see how profitable implants could be. Big boobs were sold to women constantly, via the ever-flourishing porn industry to celebrity culture, to the fashion industry. The Wonderbra – which became a leading brand in the 1990s, with the help of the iconic 'Hello Boys' campaign featuring model Eva Herzigova – was designed to mimic the look of implants. Even naturally larger boobs were out in this era – it was all about the pushed-up, artificial look. Boobs were not your own, they were almost explicitly for the men who were supposed to want to stare at them – and needed to appear to be gravity defying and as big as possible. The problem wasn't getting bigger boobs – it was being exhorted to want them in the first place.

During the noughties, the world of glamour modelling became a more covetable and profitable career-route, with household names Jodie Marsh and her rival Jordan (Katie Price) reported to be having a competitive boob-off, getting one up on each other by increasing and decreasing their breast size. They became tabloid and celebrity magazine culture fodder and the burgeoning lad culture alongside this meant that small breasts were resolutely out and breast augmentation became more commonplace. To appeal to everyday women, the plastic surgery industry had created more natural-looking implants with a teardrop shape to appear undetectable, although lots of people still coveted the fake boob look as a status symbol. Meanwhile, in the US, cosmetic surgery history was made in 2002 when an episode of *Extreme Makeover* showed footage of a breast augmentation on TV for the first time; that year, the number of people having breast implants increased 147 per cent more than five years earlier,[37] with 24,9641 women having implant surgery that year.[38]

In 2010, breast implants were manufactured by a French company using cheaper industrial silicone which wasn't authorised for human use. These implants had more than double the rupture rate of other implants – and an estimated 50,000 British people had the implants.[39] This just goes to show how the industry can be quick to go to the market for profit and less than thorough with our safety.

In 2018 a then 23-year-old blogger called Chidera Eggerue shared pictures of her breasts with the hashtag #Saggyboobsmatter to offer an alternative to the 'perfect' breast that we see everywhere and had made her feel so self-conscious. Sex educator, model and activist Ericka Hart displayed her double mastectomy scars to challenge perceptions and empower others, particularly women of colour (she had asked her surgeon what the mastectomy scars would look like on a Black person – it took the surgeon two weeks to find one). Women are pushing back but we're dealing with a long and complex legacy of being made to feel like our breasts – unless they fit a narrow and changing Western beauty standard – need to be fixed. But there is still that pressure to live up to the heterosexual male fantasy of the large-breasted, sexually available woman. Conversely in fashion, smaller breasts are far more covetable and catered for – you just can't win.

The reasons for wanting breast surgery are many, of course, and I'm not judging anyone one for having it – though I am very much judging the industries that make us feel like we need it so they can make money. But it's telling that, just as we start to reclaim our breasts and bodies, technology is being developed to make surgeries less invasive – perhaps even without using general anaesthetic – partly so it can be sold to us as little more than a 'tweak'.

Is your face 'snatched' enough?

Slightly confusingly for us here in the UK, where the word is slang for a vulva, the trend for looking 'snatched' has become a new beauty standard to aspire to. Some of the world's most beautiful women, as proclaimed by *Forbes*, like 'Rihanna, Emily Ratajkowski, Bella Hadid, Kendall Jenner', have the 'feminine, slim, heart-shaped face, and "snatched" jawline'[40]. Hadid credits face tape – a type of aesthetic sticky tape applied to the hairline – with her look. What is 'snatched'? Skin pulled upwards to look taut, using the aforementioned tape and of course, cosmetic procedures.

One of those procedures is the 'Fox Eye' surgery I mention earlier (*see also* page 110), which is undoubtedly how some celebrities are achieving the pulled-back, taut look that Instagram filters and make-up trends for sculpting faces has also influenced. Dr Robert Flowers, who pioneered the surgery over 50 years ago, is said to have been inspired by the Asian eye. He created a treatment that combines a brow lift and blepharoplasty (surgery to remove 'excess' skin from the eyelids) to create a more taut, upwards look. It's now often done with 'thread' technology, in which threads with mini 'hooks' are inserted beneath the skin and hooked into the muscle, pulling them taut to create an effect that can last up to a year, with bruising for roughly two weeks. The latter is often labelled 'non-invasive' but involves local anaesthetic – almost like a 'facelift-lite'.

'Snatched' might be a new word to us, but that taut, gravity-defying face is one of the oldest cosmetic surgeries. Procedures to tighten the skin on the face actually date back to 1916, when a German surgeon called Erich Lexer performed the first facelift but the procedures were – as you'd imagine – pretty experimental. In the 1920s, silent movie actor Mary Pickford was so worried about ageing – fuelled by the never-changing Hollywood obsession with young women – that she underwent an early version of a facelift. Sadly, it left Pickford – credited with creating the ingénue character in film – unable to show emotions. Reports said she looked mummified; it even ended her career.

Still, the risk of facial surgery seemed worth it to many women. In 1924, the *New York Daily Mirror* ran a competition to ask: 'Who is the homeliest girl in New York?', promising the winner that a plastic surgeon would 'make a beauty of her' as the prize.[41] Faces have always been the biggest beauty focus – there's so much to leverage: you can moisturise them, paint them, tweak and change them no end. A stat from *LIFE* magazine in 1956 claimed that American women had spent $2.5bn – a sum equal to Italy's defence budget at the time – on beauty, including products, treatments and weight reduction.[42] By the 1960s, facelifts had become much more routine in Hollywood, with famed beauties like film actor Hedy Lamarr admitting to having plastic surgery to her face, including a facelift, rhinoplasty and lip augmentation.[43] By the end of her life, aged 89, Wallis Simpson was said to have had 'so many facelifts that, the rumour went, she couldn't close her eyes even when asleep'.[44] It's telling that author, French-born milliner Lilly Daché said in her 1965 book, *Glamour*, 'Today there is no excuse for a woman to grow old, unless she is ill. If you want to keep up with this modern, wonderful world, you must be young in thought, feeling, appearance and all you have to do is stretch out your hand to receive the magic bounty of glamour that modern science has prepared for you.'

The rise of youth culture at the time and the battle between tradition/conservatism and progression/liberalism could also have intensified the rise in women wanting to look younger in the 1960s. While noses, boobs and other surgeries are primarily about aesthetics, the intensive and invasive nature of a facelift signifies an intense battle against ageing. In some ways, it was a definer of wealth and status – if you had money, then you could in some way hold back time and cheat 'ugly'. It wasn't always just women: the first billionaire John Paul Getty had work done in the 1960s[45] and actor John Wayne had his crow's feet removed in the same era.

Now we know women might age differently to men due to collagen levels in the skin changing owing to hormones and lifestyle factors, but ultimately, we do tend to live longer so there's that. But there was an underlying attitude that women were bringing ageing on themselves – fuelling them to risk facelift surgeries in the post-war years. New York surgeon Murray Berger said in 1951 that wrinkles signified a 'reckless expenditure of emotion' and 'careless indulgence in tricks of unlovely expression'.[46] Of course, cosmetic surgeons were against the 'ageing gracefully' rhetoric – as facelifts were given as the answer to the problem of ageing. Robert Alan Franklyn – yes, him again – even said: 'Personally, I believe it's tragic when women who still feel youthful look old and tired. It's so unnecessary.'[47]

Patronising, silencing and inaccurate opinions like this helped cosmetic surgeons sell insecurity – and their wares.

As did the vernacular around facelifts and facial surgeries, which were rebranded with descriptions like 'neatening', 'tidying' and 'fixing up' to deemphasise the risks and make them more mass-market and appealing to the middle classes too. In the 1960s, surgeons had mostly been removing fat from along the chin and jawline with their lifts; by the 1970s, with more anatomical knowledge, they were starting to reposition the muscles beneath the fat and skin for a more taut look, as the industry and techniques progressed rapidly. In the 1980s, the traditional lift was combined with smaller lifts to the face, like brow or lip lifts, creating a much bigger transformation and wow factor, helped by fillers to plump the skin rather just stretching it. It did create a tell-tale look though, with 'always-awake' eyes that almost appeared to wear you, pixie-like ears and the skin was taut – or snatched, if you will.

In the 1990s, a new way to halt time emerged and it was far less invasive than the traditional facelift and required much less recovery time: Botulinum toxin – or 'Botox' – produced by a bacterium, the first record of which is from Germany in the late 1700s, when people died from eating sausages containing the bacteria. The poison is so potent, it's manufactured in military conditions and, at £100 trillion a kilo, is now one of the most expensive substances in the world. In the past, it was even considered for use as chemical warfare by scientists in Nazi Germany. So why would we knowingly inject this poison into our faces? Such is the pressure on women to look young and halt ageing at every turn.

An early medical use of Botox was in the 1960s and 70s, to help people with issues with their eye muscles. It wasn't actually approved to treat frown lines by the US Food and Drug Administration (FDA) until 2002 (which was when it started to become more popular in the UK too), but it was being used for cosmetic purposes under the radar in the US before it was strictly allowed. In 1998, *Allure* magazine editor

Joan Kron reported, 'FDA supplies are running out as patients are begging for more injections – in their crow's-feet, necks, or right between the eyes.'[48] As soon as people were able to get their hands on it, it became huge. Botox parties replaced Tupperware parties from decades ago and mentions were everywhere in pop culture, like Samantha from the TV series *Sex and the City*'s now-iconic line: 'I don't really believe in marriage; now Botox on the other hand, that works every time.' While there was fear of looking frozen or something going amiss – particularly with these cases being publicised by the media in ever-popular 'female vanity gone wrong' stories – the risk of reward was still seen as worth it.

The global Botulinum Toxin market was valued at $5.75 billion in 2021.[49] Botox has now become so commonplace as a procedure in Western society that it seems like a rite of passage past the age of 30 – a part of womanhood that we're expected to partake in for the benefit of looking youthful under the watchful eye of the male gaze. We're taught to fear ageing before we even experience it, as 'preventative' Botox is sold to us as a way to delay it. The fear of ageing that's being sold is just another brick to sling in our 'backpack' of beauty anxiety – it's getting pretty heavy, isn't it?

Despite a huge amount of people – particularly those in the public eye – having Botox, fillers, thread lifts and much more, so few are actually open about it. Some say nothing as their faces remain unchanged for decades, others swear it's down to genes or good diet (sure they have some impact, but not enough to eradicate ageing temporarily as 'tweakments' do). But influencers and celebrities not owning up to it is the same as airbrushing in adverts, in that it's deeply damaging to women to see somebody in their fifties with lineless skin claiming it's 'good skincare'. No one is regulating that yet – and how would they even begin?

There are the occasional few female stars – like Cindy

Crawford, Courtney Cox and Katy Perry – who have admitted to dabbling with injectables.[50] You can see why women don't want to talk about it, though. In an all-too-familiar pattern, society tells us that we will be ugly and redundant if we look older, a solution is marketed to us, but if we take that solution the implication is that we are vain or self-obsessed. Sadly, so many women who do have injectables or cosmetic surgery face a backlash. The *Daily Mail* reported in 2020: 'Gwen Stefani, 50, is accused of getting plastic surgery as fans insist her face looked "unrecognizable" and "frozen" at the Grammys.'[51] The headline was: 'Her face is 99 per cent fillers and 1 per cent skin'. Many famous women have faced similar criticism – but being expected to look half your age, combined with being in the public eye and the ageist patriarchal idea of women having a shelf life is what's ultimately to blame, although industries that profit from this undeniably play a part too.

Actor Kristin Davis received comments about her reported 'overuse' of injectables and told *New Beauty*: 'It can also be extremely stressful to be aging and to be compared to your much, much, much younger self. If I was from a regular life, I would feel fine; I would feel great! I'm healthy, I'm strong, I've got this little three-year-old son, and I carry him around and it's all good – but, no, I'm on television, where every bit of my physical being is analysed.'[52] Except she probably wouldn't feel fine in regular life – because so many people don't, and the answer offered to them is surgical or injectable, without even missing a beat.

That pressure can creep up fast. In 2012 I was new to Instagram and was essentially using it to look at cute animal memes – it was a happier time. I went on a work trip with other beauty editors and they were mostly following reality TV stars and models and talking about them. So, out of curiosity, I started to follow those people too. Every time I opened the Instagram app, I looked at how their faces appeared so different to mine, even though we were the same age (in our early 30s). How was this possible, what were they doing? A colleague told me that they used an app called Facetune – so I gave it a crack, blurring my skin, slimming down my face and making myself into an avatar, essentially. Those pictures did get more 'likes', I noticed. Over a couple of months, the combination of all of those factors started to make me spiral. Up until this point, I hadn't even considered injectables, but once I could see how I appeared after I'd been airbrushed by Facetune, that all changed. I felt lacking as I looked in the mirror each morning, and as I used the erase tool to get rid of any 'flaws' on my face I decided, without looking into any risks because it was so commonplace, to get filler underneath my eyes and a little in my lips too. It was painful – something people don't often tell you, and occasionally, it was uncomfortable around my eyes when I smiled. Initially, I felt great when I looked in the mirror but the flipside of this was that as it wore off, after four months, my old face started to creep back in and I began to hate the face I'd been happy with just months before I'd had the 'tweak'. I was deflated, my lips were wrinklier from being stretched and I felt as if I looked about 100. So I did another round of filler, went through the same experience and then just had to step away. I realised that I was looking at a lifetime of upkeep and, more importantly, I didn't want to spend my thirties hating my face.

Today's beauty standards are higher than ever and the pressure to conform, to freeze time, to look perfect has only increased. Indeed, the global market for dermal fillers is projected to grow from $5.31bn in 2022 to $8.74bn by 2029.[53] Current conversations revolve around women seen as being desperate to stave off time and going too far – and who can blame them when the scrutiny is so oppressive? Whatever way you slice it (literally, in some cases), the view that a woman's value lies within her beauty and appearance of youth is very, very helpful to the cosmetic surgery industry.

Before social media – that feels like a different geological time period, right? – the faces we saw most were real ones, belonging to the people around us. We saw how they changed with age and we generally aged alongside them. Now, those margins have shifted hugely – we can see everyone, across the planet, and see how they look. But what we don't see is any inner anguish that comes in the form of having to paint on a face each day for two hours, or feeling like we must use filters or an in-phone app like Facetune to digitally tweak – until we get the actual tweaks done because we start to hate the way our unfiltered faces look, just as we hate the way our untweaked faces look. Talk about a vicious cycle that keeps us looped in perpetual dissatisfaction with our looks.

One bad picture can be enough to make us fall into the rabbit hole of searching online and pondering what procedure might make us look better. Now we're increasingly doing much of our communication via video call software that makes us even more painfully self-conscious. Even when talking to friends I zone out and start pondering my own face – 'what's wrong with it and what could I change'. Something unnatural happens when we see images and videos of ourselves constantly, the way celebrities do. After lockdown forced us to Zoom continuously, many clinics saw an increased demand for surgery and treatments on facial features most visible on video calls – like lower facelifts and filler to plump up the under-eye area.

Research on social media and its effects on our self-esteem has found that people who use image-heavy social media platforms are more likely to consider cosmetic surgery. In 2017, a huge 55 per cent of plastic surgeons said their patients wanted to look better in selfies as a motivation.[54] None of this is shocking when we look at how technology has evolved so quickly – even ten years ago, we'd see occasional pictures of ourselves. Now we see them on multiple platforms and take them daily – that makes it impossible not to scrutinise ourselves and compare ourselves to others.

Cosmetic treatments have created a new beauty divide – or perhaps just highlight one of the oldest ones in a new way. On the TV show *Made in Chelsea*, for example, we can't necessarily *see* evidence that the upper-class members of the cast are having cosmetic work done but we can make an educated guess that it's happening. 'Natural', effortless, glossy beauty is the goal here and no one really wants it to be obvious they've had work done. However, when we look at the aesthetic of reality TV show *TOWIE*, the cosmetic work – like breast implants, visible veneers and pronounced filled lips – is more deliberately obvious. Throughout British history looking working-class has often been treated with disdain and considered 'over the top'. But if you had to work hard to afford something, it follows that you might see it as a visible status symbol, akin to a Gucci bag or fancy car. Social media and reality TV have become interchangeable mediums for getting rich quick and then using that to 'achieve' the look of wealth.

It might be that to get the very best, barely detectable cosmetic treatments, you do just have to be very wealthy. The 'I'm not ugly, I'm just poor' memes featuring celebrities like Bella Hadid and Kylie Jenner reported to have had cosmetic procedures, demonstrate that money can buy you into the 'beautiful class'. But what's a really pressing issue is that this fuels a demand for cheaper procedures among fans who look up to these stars. Although it is illegal to advertise prescription-only treatments like Botox, aesthetic clinics have used TikTok's trending 'sounds' – which provide an audio clip to be used on a TikTok video that often trends – to promote the rhetoric of preventative Botox to younger and younger people. This has led to those who cannot afford the treatment by knowledgeable professionals injecting themselves or going to people inadequately trained for the treatment. A BBC Three documentary called *Under the Skin: The Botched Beauty Business* (2021) showed a nurse training people to do thread lifts on a one-day course, and a young woman explained how she had necrosis of the skin (death of body tissue) after a badly done 'temporary' injectable nose job.

When we fall short of a beauty ideal and decide to fix it, our decisions are so often cloaked in the guise of it being 'personal choice' – which has now been enmeshed with empowerment and women doing 'what we want'. If I've learned anything working in the beauty industry, through my own experiences of feeling ugly and the hundreds of hours of research I've done for this book, it's that nothing is ever just *our* choice. And that should be as haunting as it sounds. The desire for larger breasts comes from the male gaze, the kind we saw create the Venus figurines, and has fuelled everything from the fashion for bullet bras to 1980s fictional character Jessica Rabbit.

The desire to remain looking foetal until we die comes from a patriarchal history where a woman's value was as a wife and an ability to be a mother. After that, you don't matter. The desire for small noses and rounded eyes to make us look like Instagram filters comes from the legacy of white supremacy. The desire to have straighter, smooth hair originates from colonialism. These are huge cultural and historical truths that we shy from because they're uncomfortable, we want to fit in and we can't see who is pulling the puppet strings. And those making money from our malaise would rather we didn't think about any of this – and so it ends up being 'our choice' when it's anything but. If I'm honest, when I wanted cosmetic surgery in my teens, it was to fit in and to feel less ugly. And fitting in meant a slim white nose, straight hair, lighter skin and a thin white body.

I'd love it not to be the case but the inescapable fact is that we live in a patriarchal, ageist society, so these treatments can give women a sort of confidence and therefore freedom that they may feel they wouldn't have otherwise. In an ideal world, we wouldn't need or have any of it, perhaps. But we do need the reality check that reminds us that cosmetic surgery and 'tweakments' are part of an industry that, whichever way you look at it, is making money out of women's insecurities and our fear of visibly ageing. It's nonsensical – and deeply damaging – for us to just leap into cosmetic surgeries and procedures without considering the lasting effects on our mental and physical health. Increasingly, seeing women ageing without intervention – or those embracing their unique beauty – is hard to find, let alone to see celebrated, but perhaps if we see this more we'd feel like there was a choice.

There are so many opinion pieces declaring 'I'm a feminist but I have Botox' – which might suggest that we're struggling with this more than we let on, or we're letting the side down. We're not. I'm not against cosmetic surgery or cosmetic procedures at all – I might consider them again in the future – but I do think we must have our eyes open and be fully present when we make those decisions, so that they are actually empowering. Maybe it's finally time to see what else we are being sold along with our 'tweaks'?

Informed consent means having all the information to make an informed decision and currently that's not being delivered by the media and influencers, sources which give us information about cosmetic procedures, but fail to account for the history above and how that could still be affecting beauty standards. I'd always suggest that you consult a therapist before any cosmetic surgery; the psychology review before procedures isn't standardised. Here are a few questions to ask yourself before you have your first, or next procedure. I'm not a medical professional or psychologist and they are based on the findings in this chapter and what I wish I'd considered before I booked in for something I wasn't mentally prepared for.

1) Can you identify when this became an issue – and why? Often issues with our looks start with a comment made by somebody else. Go deep on what might have been happening in their life to make them behave so poorly, or why it's impacted on you so much. Was it also combined with the whiter-than-white beauty standards of the era you grew up in? Or wanting to fit in with how friends looked at school? Maybe it was large-breasted, tiny-waisted dolls that made you want a boob job as soon as you hit puberty? If it's more recent, can you pinpoint exactly why you started to feel this way? Make a timeline of when the issue started for you – and what made it worse.

2) Is there someone or something in your life that makes you feel worse about your appearance? Like social media accounts you follow or reality TV shows. Or even a friend who constantly talks about how they want to improve their appearance. If so, the first step before spending money on changing something on your body is to try to remove these negative influences from your life (where possible) and see how you feel as a result.

3) Who do you want to look like and why? Is it a younger version of yourself – and if so, what does that really represent? Is it freedom and excitement? Is that possible to achieve by changing something in your life first? If it's an influencer/celebrity, have they had work done? (Unsure? Ask a friend or somebody who is good at spotting these things.) Why do you think they had that done? Is it the pressure to fit in or to look a certain way or did they just get it for free? Have a good think about it – and where the systems of capitalism, patriarchy, colonisation and ageism might come into it.

4) If it's permanent, how will you feel if the 'style' changes? Think back to those early eyebrow tattoos with a blueish tinge and huge 2000s breast implants. Some cosmetic procedures can 'age' quickly. Will you care? Will you feel out of place and compelled then to get more work? If so, factor in the cost (plus inflation) of updating your look every decade, as well as the mental toll.

5) Is there something else going on for you that you might need some help with? This isn't me being an amateur life coach here, I just know from experience that when one area of our life takes our focus, it can mean that actually something else is making us unhappy. When my career has felt unstable or I've been in a toxic relationship, I've often over-obsessed about my appearance. If that sounds even a little bit like it might be true for you, I really think it's a good idea to try to get to the source of what's actually wrong before diving into cosmetic procedures that probably won't make you feel better in the way you hope they will. Can you speak to a trauma-informed therapist to help you get to the root of it?

6) What do you imagine life to be like afterwards? Often, we employ a 'happily ever after' ending to cosmetic procedures – do you think it will make everything in your life better? How would you cope if it didn't look as you wanted it to? Do you have any feelings around the 'upkeep' of 'tweakments' or potentially having to 'update' surgeries? Think about all the possible outcomes you can, rather than being seduced by the idea of 'fixing' a 'problem' and everything being rosy for ever after.

7) Can you afford it – and to have it done safely? My filler only lasted four to five months – if I were to have continued, it would have cost me £1,500 a year, £15,000 a decade (and that's at the time of writing). That's the bare minimum, and doesn't even include the cost of corrective procedures if something went wrong. Factor in what it costs for the next five years, with inflation, and the possibility of having other 'tweakments' too. Do the same for surgery too – cost out if it can be done affordably and safely by somebody reputable, who is experienced enough to deal with any complications – while many treatments are sound, there is no such thing as a completely risk-free procedure. If you feel uneasy in any way, or like you're being upsold: leave.

8) Who do you influence? We all have someone who looks up to us. Family, friends, siblings, social media followers and children. Would you be comfortable being honest about what you've had done? If not, why? What damage could that perhaps do to others if you kept it hidden and didn't speak about it honestly? How would you tell your children – if you have them – about it? And what would it perhaps signal to them about female beauty and society? If they wanted cosmetic procedures, how would you handle that? This isn't a guilt trip, it's just considering any collective impact.

Legal note: The British Association of Aesthetic Plastic Surgeons (BAAPS) told me on an email dated 20 October 2022: 'at the current time BAAPS have no standardised evaluation, but strongly encourage all members to attend the BAAPS psychology course, to further improve and enhance their pre-existing psychological aspects of training they have received throughout their plastic surgery training. Some members additionally use various psychological profiling questionnaires, and body dysmorphic screening questionnaires.'

OLD AND UGLY

'I don't see why there should be a point where everyone decides you're too old. I'm not too old, and until I decide I'm too old, I'll never be too fucking old.'

– Motörhead founder Lemmy Kilmister

I DID A SEISMIC PROCRASTINATE when penning this chapter. Every time I'd start writing the proximity would feel too real and I'd feel too vulnerable (feelings ... they're *so* gross). When I started to consider how ageing affects us, with societal expectations and changes in how we're perceived, my own feelings about this would surge up from nowhere, like the apprehension you might feel watching the paranormal TV series *Most Haunted*. Everything *seems* OK, presenter Yvette Fielding is there to protect us after all. Then just as you start to feel safe, that's when the spooks appear. But here I am, anxiously avoiding the topic again by musing on the undead, which is ironic when I'm faced with a chapter on the conundrum humanity has dealt with since the dawn of time: how do we deal with getting older?

I have a theory. Each time we embark on a new diet, skincare regime, workout plan or 'new year, new you' resolution what we're actually trying to do is recapture a singular moment in time where we believe that we looked our best and maybe we felt it, too. Either way, we have decided that it's our baseline, the point we're always trying to claw our way back to. Often that moment is a physical picture that replays in our mind like the most broken of all records, reminding us of how we looked, who we were and all that lay ahead of us. I call it our 'perfect me' photo – and its pull is both undeniable and visceral. Unlike comparing ourselves to a cosmetically enhanced celebrity or an overly filtered influencer, the person in our 'perfect me' photo was us, they were real. It feels like a yearning for something that's been lost or squandered and it's our fault. But when we see that picture or think of it, we know what we're 'aiming' for and that's to get back to that very moment and look like we did then.

The snap at the start of this chapter taken in 2008 is my very own 'perfect me' photo. Everything about it felt like it was the 'real' me – from my glowing, taught skin through to my weight. I had actual collarbones which haven't been seen since, at least 2008. At one point I even had this picture stuck to my fridge door to remind me to NOT EAT – 1950s Barbie would be so proud. Chances are, you have your version of this photo too, or at least an image of it in your head. Sometimes it's represented by an item of clothing, like a pair of jeans three sizes smaller in your wardrobe, or there was an age when you just felt like your very best self. But the perplexing thing is that even though we're 'working' towards recapturing that moment – maybe by losing weight or freezing time with Botox – the moment has gone. It literally doesn't exist anymore and neither do we in that exact same form, if we're being scientific – the average age of our cells is around seven to ten years so we're different people on a cellular level.[1]

What we're really doing is trying to pedal backwards, to be or achieve something that is entirely gone. This is the first clue that something is not right; after all, when are you actively encouraged to work towards the past rather than a glorious future? We don't mourn our crappy first jobs or our clumsy first loves in the way we do our appearance. Sure, we might have been this perfect-looking person for a moment and they may *feel* like our authentic selves, but is that honestly the case, or have we sugar-coated them and dipped them in rainbow sprinkles to beat ourselves up for daring to change? We have to consider the whole picture without selective amnesia.

Sure, I look nice in that picture but I was also a scared intern, terrified about my job prospects in a recession; I had also just lost three stone on a meal replacement diet, but had no idea how to eat to keep it off. As a result, my weight was going up and that was causing me so much anxiety and fuelling binge eating and purges. My self-esteem was so low that I put up with terrible treatment on those internships and behaved like a doormat in relationships. I believed the idea of perfection I was sold that everything would magically be OK if I was thinner and prettier. Realistically, I hated myself but I didn't see *that* when I had this image stuck up in my kitchen – I just saw what I wanted to see: a fake version of myself that never existed rather than a young woman who was abjectly miserable. But it's easier to look back and rose-tint our former selves rather than ease into changes to our bodies as we age and actively dissect what's causing any negative thoughts we might have about ageing.

Social media makes idealising our former selves a breeze and it does the 'reminding' for us. Facebook gives us daily picture memories of years gone by, showing us what we looked like. Instantly, we're comparing our current selves to our old selves without the real story or considering our true feelings at that time. In the past, photos lived in photo albums, tucked away for curated moments of nostalgia, but now there are daily, unasked-for reminders of our physical changes and the passing of time.

If we're not pitted against our younger selves then we're held up against other women. Just look at how female celebrities have been the fodder for the 'sidebar of shame' on tabloid websites, accused of having 'let themselves go' for daring to gain a few pounds or step outside without make-up. New mothers might be pictured alongside a snap of themselves pre-kids to exalt those who achieve their 'pre-baby body' – and look like they didn't ever expel a human from their physical being – and condemn or shame those who don't snap back. It all comes back to the two ways women are traditionally 'allowed' to be in society – we can be 'young' and decorative or we can be 'useful' by means of reproduction and raising children. Once we're seen as old, often we're none of these things. To stay visible in the dominant male gaze of society would mean we have to cling to one or more. And if we don't – we get this:

'Will Americans want to watch a woman get older before their eyes on a daily basis?'[2] That was the question asked about Hillary Clinton on a radio show when she ran for presidential nomination. When she was secretary of state, a photo of her without make-up on went viral – people thought she looked tired. But had she made too much effort, perhaps that too would have received 'feedback'.

We exist in a world that tells women that after 20 it's all 'downhill from here'. Approaching 30 has its own panic: the 'clock is ticking' and 'you must find a partner'. No wonder so many want to surgically turn back the clock because it's how we've been programmed to see ourselves: with a shelf life. Our desire to look younger might seem focused around lines or wrinkles, but that hides a bigger truth: it's about how we are more visible and admired when we are young, how youth is celebrated in all areas of society. Male ageing is referred to in terms of 'silver foxes', 'DILFs' and 'dad bods', while women are 'hags', 'crones', 'mutton dressed as lamb' and even 'cougars'. Of course, men deal with this in their own way – take the inherited condition male pattern hair loss, for example – but still their 'value' in society often goes up. Ageing in men is linked more heavily with money and power, with increased status.

Of course, on a fundamental level, ageing is a process that signifies and is symptomatic of – brace yourself – the inescapable truth that we're all going to expire. That's scarier than any of the ghouls on *Most Haunted*, am I right? Jokes aside, ageing does mark a passage of time and alongside physical and mental changes, regret and nostalgia can creep in as we mourn the time gone by. I've behaved ludicrously due to my fear of ageing and would like to take this opportunity to apologise to my former features director. Every week for six months before turning 30, I pitched her a different version of a 'leaving my twenties existential freak-out feature' – stemming from my panic that I didn't have a husband, house, baby, make as much money as I'd hoped, *still* wasn't thin. All those things I thought I was supposed to have or to be. I wasn't scared of the age, I've now realised; it was the expectations of what that age meant: I was now a grown-up and I didn't feel like it or want to be.

On my office birthday card, she wrote, 'See, it wasn't so bad!' After the day passed, I realised she was right. Now, approaching a similar milestone a decade later, I realise it isn't the age itself, it's how we've come to define it – or rather, how society has defined it for us. The pressure put upon us to conform and tick off items on a list by certain ages is limiting our autonomy and individuality but it's also how age, ageing and milestones are marketed to us. Youth culture has been elevated since the 1960s but in addition there is the obsession with naming and marketing at new generations (Millennials quickly got booted out for Gen Z, who are on their way out to make way for Generation Alpha and whoever else is next) to make us easier to sell to. Or take those '30 Under 30' lists that, while admirable, celebrate speedy ascension to fame and fortune, but often aren't entirely honest about those individuals' access to contacts, financial backing and privileges – nor do they acknowledge that we stand on the shoulders of our predecessors who pave the way for us (would I have been a beauty editor if I hadn't read Hannah Pool's iconic 'The New Black' beauty column in the *Guardian*? Maybe not).[3] Across the board, everything tells us young is the ultimate state.

Of course, the human brain is broadly wired to hate change so that factors into how we deal with ageing too, because it's destabilising and it takes away what we know. Plus, what's ageing if not change that's difficult to control no matter how much we try? I recently stumbled across a simple formula that was popularised by Richard Beckhard and Reuben T. Harris in 1987 in 'Organizational Transitions: Managing Complex Change' that examined and quantified change and offered a way to embrace it.[4] Though originally used as a business management tool, I think we can stealthily co-opt it to navigate those tricky changes as we age. Behold, the formula: Dissatisfaction x Vision x First Concrete Steps > Resistance. OK, so what does that mean practically? If we target our dissatisfaction about ageing with inspiration and positive action, this could be *greater* than our resistance to changing how we feel about it. Let me try to explain what I mean.

First of all, why might we be resistant to changing how we feel about ageing? Or, in other words, reluctant to challenge the narrative that looking older is intrinsically bad? When society makes us feel like it's natural for women to 'freak out' about ageing, in many ways it is actually easier to stick with the feeling of panic. Humans are social animals who are programmed to stay with the herd; this is more comfortable and feels safer than actively shifting your thinking, which involves a little inner exploration and mind rejigging (that's the scientific term). But accepting the status quo around ageing also makes us feel bad because you can't *not* age, can you? Which leads us to ...

Dissatisfaction: You look in the mirror and feel dissatisfied by your looks. The trigger might be a friend who you think is ageing better or seeing a celebrity who you know is a similar age but who appears ageless on social media. Or anything that makes you feel bad about a certain age and about how you look. That's the dissatisfaction trigger point – and we first need to clock when it's happening. However ...

Vison: If we can present ourselves with an alternative view to the above trigger point and counteract the negativity, this can have a positive impact on our mindset. This could take the form of seeing amazing older women embracing their changing faces naturally or mature women being celebrated on TV as sexy and cool. Anything that gives us the alternate view to how we're being made to feel. We need a lot of the vision because society provides us with so much of the opposite. This leads to ...

First concrete steps: We need to take some action to undermine the negativity society has created around ageing women. That could be filling your feed with badass mature women who embrace life on their own terms and, even better, finding those people in real life too. You do have to seek them out though, especially digitally. The algorithms sell us the opposite because, y'know, capitalism and patriarchy made them that way.

However, what the above formula doesn't account for is that while we may want to change and to ease into ageing in a happier state of mind, there are powerful external factors that keep us in resistance and stuck in a loop of negativity. The kind that sends us spiralling when our faces seem more lined than usual one day. Those factors are plentiful and you don't need to search too hard to find them: they are the filters on social media that we feel we can't post without using, or comparing how we age to others or our 'perfect me' picture (*see also* page 195). It could be struggling to find clothes we like when everything in the shops feels as though it's aimed at 20-year-olds (my current malaise, I've done Y2K fashion, it was bad enough the first time around). But the kicker is that while our yearning to get back the faces and bodies of our long-gone selves *feels* like it comes from deep within us, like it's an inherent, naturally thought-out process, so much of it is the result of how patriarchy has fetishised youth to the point where it's created entire markets to support it – as we've explored in previous chapters. One sells despair and beauty anxiety by exalting youth and the other sells a repair by selling us something to fix our lack of it – it's a tired old pattern. So, my two cents' worth is this: we have a choice to make. Do we really want to fear every encroaching line or change in our appearance as an attack from a brutal unwelcome enemy, or shall we at least try to find another way? I know I don't want to feel like this anymore. Really, do you?

So how could we do this? Let's consider the vision part of the equation: if our reality is what we're exposed to, surely changing those external factors can make a difference to how we feel about getting older? Or at the very least, make us more aware of these factors and their potential influence on our self-esteem ...

I conducted a highly scientific analysis on ageing by posting a question on Facebook in 2021. I asked my circle – a cross-section of ages, cultures, ethnicities, genders, identities, political beliefs and sexualities – about how they felt about getting older. As you might perhaps expect, cisgender men seemed to take it more in their stride (or at least they claimed to). Though some said the loss of signifiers of youth, like hair and muscle tone, was a struggle. However, the women largely deplored ageing with a palpable panic that I recognise. Those who are non-binary mentioned that their issues felt more societal and acceptance-based rather than directly connected to the process of ageing and their looks changing, but this too played a part for some in this group.

By far the most common theme for the women was feeling 'invisible' in society. This included no longer being seen as desirable or hot, the lack of representation in advertising campaigns for women over 40 and physical changes to their faces and bodies. Some spoke about their 'role' in life at certain times, how they felt like that defined them and how factors such as menopause, pregnancy, being single or child-free impacted how they saw themselves because of how society in turn saw them. Some felt too old to do things they once loved, others could feel the ticking of fertility time clocks and some said they felt 'out of date'. Some struggled with what feels 'acceptable' for their age and feeling obliged to look a certain way. Many also felt that relatable shock of looking in the mirror and not feeling like *you* anymore. This affected their attitude to having their photo taken, something I've had a tough relationship with myself as I'm photographed often for work.

These pressures can certainly add up to a sense of anxiety and inferiority and then all it takes is a friend pointing out a 'flaw' in themselves to make you think you have to fix it too, or seeing an ad campaign promising to help target 'problem' areas on the side of a bus for us to notice something in ourselves and obsess over it. Then we *really* notice it – our brains hone in on it with a force akin to that scene in Alfred Hitchcock's *The Birds* – it feels like an inescapable horror. That same negative message then pops up every time we look in the mirror and before you know it, that loop becomes a fixation and then a constant source of beauty anxiety. What adds to that anxiety? The constant reinforcement of women becoming less visible after 30 than their younger counterparts and it's everywhere: film, TV, beauty advertising... The list goes on. And it's so exhausting: no wonder we think we look 'so tired' all the time. Our beauty anxiety is doing that to us, it adds to the weight in that backpack of self-loathing we carry around with us.

I don't think we have to *love* how our faces and bodies are changing as we get older – that's such a big goal to aspire to when you consider how many centuries of beauty conditioning women have gone through. Although if you do feel like that, please go ahead and share that secret, people need to hear it and be inspired. But I think we can get to a place that feels less reactive, less hopeless and less like we've externalised our self-worth when it comes to the ageing process. So, imagine I'm a brown Carrie Bradshaw, looking out from my apartment window (that I'd never be able to afford on an actual journalist salary), asking myself rhetorical questions like: 'Why are we so darn unhappy about our appearance and getting older?' My first imaginary answer, to myself, is that there is no single reason but several causes that seem relatively harmless – and they might surprise you. Let's take a look at them now …

Reason 1: Women have been *sold* the fear of ageing

The fear of looking older is something everyone struggles with, but that age-old double standard has it that men get more handsome, while women become less attractive after a certain point. As we've seen again and again, we're still living in a society where women are judged by how they look before anything else. As we age, it's seen as fading beauty, rather than an evolving beauty. And history has plenty of examples of women feeling the pressure to stave off ageing, from the fairly tame way Elizabethan women used raw meat slices on their faces to ward off wrinkles to French women in the 1700s using aged wine on the face as an exfoliator.[5] It's rumoured that reputed serial killer Countess Elizabeth Báthory slaughtered virgins, partly because drinking and bathing in their blood, she felt, preserved her youth.[6]

In *I Feel Bad About My Neck*, Nora Ephron said: 'If anyone young is reading this, go, right this minute, put on a bikini and don't take it off until you're 34.' Even women, smart, successful women, like Ephron, can assume a woman is 'old' at 35, though she was writing this in the noughties. Why? Is it a hangover from the past when life expectancies were so much lower, so if you lived to 35 you were actually doing pretty well? Or maybe youth and fertility are still so tied up together in our collective subconscious that once we're at the 'fertility cliff' of 35, it's 'all over'. (It's worth noting that though experts often disagree on this age being the sole fertility marker, it's also now recognised that there are other factors affecting fertility.) Yet pregnant women over 35 are still often referred to in medicine as 'geriatric mothers'.[7] While it is a medical term, it sounds a bit dystopian, *Handmaid's-Tale*-esque to me – and it's certainly not helpful.

Let's now return to one of our favourite themes: patriarchal society's fear of female power. What has happened historically when a woman has sought to embrace her own power, after an age she's no longer 'useful' to men? During the Middle Ages, the belief in magic and witchcraft was common until around the 11th century, when it was seen as the enemy of Christian society.[8] The first records of systematic European witch-hunts are from 1428, which started in Valais, Switzerland, though they soon spread across Europe.[9] How would one define a witch? You might ask. You can choose almost anything that marks someone out – sometimes having red hair was enough. However, many of those persecuted were older, disabled or lived on the fringes of their societies and most often they were poor. Usually, they were female. A German book from c. 1486 called the *Malleus Maleficarum* (usually translated as 'Hammer of Witches')[10] helped create a fear around witchcraft across many parts of Europe, not least because witches were said to be able to make women sterile and men impotent.[11]

Witch mania continued during the 16th and 17th centuries, but even when people stopped hunting witches and blaming them for everything from failed crops to extreme weather, the legacy remained. In the artworks from the era, witches are often shown as old and ugly (and outside the use of men) and perhaps bitter about losing their youth (much as the Evil Queen in *Snow White*, in fact). It's a very powerful motif for the conditioning around 'fearing' older women. When Deanna Petherbridge, curator of the Scottish National Gallery of Modern Art's exhibition 'Witches and Wicked Bodies', was researching the 2013 show, she came across stereotypes of crones and hags dating back over 500 years. She told *The Herald*: 'They are extremely thin with long hanging dugs, a nude figure almost always showing the breasts, so I realised how important it was [for the artists] to show these shrivelled breasts. I realised how important it was that she was no longer attractive or fertile.'[12] Witches were outside of the control of men, which gave them a freedom that patriarchal forces sought to punish and take away.

Of course, the image of the witch – the subversive woman with access to unusual power – is still a much-loved trope in pop culture today. Disney has its fair share of 'witchy' female characters, as we discussed back in An Ugly Start, where I touched on how much of the film and TV aimed at children has a set of views about female beauty that are negative, archaic and damaging narratives to impressionable minds (*see also* page 49). It's so often the case that older women are shown as destructive and jealous of youth, which mirrors the way that society treats older women now too. Cinderella's evil stepmother is jealous and scheming in contrast to Cinderella's sweetness and youth. In *101 Dalmatians*, Cruella de Vil is the ageing heiress who wants to inflict harm on puppies to make soft fur coats – she's a symbol of vanity, lost youth and greed. In *Game of Thrones*, Melisandre is said to be a 400-year-old crone who uses magic to disguise her age and some say uses sex as a way to manipulate men. Grotbags, a witch from the popular 1990s show of the same name, doesn't look too dissimilar from Looney Tunes character Witch Hazel, with her large nose and protruding chin, who first appeared in 1954 – both are 'green' with envy for those who are youthful. We're shown that older women are to be feared and we should fear looking like them too – with everything that implies. Talk about setting up a damaging and long-lasting beauty standard.

From looking at folklore while researching this book, and just from my own interest in pagan culture, the 'divine' power was so often an older female. In Gaelic pagan myth the Cailleach is a divine ancestor associated with the creation of the landscape and known as the weather witch.[13] And yet, over time that reverence for experience and wisdom in older women has diminished to the point where they go from young and beautiful to old and wicked in a heartbeat. Despite once being known as respected healers in their communities, these wise women started to become known as hags (a 'repulsive old woman') and crones ('a feeble withered old woman') around the 13th and 14th centuries.[14] There's no equivalent for men, which is crucial to note. Wizards tend to be wise and cerebral, and from Merlin to Gandalf are often shown to be on the side of good, supporting the established order; whereas women who are experienced, wise and autonomous, on the other hand, have been viewed as a threat to patriarchy and we're still living with the effects of this toxic ageism. We have been shown older women as evil and resentful, and this idea has become embedded in our culture – but really it has just served to diminish our independence and our spirit, to make us easier to manipulate by capitalism and to control. And we're still losing out because we don't have enough visible older female role models.

Reason 2: Pop culture perpetuates the myth that our worth lies in our youth...

Pop culture would have us believe that we're all terrified of getting older and have to fight it with every ounce of courage (and pound) we have, but research in 2017 from Melbourne

University suggests that in many ways, we actually become happier as we get older, particularly between the ages of 50 and 70, which includes embracing the way we are ageing.[15]

Yet, still, as age 30 approaches a panic sets in: we think we should be considering Botox to freeze those laughter lines that were once sweet but are now 'crow's feet'. We must now use retinol, watch what we eat (because, y'know, your metabolism is slowing down as you get older) and might encounter some grey hairs, which feel like a salute from the Grim Reaper, telling you the big news: you're no longer young and beautiful to society. As 40 approaches, for many of us, anti-ageing routines become almost like an extra job on top of our many other roles in life. It's a huge area that can be capitalised on: the global anti-ageing market is projected to reach a value of 191.6 billion dollars by 2030[16] while 'wrinkles' and 'anti-ageing' are both currently among the more highly searched-for beauty terms online.[17]

So how did this happen? At the end of the 19th century, anti-ageing was gradually becoming more of a priority for women. For example, in 1889, Margaret Kroesen developed Frownies patches,[18] which you stick to your face to apparently 'train' your muscles to relax (they are still around today), after she discovered her daughter Alice (a concert pianist) had developed 'unsightly' frown lines. Would she have created them for a son? Perhaps not. James F. Stark, professor of medical humanities at the University of Leeds and author of *The Cult of Youth: Anti-Ageing in Modern Britain*, wrote for *The Conversation*: 'Although humans had long been trying to cheat ageing, the period immediately after the First World War saw new strategies to rejuvenate the body and mind gain popularity. These included everything from surgical procedures that aimed to manipulate sex hormones to everyday beauty products, like skin "foods" and moisturising creams. All of these methods promised wildly different results. In the case of male hormone treatments, a patient might expect to regain lost fertility as well as energy. Everyday cosmetic products, marketed almost exclusively to women, promised a restored youthful appearance.'[19]

In a 1923 book called *Rejuvenation*, Jean Frumusan – a French, self-defined 'anti-ageing specialist' – advocated lifestyle hacks to preserve age through periodic fasting, slow eating and being 'carnivorous at one meal, vegetarian at the next'.[20] From the 1920s, electrotherapy devices, like the Overbeck Rejuvenator (invented by Otto Overbeck, a brewing chemist), claimed to repair anything – infectious diseases and 'deformities' aside – by replenishing the body's electrical energy reserves.[21] The beauty industry was in on it too: Helena Rubinstein launched a skincare solution called 'Hormone Twin Youthifiers' in the United States in 1931 that were day and night creams with oestrogen to replace 'the vital glandular secretions of youth'; and Elizabeth Arden introduced her 'Vienna Youth Mask' in 1927 – which doesn't look too dissimilar to the terrifying cyborg LED mask I have, which uses red light therapy to help reduce inflammation in the skin. But Arden's mask was, rather sweetly, made of tin foil and papier-mâché, and used electrical currents to warm up the facial tissues. It was inspired by influential Viennese physiologist Dr Eugen Steinach, who was known for introducing partial vasectomies as a way of rejuvenating his patients' virility.[22]

Magazines of the time reflected the pressure that Hollywood's female stars faced, passing on 'second-hand anxiety' to their readers. The stars were subject to incredible pressure to stay looking young at any cost, lest they be 'retired' by the movie studios – which is what happened to Greta Garbo, aged 36.[23] As such, beauty experts in Hollywood flourished.

The correlation between the rise of Hollywood and the rise of the anti-ageing industry is no coincidence. Nobody would go further to pursue eternal youth than a Hollywood starlet and it's no happy surprise that Hollywood and cosmetic surgery go hand in hand – it's woven into its dark history. The studios ran a 'looks over talent' philosophy and anyone that the studio heads thought needed cosmetic surgery was instructed to have it.[24] As Metro-Goldwyn-Mayer co-founder Louis B. Mayer reportedly said: 'A star is made, created; carefully and cold-bloodedly built up from nothing ... All I ever looked for was a face. If someone looked good to me, I'd have him tested. If a person looked good on film, if he photographed well, we could do the rest.'[25]

From the early 1900s, Hollywood's youthful faces had often been ambassadors for beauty brands, albeit with the same 'invisible' age limit the film industry had imposed on them. Actor Isabella Rossellini became the face of Lancôme in 1982 but was dropped 14 years later at 42. She told *Harper's Bazaar*: 'When I spoke to them at the time, they explained it to me saying, "Yes, you are very successful and when we do research, women say that they are very grateful to have a woman in her forties representing them." But they said that in advertising, we don't represent reality, we represent women's dreams and a woman's dream is to be young – and that's why you can't represent that dream.'[26] Rossellini's comments embody the conflict that plagues almost every form of capitalist media out there: what women want and what advertisers want are two very different things. To apply our formula for change, the advertisers create the dissatisfaction, which sells beauty anxiety. What women want is freedom, happiness and peace from being continually made to feel bad about themselves, ideally through representation of their actual selves, rather than some unattainable ideal – but that doesn't result in fear buying.

Across the spectrum of film and TV, young women are almost exclusively depicted as the object of desire.

A report by Martha Lauzen, executive director of the Center for the Study of Women in Television and Film at San Diego State University, looked at the speaking roles in Hollywood movies between 2019 and 2020. Researchers found that the majority of female characters were in their twenties and thirties while most of the men were in their thirties and forties.[27] It's telling, as the report said, that: 'At about the age of 40, female characters begin to disappear in substantial numbers from both broadcast and streaming programs.'[28] A statement by Lauzen accompanying the report said that although there are a few well-known mature female actors in Hollywood, they are still the exceptions and that: 'The tendency to feature younger female characters in films emphasizes the value of their youth and appearance at the expense of allowing females to age into positions of personal and professional power.'[29] Art is said to imitate life – but in this case, it's hard to know where one starts and the other begins.

Is it any wonder that historically, female actors have disguised their ages in order to work for longer? And it's still happening. Rebel Wilson was 'outed' by a former classmate who said she was seven years older than she'd let on[30] – but when we consider the stats above and the 'shelf life' of a woman in Hollywood, who can blame her? Older women are rarely portrayed as desirable; instead we're sold the anxiety that we must be young to be seen as attractive – and it's a mainstay of the film culture we love. If the female star is older, that's usually a major plot point, as in 1967's *The Graduate* – famed for an age-gap relationship between an older female and a younger male. However, unbelievably, in reality, Dustin Hoffman was 29 at the time, while Anne Bancroft, who played the famed Mrs Robinson, was just six years older at 35 – yet more proof of Hollywood's enduring ageism towards women over 30.

It is of course completely usual to see a much younger woman cast as the love interest of an older male co-star – and it can be uncomfortable viewing. Take some of the classics: when filming 1939's *Gone with the Wind*, Vivien Leigh was 25; her co-star Clark Gable was 13 years older. In *Roman Holiday* (1953), Gregory Peck was 37, while Audrey Hepburn was 24. In 1958's *Vertigo*, Kim Novak was half the age of love interest James Stewart. In *Manhattan* (1979), Woody Allen is 26 years older than his co-star Mariel Hemingway. But how much has changed in more recent years? In 2003's *Love Actually*, when Andrew Lincoln's character knocks on the door to tell his mate's wife that he fancies her via the medium of large cards, he was 29 while Keira Knightley was 17. In 2015, Maggie Gyllenhaal said: 'I'm 37 and I was told recently I was too old to play the lover of a man who was 55. It was astonishing to me. It made me feel bad, and then it made feel angry, and then it made me laugh.'[31] Except it's not funny anymore. It's pretty sad because it's designed to make us feel small and feeds into the beauty anxiety about getting older.

We're so used to these age disparities that we just expect them to be carried over into real life too. Look at how the internet did a collective double-take when it was revealed that Keanu Reeves (58) wasn't dating somebody half his age, though his girlfriend, artist Alexandra Grand, was still nine years younger than him. Or the confusion caused by the fact that Hugh Jackman is married to Deborra-Lee Furness, who is 13 years his senior. It's just not the norm in Hollywood, sadly.

This older man–younger woman trope persists in our TV too; research published in 2019 found that male TV presenters are twice as likely to be employed past the age of 50 as their female counterparts.[32] Two of the longest-standing daytime British TV presenters, Holly Willoughby and Phillip

Schofield, have an age gap of almost two decades. Would we expect to see a woman in her sixties co-presenting with a man in his early forties? It seems far less likely.

We have the internet, electric cars and robot vacuum cleaners yet still this archaic view of a woman's beauty depending on her age persists. Worse than that, it's an accepted part of our culture and our regular Friday night viewing. Talk about sneaky propaganda regarding female beauty, age and worth – and a way to universalise ageist, anti-women beauty standards. The fact that such a big deal was made of Clare Crawley becoming the 'oldest' Bachelorette in the US dating show at 39 in 2020 is revealing as to what society tells women to feel about their ageing and their overall value. While shows like Netflix's *Grace and Frankie*, featuring octogenarians talking about sex and dating, are starting to push back, it feels like it will be a long time until this is unexceptional. Though there are some great examples of women breaking through that glass ceiling, like *Strictly Come Dancing* presenter Claudia Winkleman, who is one of the highest-paid earners on the BBC at aged 50, there just doesn't seem to be enough – or enough variety of appearance. When our entertainment sets up youth as the only form of beauty, there's no way that it doesn't affect how and what we think about ageing. If we don't see ourselves represented at every age, of course we start to feel invisible. It's no wonder we fear looking older and getting older when our entertainment is in many cases culturally programming us to hate ourselves.

Now there is a never-ending list of things you can do to apparently ward off ageing, from placenta capsules to vampire facials – there's even a menopause-delaying surgery that involves removing and freezing chunks of ovarian tissue, which can then be transplanted back into the body in later life to slow the onset of menopause. Often it's Hollywood's stars who try these procedures first, which comes from a desire to stay in work, to look younger and feel relevant in a patriarchal industry. Then we hear about these treatments as miracles in halting anti-ageing as that information gets passed down to us.

Attitudes to stars ageing have changed – sort of. Lancôme hired Isabella Rossellini back in 2016, but often we still see Hollywood stars in their twenties fronting anti-ageing skincare campaigns, which seems somewhat farcical. We need to be mindful of what we watch and aware of what beauty ideals we're being sold – even when we're on the sofa with a takeaway and wine. It's not always just entertainment, it's anti-women propaganda. Perhaps it's time to look to those who do it better. French brands often choose more mature models and stars for their campaigns: Catherine Deneuve in her late 70s featured in a 2021 campaign for YSL,[33] while in 2022 at age 54, Carla Bruni appeared in a Balmain campaign.[34] Typically, in French cinema sex appeal is an intrinsic quality that doesn't devalue with age – more of that, please.

Reason 3: We are *told* how to age...

When it comes to ageing well we're *told* implicitly what this looks like – and that's lineless and appearing to be half our actual age. Inside the industry, I've been overlooked for influencer campaigns for being over 30 (though perhaps because I'm a sweary goth too) and have heard how older beauty editors and publications aimed at older women are sometimes ignored by beauty and fashion brands. It's easy to shrug this off as being 'life' or as a part of society but it isn't: it's ageism and discrimination.

Even when somebody over 40 is celebrated for their looks or chosen for an ad campaign, it's *despite* their age –

which so rarely happens for men. A tabloid headline reads: 'Sharon Stone, 63, looks 20 years younger in au natural photoshoot' with her beauty labelled 'age-defying',[35] for example. Beautiful women over 60 are often seen as ageing 'outliers' – and just look at which older actors are chosen for advertising campaigns: invariably they're the ones who look palatable to the white gaze, with long straight white hair; they're always thin and often former models. Swedish model and actor Paulina Porizkova had a magazine cover that called her the 'supermodel that dared to look her age'.[36] Though admirable, she 'dared' to look her age while still being acceptable to the Eurocentric beauty ideals. We just don't see older women with other body types and other ethnicities celebrated in the same way or on the same scale – unless 'they look good, for their age' which needs to be struck off our parlance as it is deeply damaging. 'Ageless' is often a coded word meaning 'still hot to men'. The recognition of older female celebrity beauty is often in the context of their faces 10 or even 20 years ago – if they still look similar to how they did over a decade ago, then women are ageing gracefully and they look good. But think how much we change and lives change over that sort of period and what we might have gone through. Can we really only ever be beautiful if our faces and bodies remain as they were?

Sure, there are people whose faces do not change as much as those of others in their peer group as they get older due to heritage, genes, lifestyle, etc. But there is no such thing as the fountain of eternal youth (although Juan Ponce de León, a 16th-century Spanish explorer, believed it was in Florida)[37] and so often surgical or cosmetic intervention is behind an unusually ageless face. But, and I know this first-hand, we see so little of what celebrities and influencers do to achieve this because – as we've witnessed again and again, and all through history – women in the public eye can't be seen to be going to great efforts to appear conventionally beautiful, but they will be devalued if they are not deemed so. So, the next time you compare yourself to a celebrity, here's a heads-up from somebody who has seen this, up close. Their beauty and body regimes are pulverising and include a mix of many of the following: a personal chef, nutritionists, personal trainers, weekly facials, masseurs, hairstylists for every event, hair extensions and colour, including clip-in pieces and wefts for photo shoots, make-up artists before every picture taken, lash extensions as a standard, a variety of cosmetic enhancements (fillers, Botox), cosmetic surgery (often so slight, you can't always see it) and intensive skincare treatments. While magazines now have strict guidelines around OTT airbrushing, suffice to say, it's often celebrities themselves who ask for much more extreme retouching. But realistically, they're caught up in the same crossfire we all are – just with access to the best surgeons and the pressure to use them.

The 'has she, hasn't she had surgery?' game is a form of clickbait in itself. So much is designed to cut women down when they are in their powerful prime. We've become conditioned to think it's 'bad' to look our age and to want to erase every line that says we've lived and survived. Think about the old saying to 'never ask a woman her age', which sometimes comes with 'or a man his salary', which offers up the slice of toxic societal conditioning we just can't seem to shake off: men's value comes from their careers and bank balance, women's their beauty, youth and ability to reproduce. We're shocked when somebody is older than we think they are – our vision of what 40 or 50 looks like in our minds and how we've been shown it through the media is totally different to the reality. After *Friends: The Reunion* aired in 2021, I heard nothing of the plot and everything about how great actor Matt LeBlanc (Joey) looked and how overboard the show's female stars had gone with aesthetic treatments.

What's funny is when I think about my male pals, in their thirties and forties, many of whom I've known since school or uni: they largely dress the same, in band tees, vintage clothes, gothic attire. Nobody at any point says to them 'you're mutton dressed as lamb'. Of course, men have their own woes, but they're not usually the target of magazine articles like '20 items you need to toss by 30', 'Fashion for over 60' or 'Dressing right after 40' – all pieces I've just found on popular media brands, which we anxiously click to read in case we are doing something wrong or making ourselves ridiculous in the eyes of society by wearing something 'age inappropriate'. This serves to curb our individuality and diminish our self-expression. Imposing age-based beauty and fashion 'rules' is rampant – for example, cut your hair short after 50, choose between your face or your body as you age, no bright or glittery make-up after 30, being too old for red lipstick – and reinforces the edict that ageing is a bad thing. When it's not, it's a privilege. 'Age-appropriate' is patriarchy keeping us small. And boxed in. As if resisting this pressure wasn't hard enough, we are also increasingly told that we should love ourselves and be comfortable in our own skin by the fashion and beauty worlds that still sell us the opposite. Talk about mixed messages: to me it feels exactly like the push and pull between feminism and the patriarchy in a nutshell.

When I did my highly scientific Facebook research, it was really highlighted to me how men have a different lens, culture, value and philosophy towards ageing. While many lamented hair and physical changes, our culture has made it easier for them to grow old 'gracefully'. Women rarely get that freedom – they become objectified as soon as they hit puberty (fuelled by societal programming that their worth mostly lies in their beauty) – then have a space of 10 to 20 years before they're old maids, hags, spinsters and the like. For us to age 'gracefully', we're exhorted to maintain our looks, be age-appropriate, still be aesthetically pleasing and not go overboard – or fear the repercussions. We can age gracefully like Helen Mirren or inspirationally like J.Lo. Alternatively, we can 'let ourselves go' or even age 'disgracefully'. For example, Madonna is often cast as a figure of pity for not acting as she 'should' for her age, with detractors like presenter Piers Morgan saying she should 'put it away'[38]. Everywhere we turn, we're assailed by insecurities not just about our age but how we're ageing – men in the public eye so rarely face the same scrutiny.

However we want to age, or choose to age, we have more than one, white-knuckle, fear-filled option – but we have to seek it and start defining ourselves as valuable in society, aside from our appearance. That might mean looking to those who have had work done, but are honest about it, like Jane Fonda, who has taken the candid approach, ascribing her looks to 'good genes and a lot of money'.[39] Or finding people who have embraced it more naturally, though it's worth just noting that this is tricky too. Not having anything 'done', letting your hair go grey and embracing ageing without cosmetic intervention is now the radical act.

There *has* to be another way to age that doesn't feel quite so all-consuming and terrifying. As each decade rolls on, I don't want to feel as though my worth is diminishing with my collagen or oestrogen levels. It's OK to want to look great, whatever that means to us as individuals, and as youthful as we feel – but that's not always about beauty or our looks. One way of reframing it is that if anything, our confidence should increase as we get older. After all, the more you have experienced, the more you know. Cultures outside of the West often have a much greater appreciation of older generations than we have. In Japan, the title 'Living National Treasure' is awarded to those who are masters of traditional Japanese arts towards the ends of their lives[40] and I've seen how my Indian culture often reveres its elders. In the Western world, we seem to push older women aside, particularly as their beauty 'fades'. It's worth repeating that ageing is a privilege – to quote my funeral director friend who has a healthy attitude towards it: 'What's the alternative to getting older? It's dying young, and that's deeply tragic. So we need to embrace getting older, because we *get* to.'

So how can we ensure we protect ourselves and we protect other women – our peers, our children and our mothers – from the obsession with the epidemic of 'hot for her age'? Here's a few suggestions that might help us to begin to break the cycle and embrace Lemmy's whisky-soaked point of view …

Get conscious: I'd like to challenge you to take note of how many messages about anti-ageing you give yourself or see around you over the course of a week (tag me with them on social media if you like). When you recognise every single message you receive about how women should try to look as young as possible you'll be shocked. I'm sat at my desk now and I can see a plumping serum (to 'replace' the volume we lose as we age – which isn't really doable with a serum, just FYI, though it's good for hydration and environmental protection). The magazine to my right has a female celebrity on the cover looking 'fresh-faced', apparently. I just listened to a comedy podcast that had an anti-ageing skincare advert right in the middle of it and a mate just texted to ask for a recommendation for an anti-ageing facial/Botox/something because she 'hates her face' today. That's without even leaving my home. Then, when I looked in the mirror just now, my first thought was 'Man, you look tired … how can I fix this?' Even noticing these things – and their effects – and questioning them gets our cognitive juices flowing. When we interrupt our negative automatic thoughts about our looks – which is hard – it could create a small, but definite change in how we view the ageing anxiety we're being sold.

Beware of second-hand ageing anxiety: You may know this scenario well: you're feeling good, have a Frappuccino in hand, the sun is shining, things are excellent. Then you bump into a pal, who tells you about their own worries, their fears, their big anxiety. You walk away and suddenly your 9/10 day looks like a 5/10 and you're not sure why. Your delicious iced beverage is now an unappetising pile of mush, your mind now ruminating about what they said and its relation to your life. Someone else's anxieties have latched on to us and our negatively wired caveman brains, which are perennially but often unhelpfully looking out for any ways to keep us safe by considering potential 'dangers'. Before you know it, their issue is now your issue. Not even a sugary beverage can save the day.

There's another part to this too. Our mirror neurons (cells in our brain which create an empathetic response to any behaviours we see) are said to gear up when we see something happen to someone else in a process called 'emotional contagion'.[41] So when we see somebody fall over, we wince for their pain, or if someone jumps with fright, so do we. But studies also suggest that we do the same with emotions, even increasing our own cortisol levels as we do so and so when we hear somebody lamenting their grey hair or wrinkles, and if they are someone we care about, this second-hand anxiety could affect us too.[42] So, what can we do about it? Of course we empathise and feel concern for our friends but if a mate bemoans her wrinkles or age, you can explain it's making you feel a bit rubbish and maybe suggest a way for her to break her cycle of anxiety. The age-old cognitive behavioural therapy (CBT) technique of 'what's the evidence for this thought?' might help them think a little deeper about it themselves and make you feel more active in the conversation, as would finding an example of someone loving themselves as they age. We can help each other unpack and neutralise our beauty anxiety, but so too could doing something fun to break the cycle. Psychologist and TED speaker Guy Winch also says that identifying what you're good at and doing more of it can help – for example, having more dinner parties if you like cooking. As does mitigating self-criticism with self-compassion to help raise our self-esteem.[43] All of which might mean we focus less on how our face is changing and more on finding joy.

Ditch the categories and age groups: Cross-generational friendships are so rewarding and we may have more in common with somebody who likes the same music, films or hobbies as us than we do with someone born the same year as us. Expanding our social groups also means we get to hear other viewpoints and a variety of opinions. Book clubs or volunteering can be a brilliant way to do this. I also think there's so much inspiration in filling our social media feeds, Pinterest boards and TV screens with women who live life on their own terms, rocking bright make-up, getting tattoos, going off on their own adventure, amid the foghorn of society telling them to 'be quiet and age appropriately'.

Actively celebrate older women: Women are not supposed to get angry, so the patriarchy tells us. Which, to me, seems like a clear message that it's exactly what we need to do. We are being done a huge disservice in how we are treated as we go through our life stages. Let brands know that you want women of all ages in their campaigns and not just the usual faces of acceptable ageing. We need to see more and more people who can show us another way to age from what we're usually sold. Every time I've told a woman over 50 she looks amazing, there's a palpable sense of disbelief, which is such a heartbreaking indictment of how society makes us feel as we get older. Go out of your way to tell other women how great they look or how much you admire them. Our biggest problem isn't the fight against ageing, nor the lines on our faces – it's the fight against being defined by them.

Reclaim your relationship to beauty: How much of your beauty routine pertains to actively looking younger? It's fine to use that stuff of course, but could you focus more on the sensorial aspects of it, the smell, the feeling, the joy you get from the packaging – rather than it feeling like a 'jar of hope' each morning? When you think you look 'old and tired', it's not a signal you need more concealer – maybe you just need a rest (a physical one, plus a break from the never-ending shitstorm us women are subjected to about looking fresh-faced and youthful.) Reclaiming what you loved about beauty before it became about 'the battle with ageing' is one of the most joyful ways to repair your relationship with your appearance too. So, hear me out ... What aspects of beauty did you used to love that you don't do anymore? Did you spend your teens wearing multi-coloured shadows? Find a palette that 'sparks joy' and try wearing a little colour again each day. If you were a noughties emo kid, maybe go heavier on the eyeliner while playing Paramore and use that to express yourself. When we're focusing so much on looking young, I think it's often the parts of us that feel unexpressed that we're trying to recapture rather than our 'perfect me' pictures. Whenever that 'I look old' rhetoric starts to slip in, I think it's a sign we need to reconnect to feeling more authentically us. Use beauty to remind yourself of who you are inside, on the outside.

THE UGLY SIDE OF WELLNESS

'Caring for myself is not self-indulgence.'

– A Burst of Light: and Other Essays,

Audre Lorde, 1988

TEN YEARS AGO, 'WELLNESS' was a word we seldom heard. 'Beauty' – yes. Health – sure. But 'wellness', a murky segue between the two, was relatively unheard of. Now, large corporations have wellness programmes for their employees, our social media feeds are awash with people doing ice baths and we are exhorted to choose the wholly beneficial path of wellness at every turn. Wellness, we are told, allows us to be our best 'well' selves through hacking and improving our way to a place of happiness.

The word itself is derived from 'wellbeing', which describes our state of health and happiness, both personally and as a community. But wellness has a slightly different meaning and is the quality of that state of health and happiness as the result of 'deliberate effort'. That's because wellbeing is the goal, but wellness is the marketing buzzword for an industry that promises to get us there. Wellness keeps us accountable with tracking devices and gym memberships – but one thing it rarely mentions? Community. Wellness cares deeply... about itself. And it exhorts us to do the same. It's easy to forget as we rely on meditation apps or knock back protein shakes, that wellness, like beauty, fashion, diet or cosmetic surgery, is a profit-driven industry. We all deserve to feel any combination of happy/calm/healthy/joyful/present that we desire but there is a curious paradox here: if we have so much wellness at our fingertips, then why have we, generally speaking, become so 'unwell'? Why are mental health statistics getting worse? Why is our self-esteem in the gutter? Why are we still so unhappy with our appearance? That poses the biggest question of them all: does 'wellness' genuinely want us to be well? After all, the worse we feel, the more we need it and the more profitable it can be for those in the industry.

I wanted to write about wellness in a book on beauty standards because the two have become inextricably interlinked. Lifestyle and beauty brands have seized on the trend for wellness and run with it to the point where it now encompasses everything from watered-down spirituality to health and nutrition, to how we choose to relax and – crucially – how good we look doing it. As the modern wellness industry has grown exponentially in the last decade, it has pulled so far from its origins to the point where it has become something of a two-headed serpent – one beast cuddles up to us like a friend while the other is ready to kick us when we're down. And because this boom has happened so fast, we've not had enough distance or time to reflect on what we're really being sold as we're encouraged to 'be our best selves'. The wellness industry still feels shiny and new, that's what makes its real intentions harder to identify – but we just have to scratch the Lycra-clad surface.

We're constantly being shown how wellness can make you feel like a winner and help you succeed, from the elaborate morning routines of CEOs rising at 4am to work out/hike/meditate and having most of their day nailed by 7am (with no mention of support staff, personal chefs and trainers and maybe self-help guru Deepak Chopra on speed dial). It's things like this (and many others, as we will discuss) that have made being 'well' seem like a privilege in itself. Just as with beauty ideals, the bar has been set so very high that it keeps some protected and others always feeling like they never measure up – if they can even access it at all. Often, we fail at wellness before we even get started. Despite its green-juice quaffing, reishi-snaffling exterior, wellness hides some truly ugly beauty standards behind some ludicrously expensive leggings; in fact, wellness has become quite unwell itself.

A big part of the message has become focused on looking like we have good health by being in the right luxury kit, hanging out at the most exclusive wellness locations and having the 'right bodies' – that's obvious with how wellness brands market themselves across the board. Search online for 'yoga' and you get all manner of mostly blonde, white, lean-limbed yoga bunnies on pristine beaches and that's because looking 'well' has now become intwined with the Eurocentric beauty ideal in itself. These are the images brands sell us on our feeds, their ad campaigns, or that we see embedded in articles on wellness to the point where that's what I imagine when I think of a woman doing yoga and I'm *Indian* – how messed up is that? (My ancestors are likely cursing me as I type this.)

This is probably starting to sound pretty familiar. Wellness promises us so much – a longer life, a healthy body, mental clarity, and alongside this, clear skin, thick, shiny hair and bright eyes. The message is clear: wellness will make you feel better *and* look better. What is that, if not a beauty standard? The wellness poster girl is largely slim, white, able-bodied, practising a yoga pose on a beach – we are sold her 'wellthy' lifestyle. Look at the leading influencers with best-selling books, their own wellness brands or millions of followers – there is a clear aesthetic designed for us to emulate. Or take the TikTok archetype of #Thatgirl that has been viewed over 800m times. Who is 'that girl'? The newest incarnation of the noughties 'it girl', she's the #Girlboss who wakes up early, has a green juice breakfast, writes in her journal and reflects from a sun-drenched location – she's the vision of perfection. But are you even 'that girl' if you don't post about it on social media? Can you be 'that girl' if you miss a spin class because you're exhausted from being a single parent or if you have a McMuffin because it's half the price of a smoothie bowl? Can you ever be 'that girl' and win at wellness unless you have all the pastel-toned matching kit? Social media, advertising and the way the wellness industry markets itself would suggest not. Why we're putting smoothies in bowls and not glasses is a pertinent question because it makes *zero* sense, but the bigger question is this:

are we allowing the same beauty standards to be forced on us by capitalism, white supremacy and classism (and much more) in the new guise of being 'well'?

Everyone wants a part of the glossy allure of wellness, from the fashion industry (sportswear is the new casual when ten years ago, people didn't want to be seen 'out' in gym kit, let alone clubbing in it) to the beauty industry, intent on adding superfoods and crystals to *everything* (is there rose quartz in my toothpaste – sure, I'll try that!), through to the food industry (where do we begin ... isn't that ludicrously expensive bone broth just stock?). The global wellness industry is now worth a colossal $4.2 trillion, while meditation app Headspace has over 30m users and has recently merged with mental health tech company Ginger for a reported $1billion[1], and SoulCycle – the mindfulness-meets-spin fitness class – has been valued at more than $900million. When you look at the money involved, it's not surprising that everyone wants a bit of the wellness buzz: in 2020 dating app Hinge even partnered with Headspace to create 'pre-date' meditations.[2] Add a little splash of wellness to anything you're selling and it feels like it's 'good for you' – it's a really smart marketing technique.

Over the last 15 years I've tried every conceivable health trend from urotherapy (which is, indeed, drinking your own wee to harness its reportedly 'bioavailable' vitamin content – I wasn't paid enough to do that) to intense detoxes to vagina steaming and wiping actual fresh snail slime on my face. 'Wellness' is a world I've always been *obsessed* with and, like so many, I've spent so much time believing I was just one raw cleanse, self-help seminar or boot camp away from being prettier/thinner/happier. I've given wellness everything and yet at times it's made me feel a lot worse. Like 'beauty anxiety', our 'wellness worry' now ensures that we never feel like we're doing enough to take care of ourselves. It keeps us in pursuit of trying whatever is sold to us as the new method to 'fix' our woes.

Around a decade ago, I started working at a big health magazine in a time when nobody outside of LA – the long-time mothership of many toxic beauty and wellness standards – cared that much about green juices, breathwork or mindfulness. If anything, it was all a bit niche. The covers talked about 'buff bodies' and 'getting shredded' and our features covered blitzing fat, tracking your macros and everything that went with 'bullet-proofing' your health. Here, it was normal to work out twice a day, for a chocolate bar to feel like a contraband drug and to treat every new health fad as life-changing. I was the only plus-sized member of the team (i.e. in desperate need of fixing) and responsible for all the magazine's health and beauty content. When I 'failed' a body makeover challenge because I didn't lose the three stone in three months, it felt like I'd fundamentally let myself down by not being able to transform into a coveted 'after' shot. I was not #Winning at wellness – and it wasn't the first time I'd felt that way.

Who is well-come, and who isn't?

So how do we learn what it entails to be 'well'? Often our first brush with 'wellness' of any kind comes in the form of physical education (PE) and physical fitness at school, including much-hated cross-country sessions. As in the world of beauty, it's not a level playing field – often we're divided into two camps, the sporty elite and unsporty leftovers. While I'd like to think PE has modernised and become more inclusive since those days, for many of us our early experiences left a lasting impact.

My first memory of PE, aged six, left me feeling anything but well. As with beauty shaming for braces or sticking-out ears, we're often fitness-shamed at a young age. Mine involved wedging myself into awkward gym shorts and plimsolls, which was bad enough, but the real humiliation was then having to climb up a thick rope in our school gymnasium, one by one, as everyone else watched. I knew my ascent was doomed – I couldn't coordinate myself to hang on with my legs and move my hands simultaneously so I made it a quarter of the way up before freezing as the teacher barked, 'Keep moving!' I was just hanging on to that rope for what seemed like an eternity, as my classmates watched, until I gave up and slid down as the coir burned my legs. I didn't feel breathless from the exertion but I did feel winded from the shame of being unable to reach this seemingly important milestone.

I found zero joy in this, only unexpressed dread. What I wanted to do instead was ballet classes, but my passion was thwarted because there were no leotards in my size available (which wasn't that big at all, by the way – not that it matters or should ever matter). I'd peer in the frosted glass doors as everyone stayed after school for ballet, watching the tiny ballerinas twirl in their pink tutus with sadness. As PE turned to athletics as I grew older, I experienced the same anxiety as trying to leap over a hurdle was forcible torture and two-hour cross-country runs every week felt like the work of Satan.

Without choice or consideration for different skill sets and interests, it can mean that PE becomes a source of anguish for kids. Studies have shown that it can be a point of distress, particularly for teenage girls, leading to low confidence and body image issues.[3] In my head I compared myself to my friends and came up with reasons for my lack of prowess: 'you're fat, you're slow, you have no coordination and even you're not good enough'. To me it felt like PE set some kids up as heroes while everyone else was a loser by comparison. It's meant that any form of fitness for me has since been laced with fear and dread; I'll always be that six-year-old, looking up at the rope, waiting for the shame to be over – but in wellness, it never is.

When we're 'labelled' so young it can affect our approach to movement throughout our entire lives. It also means that PE fails to do what it should do and that's to teach *all* children to enjoy movement, fitness, sports and being part of a team in a way that builds up their confidence and doesn't destroy it. A US study found that making children do PE every day actually increased discipline issues and absence rates. Co-author Analisa Packham, an economics professor at Miami University, Ohio, cites bullying, changing-room anxiety and the teasing of kids not deemed 'athletic' enough as likely causes.[4] Just as magazines, reality TV and social media dictate to children who is pretty and who isn't, the same approach happens in our earliest encounters with wellness and creates a serious divide. So often sporty kids are some of the most popular too.

The awkwardly fitting kit, our changing bodies and the policing of them through arbitrary definitions (does anyone *need* to do the bleep test every week like we did in school?) can not only threaten our self-esteem – which we know is delicate at a young age – but also affects how we see our bodies and our capabilities in the future. As we become adults, we see the same idealisation of one kind of 'fit' – which can also be 'thin' in another guise. Not only does the wellness industry mirror our childhoods back at us with the narrative of 'if you don't fit into the pricey gym kit, you can't sit with us', it so often sells Eurocentric beauty standards at us too – through thinness, whiteness and wealth. Sure, you occasionally see a person who is 'acceptably fat' – that is, hourglass, between a size 14 and 20 with a slim face – in a gym ad to make it seem less intimidating, but the archetype of a fit person largely remains as it always has been.

As journalist Poorna Bell writes in her book *Stronger: Changing Everything I Knew About Women's Strength*: 'An old defence the fitness and entertainment industry clings to around promoting larger bodies is "Well, we don't want to encourage obesity" – but it is baseless and without merit. Where is the scientific evidence to show that this is what happens when you advertise plus-size bodies working out and being active? On the other hand, consider the evidence that is there.'[5] The evidence she refers to is that worldwide obesity has tripled since 1975, according to the World Health Organization, which also says that supportive environments and communities are key to allowing people to make healthier decisions. Yet support is often the opposite of what wellness sells anyone in a larger body: as I've said earlier in The Weight of Ugly, Nike didn't launch a plus range until 2017 (and when it introduced plus-size mannequins, there was some backlash)[6] and Adidas didn't launch theirs until 2019.

The beauty standards that control our bodies often fail the athletic elite too: in 2021 the Norwegian handball team were fined 1,500 euros by the European Beach Handball Championships. Did they throw an all-night rave and snort substances off the umpire's whistle? I jest, of course – it was for far less. They broke the strict uniform rules that state female players must wear bottoms that do not cover 'more than 10cm on any sides … with a close fit and cut on an upward angle towards the top of the leg'. Essentially, those athletes must wear a bikini while the men's uniform is a vest and long shorts. Earlier, in 2011, the Badminton World Federation was criticised for its dress code, which insisted all female players wear a dress or skirt to 'ensure attractive presentation'. Wimbledon's rules around visible and non-white bras have meant that players in violation of its strict dress code have had to change bras before matches or even go braless.[7]

The skirts we *had* to wear for netball when I was a teenager only came in small sizes and mine was so tight, it threatened to fly off at any moment, exposing my weird grey netball knickers. Not only that, they just didn't feel as comfortable or protective as jogging bottoms. For women there is often a 'decorative' aspect to any kind of sport or fitness; it's always under the watchful eye of the male gaze to ensure that it's 'sexy'. And now, just as women are getting more into fitness and being accepted into traditionally male-centred spaces, our gym clothing has become tighter, smaller and more revealing than ever before (let alone the vast array of make-up and skincare designed 'for the gym'). Of course, it's fine to do or wear anything you like to the gym – but the timing of this trend is more than suspect. Though there are codes of behaviour in some gyms and not all men who work out think this of course, the underlying patriarchal message is that women should be decorative, even when they work out. And then, there are those who complain about women wearing too much make-up and hairspray to the gym. Whatever we do, we are yet again judged on our appearance.

The mantra 'strong is the new skinny' is pitched as a way of offering women emancipation from 'weight loss' but often it's still selling us an ideal body shape. When we're shown what a 'strong woman' looks like on social media, she is invariably toned but never so ripped that she could take a man down in an arm wrestle. Her proportions are often a muscular hourglass and she's usually white or light-skinned too. The way whiteness is sold through wellness is so cunningly veiled. Take the way the tennis superstars Venus and Serena Williams are spoken about: a US radio host called Sid Rosenberg called Serena an 'animal' (dehumanising much?)[8] while Russian Tennis Federation President Shamil Tarpischev referred to them as 'the Williams brothers'[9] on a talk show, referencing a tired narrative of strong, Black female bodies not being seen as attractive to the dominant white male gaze. It's a common trope that Black women who are perceived as too 'masculine' have their womanhood withheld from them (see also South African runner Caster Semenya), because white women are the ultimate arbiters of who gets to be considered a woman and who is denied that. I was told by the digital teams on two different women's titles I worked at that the sisters did particularly poorly for web traffic compared to any other female-focused fitness content or athletes on the site. So maybe it isn't always just the male gaze perpetrating it and more proof that an aspirational fit body usually conforms to Eurocentric beauty standards.

Wellness standards – like beauty standards – act like a private members' club, admitting people, vetting or excluding them, depending on a set of subjective, harmful constructs around appearance and their perceived value. It ensures that elite wellness spaces can make anyone who doesn't fit the criteria feel out of place. I've lost count of the number of classes I've been to where I've felt that I was being stared at for not fitting the 'yoga bunny' ideal or singled out in a room to push harder. Even those working in wellness have struggled: female personal trainers have told me that despite their lengthy experience, they've been rejected from teaching the buzziest group cycle classes because they 'don't have the right look' – which translates as not being thin enough, young enough or 'feminine' enough (and all the stereotypes that entails). There are so many aspects of wellness being gatekept, but because wellness is so glossy and its veneer hasn't eroded yet, we just can't see them.

Like beauty, you need to be able to afford to be part of wellness in the first place to even be given a members' application form. First, it helps if your childhood involved organic, fresh meals and space to run around, perhaps the money to buy sports kit and attend afterschool classes, as this is likely to make you more comfortable in the wellness space as an adult, not least because your parents probably also had the money to join exclusive sports clubs for themselves, so the idea was familiar. But that's not the case for everyone. If your caregivers are working extra hours to provide for your family they may be unlikely to have a lot of time to prepare healthy food from scratch and drive you to football or dance class every other day. We receive such different messages around wellness from a young age, but often they stay with us. Socioeconomics and cultural heritage are so rarely offered up as a reason for any disparity. Often, anyone who can't afford to engage in wellness is excluded, shamed or told 'try harder' – just as in diet culture. There are also practical reasons why some who might want to try sometimes just can't – of the 7,200 health and fitness clubs currently in the UK, only 68 are accessible to disabled people, according to the Inclusive Fitness Initiative (IFI).[10]

There's also a lack of accounting for who feels safe in those spaces in which we are supposed to be practising health and wellness. Feeling out of place at a fitness class is one thing, but physical safety is another. Dianne Bondy, a Black Canadian yoga teacher and activist, told me that during a run in a white affluent Canadian neighbourhood, she was, in no uncertain terms, told to 'go back to Africa'. Being in nature and walking are cited as the cure-all, cost-free wellness solution that everyone can enjoy but they're not something that comes naturally to all of us. Friends of mine never seem to understand why I don't share their love of parks or long countryside walks, but here there's another safety aspect that goes unrecognised. Playing outside as kids wasn't the same experience for everyone. I grew up with stories about Asian children being physically assaulted or picked on while playing outside. It meant that I was constantly on guard and wary of danger away from the safety of my family home, and there was always the looming threat of being called a 'Paki', which, for the record, did happen a couple of times. It was only a couple of years after the picture of me enjoying the wild (see page 225) was taken.

For Aaron Jones from Chicago, it was historical precedent that made him uncomfortable being in nature. As he told the *Guardian*: 'A few years ago, a white friend suggested we go on a hike. All the fears I had about being in nature hit me in the face. It's a very real fear for black people, especially those from urban communities, that bad things happen to black people in the woods, like lynching. It's something that you see again and again when you look at the history of the civil rights movement and slavery: black people going into the woods and not coming back.'[11] A 2017 study in the UK found that while 60 per cent of white people had 'visited the natural environment at least once a week', that number was 40 per cent for all other ethnic groups combined.[12]

Speaking to BBC One's *Countryfile*, psychotherapist Beth Collier explained 'rural racism'. Older generations of ethnic minorities felt intimidated when in the countryside and encountering people who hadn't seen many non-white faces. As a result, their children were raised to believe they'd be unsafe if they visited the country – a 'generational disconnect' meant that non-white urban Britons had little contact with the countryside, which has in turn created the idea that being in nature and the country 'is a white thing to do'.[13] Sometimes those fears remain legitimate. The countryside can feel elitist, with a lingering sense of patriotism, and Britishness that can feel unwelcoming. As I write this book, my parents tell me that they stood behind two white women at the RHS Malvern Spring Festival and overheard them lament how 'there were not enough British people in the finals of *MasterChef* this year'. All the finalists were in fact British nationals – what these women meant was that all three of them were non-white.[14] That's not to say everyone in the countryside is racist and our towns are full of the enlightened (the chaos of central London on a Friday night is sufficient evidence of this) but often there is a divide and a tension that as a non-white person you can be made to feel.

It does warrant a pause to remember that what's offered to all as a 'free' wellness solution isn't necessarily universal, but community provides the solution. Groups like Diversify Outdoors aim to promote diversity in outdoor recreation and provide insights around issues like the stigma of colourism that can mean some are taught to avoid sun exposure for fear of getting darker, influencing the lack of diversity in outdoor pursuits. Likewise, Black Girls Hike C.I.C. was founded in 2019 to create a safe space for Black women to explore the outdoors after founder Rhiane Fatinikun set up an Instagram account to chart the journey. The group was featured on a *Countryfile* episode on representation. Presenter Dwayne Fields said: 'When I talk to people from the BAME community, it's clear that they don't view the UK countryside as somewhere that's for them.' The programme received 572 complaints from those who felt it 'to be inaccurate'. One Twitter user said: 'This is absurd. To imply that the countryside – a passive, welcoming phenomenon – is somehow racist is ridiculous.'[15]

Perhaps this is due, yet again, to the lack of historical context in school education about the realities of colonisation and slavery, which could provide insight into how and why certain spaces like the countryside might not feel accessible to all. But on a ground level, these conversations getting airtime and initiatives like Black Girls Hike serve as a reminder that the countryside is, and should be for everyone to enjoy, as a nurturing and free wellness resource.

How did relaxation become elitist?

How many of our modern woes – stress, anxiety, too much time in front of screens – would be eased even a smidgen if we had the time and space to relax a little more? We're increasingly so spent that we need this time away from reality to calm burnout from our progressively plugged-in lives.

Perhaps this is where other cultures have nailed this. Trips to local Ayurvedic spas in India with family have felt both healing and noticeably accessible to people from a wider range of socio-economic backgrounds. In Japan, the traditional Onsen culture – which involves bathing in hot springs – goes back centuries, with evidence suggesting the famous Dogo Onsen on the island of Shikoku may have been used as a spa over 3,000 years ago. And they're still popular, relatively inexpensive and found all over the country. That they're frequent forms of relaxation in so many countries and cultures is proof alone there is something particularly healing within spa culture.

In Korea, traditional bathhouses *(jimjilbang)* are also still part of modern life and are used as a place for people to meet and socialise while relaxing. I interviewed a group of women in Seoul, who told me how spas are something they often did on a Friday night with friends – akin to going to the cinema – with prices starting at around 9000 Korean won, or £6, for a visit. Russian *banyas*, which have steam rooms and saunas and are characterised by a treatment technique where you're thwacked with branches to improve circulation, can cost from £30 a day, and in Finland there are approximately 3.3m saunas (in a country of 5.5m inhabitants) and they're often a place for families to relax.

I truly believe that the apex of relaxation and taking time out is embodied in the spa. I'm not alone in my love for them and in 2020, there were over 160,000 spas globally, taking

$68 billion in revenue, projected to hit $151 billion by 2025.[16] Many now come with Michelin-star restaurants, celebrity chefs, extensive grounds and are architectural masterpieces. Prices for the most covetable start at £800 a night and even the more 'affordable' spas still come in at £200+, despite being stuck on the end of a golf hotel as a respite 'for the wives'. Sure, they divide opinion, but being allowed to wear a dressing gown *all day* sans judgement and being taken care of as an adult is incredibly appealing, you have to admit. When so many cultures have this facility available at affordable prices, was there ever a time when Britain had a more level approach to wellness and relaxation?

The spa as we know it has as its ancestor the bathhouse, which was – and still is – a feature in many cultures around the world. Which makes sense, when you think that bathrooms and even indoor running water are relatively new additions to homes. In Ancient Rome, it was common for people to visit the baths daily and most Romans, including women and enslaved people, washed at them. Crucially, admission fees to public baths were low and children got in for free, so they were accessible to almost everyone.[17] They were so popular, and so valued, that admission was even bequeathed in wills.[18] The ritual of going to the baths was much more than just a functional scrub or dip: people socialised, relaxed and did business; they were a part of daily life and not just for special occasions. The healing remedies of water, relaxation and crucially community were built into everyday life for many.

Now, the idea of us communing for relaxation anywhere other than the local pub seems unfathomable but baths retained their popularity in the medieval period and people loved steeping in soothing thermal spa waters. And it was the done thing too, as a text from the mid-1100s called *Gesta Stephani* describes: 'from all over England sick people come to wash away their infirmities in the healing waters'.[19] However, the Church became increasingly suspicious of bathhouses – and, more specifically, what all those naked people might be up to other than having a wash (like conspiring against the Church, essentially). Aided by outbreaks of plague and other diseases that made it less appealing to gather in steamy bathhouses, their popularity declined. Many bathhouses closed, or were taken over by the Church, and a shortage of firewood also meant that public baths became too expensive for most people, though the gentry still visited spring water baths.

Around the same time, a new kind of 'bathing culture' became popular in Italy after doctors recommended various treatments like mineral water drinking cures, purging, mud packs and of course dipping in the waters too. Some argued that a spa treatment really wouldn't benefit 'the poor'. Why? Because one needed comfort, quiet and good food to really feel the benefits alongside a spa trip. But practical issues also stopped them from attending the baths, namely a lack of leisure time, and the cost.[20] As Italian spa culture spread across Europe, in the UK an influential book on therapeutic bathing was published by William Turner in 1562, which discussed over 60 disorders that could benefit from bathing[21] and also popularised spa treatments in the UK. Between 1660 and 1815, 48 spas were opened in England.[22]

At points in that period, British spas – most often built around natural spring water sources – were seen as an equaliser in society too. You would often find aristocracy and the lower classes coming together to bathe in the same hot springs, relax and cure an assortment of ailments from infertility to piles, forgetfulness, worms in the belly (terrifying, much?) and the curiously named 'dullness of smelling'.[23] When Queen Elizabeth I visited Bath in 1574, she declared that the public should always have access to the thermal waters (go Team Liz!).[24]

By the 1800s spas increased in popularity as doctors lauded their curative properties and the development of guesthouses and hotels near these natural springs gradually became more common in Europe and America too. In Britain these lodgings were often ostentatious. Alongside the once affordable natural spring baths, were lounges, theatres and extensively manicured grounds to saunter through (very *Bridgerton*). They became more glamorous to attract as many elegant, monied visitors as possible – and to cater to the rising middle classes of the Georgian period. Soon spa towns like Bath and Cheltenham were the height of fashion, and then eventually racy, more debauched, sorts of places.[25]

Language has a way of revealing so much about our societal power imbalances – until this period the word 'well' (or 'wel' as it was known then) was used to describe a general sense of abundance and health but by now, it had become synonymous with wealth and the phrase we still use today – 'well-to-do'.[26] The healing power of water was still highly regarded towards the end of the 1800s and Queen Victoria would even demand bottled Malvern water during her royal tours.[27] The health-obsessed Victorians kept the tradition of spa trips going and visited Turkish baths that were popular in places like London – but only if they could afford them. Poorer people now had to make do with public baths for bathing and washhouses for clothes washing. These became more popular as a weekly occurrence, though were certainly more functional – and still price dependent. Money could buy you a warm private bath rather than an 'invigorating' cold communal wash – not quite the spa experiences the wealthy were enjoying.

Spa towns fell out of fashion in the early 20th century, partly because claims made around the medicinal benefits of healing waters had come into scientific doubt. Instead of living their best spa lives, people now travelled to the seaside for a swim, as more regulated working hours ensured that even the working classes were afforded this concept of 'leisure time'. If they could afford to take leave, that is. After the mid-century, commercial flights meant that holidays overtook the popularity of spa visits.

In the 1980s, spas staged an epic comeback and regained their status as a luxurious treat and a way to escape the hard-working culture of the era, but they started to have more of a hi-tech beauty and anti-ageing focus, which was the main mandate of the decade. Into the 21st century, the rise of party-hard banking culture saw spas become more popular for the wealthy at least and might account for the rise in prices. Since then, they've grown in popularity but retained their Georgian mantle as a pastime primarily for the well-off. In 2006, there were only 50 and now there are reportedly over 900 spas across the UK.[28] That's partly due to the rise in popularity of the wellness industry and practices but could also be linked to the high stress levels reported by Gen Z and Millennials. Our spa visits have now become much more of an emergency burnout measure due to the cost, rather than something we might do on a more regular basis.

It's fair to say that in the UK, spa culture has also become a status symbol for those who can afford a lavish break rather than the accessible, welcome-all wellness ritual it once was. You can't leave said spa without a picture in a fluffy robe, holding a champagne flute to prove you are doing #Selfcare. But maybe that's a form of 'performative wellness', where we do things for our health because we want the status of being seen to do them, or to be viewed as the 'kind' of people who do them. Though that doesn't always mean we're really reaping the rewards: on a burnout spa break, I was in a hot tub and desperately trying to coax my brain into relaxing.

The person next to me was more invested in getting the perfect spa selfie... for almost 30 minutes. Perhaps that's how she relaxes, who knows, but getting the perfect picture to post seemed to be what mattered most in that moment. In their newest reinvention, spas and posting pictures from them have become an undeniable status symbol – so much so that spas often use 'most Instagrammed pool' and the like on press releases. It's indicative of how once-simple wellness practices now come with a hefty price tag and a desired clientele.

So what's on offer if you can't afford a spa? Often, a local pool or lido filled the gap and was the equaliser of a community – plus a chance for people to mix, socialise and build community. Indoor swimming pools started to become popular in the 1800s, with new filtration and chlorination technologies making them more accessible and common. Often they functioned as public bathing too for those who didn't have running water or couldn't afford a spa visit – and gained popularity into the mid-20th century as swimming became a more popular pastime. Many of us have memories of local leisure centres in our childhood but sadly, local pools – once the centre of a town – are now a fairly unrelaxing experience and are often pretty rundown. Swim England reported that by 2033, there will be a huge reduction in swimming pools due to the need to refurbish the facilities built in the 1960s and 70s and lack of funding to do so. Jane Nickerson, Swim England Chief Executive, said in a report: 'Pools are hubs of the local community, helping people of all ages to lead healthier, happier lives and saving the NHS hundreds of millions of pounds each year.'[29] I'm inclined to agree – the closure of them is just another way that relaxation and access to leisure facilities is becoming more of a privilege than ever before.

Even if you can afford a spa break, that's not to say you'd

always feel welcome at one – if you fall short of being their 'ideal' patron. Spas are my favourite way to chill but there is a moment during any spa trip when I know I'll either love or loathe the experience, and it boils down to four words: 'one size fits all'. I'm talking about the dressing-gown moment, where you're handed a towelling robe that only fits up to a size 14 at best, as the only option to cover your modesty. That's without factoring in the tiny towels and tinier paper pants that cut off your circulation. Sometimes a massage therapist thinks that if you're bigger, you can take more pain and so they pummel you like you're a piece of unrelenting cookie dough. Sure, many spas say they are accessibility friendly – but that bar is set pretty low. All they're required to provide is a low-level entrance bell, disabled toilet and a ground-floor treatment room when really they need beds that can be lowered or raised, lifts and pool hoists, lifts between floors, wet rooms or menus in braille, for example.[30] But here's the catch again: often the ones that do have these facilities are some of the more expensive ones.[31] These details often add up to an alienating experience for anyone who doesn't fit the 'ideal customer' – who is *always* the main spa brochure image and, you've guessed it, is the beauty standard.

There's already a discrepancy in the service industry as to how non-white customers (and those with other marginalised identities) are treated that means spas might not always feel equally welcoming. So how do we create a more inclusive way to relax? There's no easy answer. Spas are a massive part of the wellness conglomerate and it's fine that they cater to higher price points (often they're expensive to build and maintain and were, like so many businesses, hit by lockdown closures), but pay-it-forward schemes could allow more people to visit them, as would prioritising accessibility measures. Hot water springs in Britain have largely been closed or privatised into luxury spas but I'd love to see a resurgence of those being available to all at a reasonable price (as they are across much of Europe still). Plus, mineral-rich spring water can be deeply healing for many health conditions, from arthritis to eczema.

But maybe the way forward is prioritising the revitalisation of communal relaxation spaces like leisure centres that desperately need funding – everyone deserves to be able to use and enjoy them. They're one of the few hubs communities have left for communal relaxation, so we need to safeguard them now more than ever. Of course I don't have all the answers to the class gap in wellness, but let's take a history lesson from the polarisation of spa culture: when wellness is reserved for a select elite group, really, we *all* fail to be well.

How wellness got whitewashed

Most often we hear about cultural appropriation – used to describe the 'taking over' of practices from another culture – in the context of fashion and beauty. Unfortunately, this is something that still seems to be happening a lot. For example, in 2019, Kim Kardashian originally named 'Skims', her shapewear brand, 'Kimono' and tried to trademark the Japanese word. In beauty, hairstyles traditionally used on afro-textured hair are being credited to white women, erasing the culture from which they actually come. As when Kardashian (maybe there's a theme here) called her new cornrows 'Bo Braids', referencing white actor Bo Derek and not the Black women who created them.

In wellness, cultural appropriation is sometimes trickier to spot. Often you see it in the aforementioned spa culture – spas are frequently decorated with Buddha statues as if they're pot plants (imagine the uproar if a spa was covered in statues of Jesus instead?). Training directives often involve no reference to the origins of the treatments being performed ('I think it's French,' one therapist told me about a Polynesian Lomi Lomi massage). I'm emailed on a daily basis about wellness trends purported to be the big 'new' thing, such as 'face rollers' hoping to improve muscle tone (derived from the traditional Chinese medicine practice of gua sha) and 'hair oiling' (a scalp health technique most often credited to Indian Ayurvedic practices) that have become popular recently. It can feel alienating and insensitive to people from those cultures when their heritage is being appropriated without care – I feel that deeply as Indian wellness traditions are a pillar of Western wellness trends. There's such an odd irony to being told you smell like 'curry' as a kid, as people sit in wellness cafés drinking turmeric-laden 'golden lattes' in peace.

Of course, cultural appropriation can be accidental, and it often is – in which case we can take the feedback, learn and evolve, but largely speaking, the wellness industry doesn't really care either way: every week there's a new wellness trend from another culture going viral online and brands supporting it, without crediting the origins. The creation of modern yoga and mindfulness culture is perhaps the best example of how the Western wellness industries swallow cultural practices, watering down and simplifying long-held traditions into a more palatable version. It makes them feel less 'new age' and, crucially, more profitable.

Yoga is an ancient Indian spiritual practice; in the West, it's become huge – worth an estimated $88 billion.[32] In the UK, there are over 10,000 yoga teachers, with 460,000 people attending a classes each week,[33] learning to do a downward dog (which is actually the Sanskrit, *adho mukha svanasana*). But if you live in the West and don't know much about yoga, you might not even realise it's Indian, thanks to many popular purveyors of modern yoga responsible for it being repackaged simply as an exercise or component of an aspirational lifestyle. Mugs with 'namastay [namaste] in bed' and yoga pants with Om symbols cash in on it further and help position it almost as a brand, so for many it is just another form of fitness – like a spin class or body pump.

That would be OK, perhaps even fine, if it hadn't become so exclusive – both to patrons wishing to attend and to those wishing to teach it. Now, the 'yoga look' neatly ties in with the beauty standards we've discussed throughout this book. Of the ten most popular yoga channels on YouTube at the time of writing, almost every teacher was white (or white passing), slim, able-bodied and fit in the Eurocentric beauty ideal, which is also – let's be honest – the wellness standard. One of the biggest yoga influencers – Adriene Mishler (of Jewish and Mexican heritage) who has 11.5m followers on YouTube – epitomises what we've come to think of as the ideal model of wellness. Often much-lauded YouTubers and teachers tend to dial down yoga's origins to make it more palatable to Western audiences for 'relatability'. Yoga is seen as 'aspirational' when taught by a white person (in the US, 77.1 per cent of all US yoga instructors identify as white),[34] but when kept in its original Indian form it's *too* spiritual – and maybe being taught by an Indian yoga teacher is just a bit 'too ethnic'.

It is 'ethnic', though – despite the number of incarnations, like 'rave yoga' or 'glowga' – a glow-in-the-dark version. Yoga dates back to roughly 1,200 BCE and is first mentioned in sacred Indian texts called the *Rig Veda*. It was defined by rishis – or sages – and is among the six schools of philosophy in Hinduism; it also became a part of Buddhist meditation practices. Swami Vivekananda, a monk from Calcutta (as it was called then), is thought have first brought yoga to the West in 1894 when he travelled to America for a lecture tour about India and Hinduism. Until that point, yoga had largely been practised by holy men and was more of spiritual fortitude and stillness, but at the turn of the century, with developments in photography, it was easier to share images of the poses and its popularity spread. By the 1960s, Western young people were on the 'hippie trail' – a 6,000-mile route from Europe to the Middle East and into Central and Southern Asia that often ended at Indian ashrams. When the Beatles visited the Maharishi Mahesh Yogi's ashram in 1968, Indian spirituality really hit the spotlight, as did yoga and meditation. The Beatles were pretty good at making sure Yogi's ashram and cultural significance were at the forefront of any of their discussion about Vedic meditation – although they eventually cut ties with him following reports of sexual assault and other allegations.

Scientific research sought to 'legitimise' the ancient Indian practice and prove its health benefits, leading to yoga becoming more widely practised – and, ultimately, becoming secularised away from its spiritual Indian origins. But this doesn't just 'happen' by accident to cultural practices. It happens when wellness trends gain popularity and Western capitalism recognises there's money to be made. This, they think, is how to sell to Western audiences, which, when you think about it, does us a disservice. It causes the erasure of the heritage of the practice and that can be seen in who 'represents' yoga and who largely profits from it. All of this makes wellness practices like yoga feel like an elite nightclub where you have to 'look right' to be able to get in.

Actor Gwyneth Paltrow, who founded wellness lifestyle brand Goop in 2008, seemed to think that she should be credited for popularising yoga. She said in 2018: 'I went to do a yoga class in LA and the 22-year-old girl behind the counter was like, "Have you ever done yoga before?" And I was like, "You have this job because I've done yoga before."'[35]

Anyone should try yoga or be able to teach it, of course. I don't own it and there's not a number to dial to ask 'India' if you're allowed to do your daily tree pose (or *Vrksasana*). The same applies to any other wellness or spiritual practices. They were created with healing at their core, which is the ultimate goal. But it's now the case with both yoga and meditation that you have to seek out those more spiritual, connected forms that pay direct homage to their ancient roots, the ones who use and pronounce terms correctly, know the history and have a deep reverence for it. There is an issue with the marginalisation of teachers from their own heritages being celebrated by the mainstream wellness companies (have you ever seen an Indian yoga teacher fronting any kind of yoga-related advert, or campaign? – I haven't). The saddest part is that the commodification of practices like yoga has meant that what makes them special is lost in this process. Doing a yoga exercise class in my local gym, and one in India, are two entirely different experiences – one is a bit of stretching, another feels like being reconnected to my soul (deep…). But you don't have to jump on a plane to Kerala to get the benefits – this is where we can seek out teachers with integrity, who are properly rooted and trained in the practice, so we really feel the benefits.

Mindfulness too has become a huge part of wellness culture in the form of apps, even being practised in some schools. But seldom are we taught where it comes from. The origins of what we now call 'mindfulness meditation' are believed to belong to ancient Indian and Chinese traditions of Hinduism and Buddhism from as early as 1500 BCE.[36] In 1979 a microbiologist at The University of Massachusetts Medical School named Jon Kabat-Zinn created a pioneering eight-week course called Mindfulness Based Stress Reduction, which aimed to reduce stress for patients with chronic pain. Kabat-Zinn had been meditating since 1965, using the fundamentals of mindful meditation in Zen Buddhism. He recalled in the *Guardian* in 2017: 'I bent over backwards to structure it and find ways to speak about it that avoided as much as possible the risk of it being seen as Buddhist, new age, eastern mysticism or just plain flakey.'[37] He followed the tried-and-tested method of de-culturalising an ancient wellness practice, backing it with Western science to give validity. But here's an interesting question to turn inwards – would we have 'accepted' mindfulness as being so impactful, if he hadn't?

Mindfulness really entered the mainstream in the UK when, in 2002, psychologist Mark Williams was part of the team that created the NHS course for mindfulness using Kabat-Zinn's US programme alongside CBT. Williams also taught comedian and mental health campaigner Ruby Wax about mindfulness, which she then popularised in her 2013 book, *Sane New World*. In 2010, former Buddhist monk Andy Puddicombe launched the Headspace app. Colouring books, magazines, emblazoned on a T-shirt… there's no end to the ways that mindfulness has been popularised and commercialised, in what Kabat-Zinn calls 'McMindfulness.'[38] Everyone can benefit from yoga and mindful meditation, of course – ultimately that was the original goal and purpose – but there's a fine line between appreciation and appropriation and what decides this is often how it can be 'repackaged' and how much profit can be made.

There's no denying that for Western culture to accept something 'foreign' it has to be diluted, secularised and 'proven' first: from a quick mindfulness pitstop on a science-backed app through to a hurried morning matcha latte – the opposite of the time-honoured traditions of tea ceremonies in Japan. They're created as ways to give us the wellness hit, fast – and sometimes that works. Often, it's also because anything that sits outside of the Western experience is automatically filed under that catch-all phrase 'woo-woo'. We need to consider how and why we use that phrase: if science is seen as the only rational and indisputable way to make something worthy of our time, how do we account for scientific racism, or the lack of studies on women's health?[39] I'm not disparaging science – it's essential and life-giving – but it's not the only way to make something 'valid' and worthy of our attention, and science too can be concerned with its profit margins.

Take turmeric, a native Indian plant which – prior to golden milk and turmeric lattes – has for centuries been a staple in cooking and known for its healing benefits in South Asian countries – so much so that in India, you often see people's skin stained yellow from applying it. Back in 1995, when researchers at the University of Mississippi were granted a patent for the use of turmeric in wound healing, India's Council of Scientific and Industrial Research (CSIR) challenged the patent. They took issue with the West capitalising on this traditional knowledge and contested the 'novelty' criteria required for acquiring a patent. After a costly year-long battle, the patent was revoked.

The cherry-picking of ancient practices as 'trends' also means that people from that culture are hidden if not completely erased – and often they can't fight back against swirling wellness trends and huge wellness companies. But the way that wellness takes from marginalised communities and wipes out the heritage is just the methodology of colonisation but under a modern guise. Under colonialism, many indigenous people were often prohibited from practising their own traditions. Smudging, a healing and spiritual practice used by many North American indigenous cultures, often uses white sage to cleanse, purify and pray. But it was illegal to practice this as recently as the 1970s and so these communities have suffered deeply from colonisation and persecution at the hands of the West. But that hasn't stopped the wellness industry from profiting. In 2018, Sephora US started selling a 'Witch Kit' with cleansing sage –

which received backlash for appropriating both Wiccan and Native-American Indian cultures for profit.

In 1833, the British-owned East India Company closed Ayurvedic colleges, banning indigenous medicine to create: 'civilised communities'.[40] Ayurveda was dismissed as 'the poor man's medicine', used only by those who couldn't access superior Western medicine. The anecdotes about the offence that the British took to Ayurveda are plentiful: 'Officers would chop off three fingers on Ayurvedic doctors so they couldn't do pulse diagnosis and after the British left India, Ayurveda was nearly wiped out,' Will Williams who teaches ancient Vedic meditation, told me for a feature in *Glamour*.[41] When India finally gained its independence back in 1947, thankfully, Ayurveda remerged and regained its popularity.[42] Nowadays, it seems like the Western wellness movement has gone from dismissing these ancient practices as 'woo-woo' to taking from them at will – only recently I was emailed about a 'trend' for using coconut oil as a mouthwash. That's actually the Ayurvedic practice of oil pulling.

We do have to remember that people's ancestors could have been hurt or imprisoned for practising spiritual aspects of their own cultures. I could fill a whole chapter with incidents where cultural appropriation has shown disregard for or even eradicated cultural practices and their people too. There was the wellness festival offering a talk in celebration of a Hindu goddess of wealth but they – and the non-Hindu/white woman doing the talk – mixed the goddess up with a different one. British sportswear brand Sweaty Betty at one point sold yoga wear named using Sanskrit words, such as the 'Brahma Yoga Bra' – named after a Hindu god, which they have since changed.[43] A smaller example: I took a yoga class on Zoom recently and the teacher had a Ganesha statue on her floor next to her feet, which, as I pointed out to her privately, and gently, is a sign of disrespect in the culture.

I'm not saying we should pile on every yoga teacher who doesn't know the practice and culture inside out – they're not the big issue here. There does, however, need to be a collective accountability of how Western wellness brands treat the cultures they profit from – the above festival could have used this opportunity to raise the profile of somebody from an Indian or minority background for this talk, for example. Cultures do and can borrow from each other, of course, but ultimately this should come with respect and knowledge of how those communities have been treated in the past and how people live with that trauma still. It can feel hard to accept appropriation against the background of overt discrimination and systemic racism that many of us endure, and considering the trauma caused by colonial occupation. The modern wellness industry seems happy to erase and appropriate cultures, all to make a quick buck. The conglomerates who can afford it – I believe – should be giving back to the culture being profited from through charity donations and celebrating/employing people from those cultures. When their profits are so big, this isn't a huge ask and it comes down to respect.

As well as holding wellness companies to higher ethical standards, we can of course take some personal accountability. Collectively, we can be a little lax when it comes to spotting cultural appropriation in wellness from the Western position of privilege because there's a sense of individualism at play – maybe the goal of being 'well' is more important than any internal moral conflict? Or perhaps we just can't see that conflict to begin with (though hopefully this chapter can help with that). We can bring awareness to our wellness choices by looking around the next time we're at a yoga class and seeing how inclusive it is or noticing where indigenous wellness is being diluted for our benefit. We can use our spending power in wellness with integrity.

And we benefit from that: as meditation teacher and author of *Take It In*, Giselle La Pompe-Moore, says: 'If we focus on the reasons behind why we're doing these practices, and have a firmer grasp of the heritage, lineage and teachings behind them, then things can change. They need to change because right now we're forgetting what spirituality and wellness actually *is*.'[44]

There is a real opportunity in many of the examples I have given in this chapter to celebrate somebody from the original culture and to broaden and deepen everyone's experience. It just doesn't seem to happen very often and that's mostly because wellness brands want to make money and want to sell something that white Western audiences can aspire to – and that is somebody who is representative of Eurocentric beauty standards.

The cult of clean

Words like 'clean', 'detox' and 'purify' are used frequently in wellness marketing and have almost a religious angle to them: darkness to light, sinner to pure. They present the illusion that we can remove anything that's bad, or at least take control of in an uncontrollable, fast-paced world. Our smoothies are 'innocent', our low-fat ice cream gives us a 'halo' – have a look the next time you're doing a food shop, the symbolism is fascinating.

At the start of my career, 'clean' wasn't quite part of our vernacular just yet, but within a few years, the 'clean eating' movement was the newest trend. In 2007, Tosca Reno, a Canadian fitness model, published *The Eat-Clean Diet* book, talking about her weight loss, which she said was achieved by avoiding processed and refined foods. And with that – and others like her – came a new way of living. This was more than a diet book: 'eating clean' and 'living clean' were synonymous

– no one was existing on kale and chicken then smashing Jägerbombs into the night. This was a lifestyle that we were being sold – and we still are. Indulgences like burgers and fries topped with 'bad' stuff were now often referred to as 'dirty', while green smoothies and juices are the opposite – they're pure, virtuous and make us feel wholesome.

We already exist in a culture where to many, food feels like a battleground after decades of toxic body standards and diet culture trends, which we are still unpicking (Slimming World calls some food 'syns' for example).[45] The wellness industry has boomed alongside the rise of social media, but having access to people's lives in such an intimate way means we can find out too much. Take YouTube, Instagram and TikTok's popular 'What I eat in a day' videos, which fuel a sense of 'should I be eating less/like her?' – which is exactly how I felt when watching what and how much people were consuming. Before I caught myself and realised what I was being sold, which is thinness in a new guise.

Looking to food as a healer isn't new – pretty much every culture has a recipe for something that promises to cure your cold – but the issue is what it is we're really being sold along with our nutritional needs – and that's a lifestyle to admire and emulate. And the people promoting this are so often young, wealthy and fit – the Eurocentric model of beauty. Many of them are writing from personal experience, often with little or no background in nutritional science, but become elevated to expert status by the wellness industry. Underpinning it all are the age-old dichotomies: us vs you. Rich vs poor. White vs dark. Self-control vs gluttony. Good vs bad. Clean vs dirty.

In an age where we're told to love ourselves as we are, clean eating seems like we're doing exactly that. We are 'doing wellness' rather than a new version of a diet (which has even become a little passé). But the trend for clean eating is weight loss, strict body standards and thinness very well disguised. It also serves us that tired delusion – that if we are thin, we are automatically healthy. At my thinnest, I was anything but healthy – I was eating six almonds a day then bingeing on takeaways at night (though maybe we'd call that a form of intermittent fasting now). The wellness and diet industries are the same beast – they want women to be in thrall to beauty standards because it's profitable, which is why it elevates those who embody it as ambassadors. In the past, cutting out entire food groups was seen as unusual and was noticeably controlling behaviour, often associated with anorexia, bulimia and other disordered eating behaviours, but it's also now become almost excusable as a form of healthy or clean eating. The term 'orthorexia' refers to an unhealthy obsession with eating foods considered 'pure' – but what this means is subjective and varies from person to person. It isn't recognised in a clinical setting yet, but is becoming more well known in our clean vs dirty eating age and as the diet and wellness industry boundaries continue to blur.

As the diet industry moves further away from the 'd-word', many companies who previously promoted dieting or diet products have rebranded – WeightWatchers is now WW or Wellness That Works, Coca-Cola and Pepsi introduced Coke Zero and Pepsi Max respectively. But these products still exist, they just morph into the newest diet trend and often elements of beauty standards creep in too, like added collagen in our snack bars. Like beauty standards, in wellness you can never be too health-obsessed or, seemingly, too thin. Chef and former *Great British Bake Off* contestant Ruby Tandoh wrote about her experiences with eating disorders and wellness culture in *Vice*: 'Wellness was alluring precisely because of the restriction it promised. There's nothing left to be fearful of when the bad food is labelled "bad food," and when what's left is a miracle cure... My eating disorder had once looked very different, and then I found wellness – but I was not well'.[46] Even tracking apps, particularly the calorie counting ones created to help us monitor our macros and eating habits, can have negative effects and links to poor mental health with people obsessing about the data.[47]

If we truly want to take care of ourselves – and others – we have to recognise what we're being sold here. And that's deprivation, thinness and self-loathing for a new generation. Haven't we had enough of this?

The dark side of self-care

Wellness comes in many guises, but the one most frequently championed is self-care. Eating clean, working out daily, affirmations, meditation – all of it – we're told is self-care. And groomed nails, glowing skin, looking well rested and just put together enough to look 'effortless' is the look that self-care wants us to aspire to. Of course, #Thatgirl could probably do all of this without ever breaking a sweat.

But if self-care is truly about feeling good on the inside, then why is there so much emphasis on 'looks' – and on 'stuff'? Self-care has also become an entire market of its own: gift shops littered with 'little books of self-care', clothes with 'you've got this' written on them, wellness journals, health tracking apps and more exhorting us to become our best selves, like a perfect butterfly emerging from the caterpillar's imperfect cocoon. It feels like anything can be labelled self-care to make us feel like we are caring for ourselves in the way we deserve, while often, all we're doing is buying stuff without the moment to decompress. Even the most basic functions have come in for a rebrand: a bath was once simply about hygiene and, of course, the healing power of water. Now it's sold to us as a self-care ritual, alongside various paraphernalia to apparently enhance our experience. We post bath selfies to prove we did relax and 'shelfies' to show off the crystals, candles and bath bombs we have – all signifiers to say: 'I take care of myself. Here's my bathtub to prove it'.

The origins of the notion of self-care give us a major clue as to what's gone wrong here. It was first used by Black feminist writer and poet Audre Lorde when fighting cancer in 1988, and featured in her *Burst of Light* essay collection. Lorde wrote: 'Caring for myself is not an act of self-indulgence, it is self-preservation, and that is an act of political warfare.' The struggle in that war she mentions is the oppression of Black women by a structurally racist society and patriarchy. The 'radical' self-care that Lorde endorsed meant that to put your own wellbeing before anything and anyone was a bold and brave protest in the face of this oppression, and yet self-care has since become a capitalist slogan for 'buy our wares for an instant dopamine hit' or 'because you deserve a treat' ('and we deserve your money').

Buying these things isn't a problem – I like a calming scented candle as much as the next person – but the act of buying one isn't self-care. It's an accoutrement to the actual practice of caring for ourselves. And it's clever wellness marketing. But there's a bigger issue here than consumerism. It's that what self-care 'looks like' is being dictated to us. Social media is awash with pictures of a nice bath and facemask as self-care and sure, they can be a form of relaxation and comfort. But those alone aren't going to cut through the toll of the mental health crisis, or systemic racism. They won't fix everything. It's the same for the endless wellness posts on social media, exhorting us to 'live our best lives' or 'transform yourself' under the guise of (toxic) self-care. 'Positive vibes only' sounds good in theory, but it could also eschew connecting to why you feel down and addressing that problem. It's one of the criticisms levelled at modern mindfulness, in that it isn't necessarily the 'cure all' for everyone.[48] Likewise, exercise is great for our mental health, but training is not therapy – that's another dangerous narrative we've been fed.

One of the newer self-care methods is using strategies like moodboards and visualisation to help make an individual's wishes come true, a technique known as 'manifesting'. Although it's not new – there have been various incarnations in the past – it has become a part of modern spirituality alongside other metaphysical practices like tarot and astrology to take back control of our own destiny. That makes sense – it feels like we have such little control over factors like politics, the economy, the job market and climate change. Using the 'law of attraction' to get what you want isn't an issue – I used manifestation practices to help me with this book, they can be useful to connect to your true desires. But as it's become more commercialised and monetised, it has conveniently ignored the role privilege – across the board – can play in getting what you want. As a poignant meme states: 'maybe you manifested it, maybe it's white privilege'. Celebrated manifestation experts exhort people to keep trying harder and harder, often pointing the finger at those who don't truly believe they're deserving of what they desire, without recognising their own privilege or considering any additional roadblocks to getting that coveted 'dream job' or the six-figure salaries that many of them boast of. Naturally, it can come with a heap of paraphernalia to buy and crucially, those who are highly profiled and profit most from it, fit (sigh…) the wellness beauty standard. Of course they do.

But wishing something into existence isn't a level playing field, nor is it a substitute for therapy or actual healing. Perhaps this is why we get 'self-care burnout' from trying to do and be it all, which is ironic because if anything, wellness is probably about doing less, not more. And it can become overwhelming – practices like manifestation, when discussed flippantly, or without integrity, can feel like a standard you'll never quite live up to. Like most parts of wellness, there's somebody who knows better, but that also drowns out the 'inner voice' we're told we should be listening to. It's hard to access when self-care and wellness are exhorting you to 'live your best life' when perhaps, staying afloat is rather more the focus. In our constant state of being overwhelmed and exhausted, self-care has never been more important, which is why it is scary how casually parts of the wellness industry turn this against us.

It can feel like we're being constantly judged by wellness's high standards and exhorted to care for ourselves to the point where it's become a badge of honour. Somewhere along the line, something has gone quite wrong. For writer Brigid Delaney, as she explained in the *Guardian*: 'The problematic nature of the term is rooted in its very linguistic structure: self. While looking after yourself is great, self-care is still an idea rooted in a neoliberal tradition of looking out for ourselves, rather than seeing ourselves, our health and our fates as inextricably linked to our fellow human beings. Wouldn't it be great if this decade we took the self out of self-care and strived instead for communal care?'[49]

To look at it another way, among all the things that are supposed to improve our wellness as part of our self-care routines, from sleep hygiene to infrared saunas, it's worth asking what doesn't get much of a mention. I'd argue that community – the kind we had at ancient spas or that inclusive outdoors groups now provide – is one example of these. And, tellingly, community is largely free and difficult to package up and sell. Yet feeling part of a community has been continuously proven to make us happy. According to Dan Buettner, author of *Blue Zones*, a book that examines the factors common to the places in the world where people live the longest, 'We're genetically hardwired to crave social interaction and when you don't have it, there's a level of subconscious stress that grates away at you.' The islands of Okinawa, Japan, have the biggest ageing population in the world. There is a variety of reasons as to why this is, but important among them is *moai*, which roughly translated, means a group of lifelong friends and a social support group. In Okinawa, it's customary to meet one's friends daily.[50] You might argue that going to your gym class is social and a form of self-care, sure. But community and social support is more than a mate to say hi to as you're in a headstand – it's being part of an extended group who look out for each other. This is not something you can order from Amazon, but it is a key to wellbeing and it's free, yet often absent from the wellbeing conversation.

Closing the wellness gap

It's not that we *shouldn't* utilise wellness or feel guilty for engaging in self-care or posting about it, but maybe we can go back to basics and do self-care and wellness in a way that feels genuinely beneficial to ourselves and our wider communities too? Maslow's Hierarchy of Needs shows that having connection from 'love and belonging' is a vital requirement for our survival after our basic needs for food, shelter and safety are met.[51]

Taking self-care offline could be one way to help achieve this. The thing with our phones, watches, Alexas and tech-dependent lives is that we almost forget to connect to ourselves (#Intuition). We're swayed by what we're seeing others do on social media before we've truly worked out what we need. Even if we have a goal, we shouldn't ignore and flagellate the version of ourselves in the present or put everything on hold until we reach an idealised future us that doesn't yet exist. We can practise self-care and wellness in myriad ways without consumption, but it's vital that we *all* have access to it. That might be in the form of countryside walks, journalling, meditation and so much more. A community-minded version of self-care could look to buying yourself a class and contributing to a pay-it-forward scheme or joining (or creating) groups that provide valuable support systems for yourself and others too.

But we do need to be accountable for ourselves – for the decisions we make and for our wider communities too. Just because it's in the wellness bubble and it's our personal form of self-care, that doesn't mean that the consciousness we have around privilege doesn't apply here. Racism, homophobia, classism, ageism and ableism cannot be soothed away with a nice scented candle, so when we pick an indigenous wellness practice, do we know where it's come from? Does it have a history of colonial oppression or other power systems? Wellness should not have to be about spending money – but if we buy wellness paraphernalia, we can ensure that it's ethically sourced, there are no sustainability issues and it's from a company that financially supports the country of origin – it's an extra step in the process, but also an empowering and community-minded action. It's actual wellness.

When we're feeling time-pushed and want a wellness or self-care hit, doing research feels like an extra block to feeling better – but we do have to consider the impact of our choices. Assuming self-care is the same for everyone erases our differences and it pays to be mindful in the spaces we have access to. Look around the room in your next fitness class – who is there? And who isn't there? How diverse is it – and why? Perhaps that's proportionally representative of where you might live, but it could be that not everyone feels welcome there.

I don't wish to ruin wellness for you or me – there's a reason the industry exists, there are elements of it that we do need and parts of it that are deeply beneficial. But perhaps, along with the suggestions for how to navigate the industry more ethically, we should look to redefine what it means to be and look well on our own terms. Try creating a personal self-care manifesto – a list of all the things you know work *for you*. And stick it somewhere you can see it and refer back to when the capitalist wellness chatter gets too much – or that self-care overwhelm kicks in ... or another vagina-scented candle hits the shelves.

PRETTY UGLY

'It is better to be looked over
than overlooked.'
– Actor Mae West

IS BEING PRETTY A privilege? We've all been taught – right from our earliest *Cinderella* watching days – that the more conventionally attractive you are, the more likely your chance of a happy ending. Cinderella came from humble circumstances, but her virtue and beauty meant that she barely needed to say a word to Prince Charming before he fell in love and married her. Such is the power of fairy-tale endings we were told and of course, appearance.

Should we just accept that, like a VIP discount card bestowed on you at birth (coupled with so much more, we'll come on to that), good looks can be a helping hand across so many areas of life? But what do they give you other than a pleasing appearance? An ease with which you can do everything from clothes shop to date more easily. If the world around you confirms that you're attractive right from birth, logically you can see the stealthy confidence that could bring as a result. Maybe you don't have to try any harder than that? In Louisa May Alcott's classic novel, *Little Women*, we get the sense that Amy March has an inherent deservingness that none of her sisters possess: like she knows she'll do well and 'marry up'. That's conveyed more directly in the 2019 film adaptation. As her sister Jo puts it: 'Amy has always had a talent for getting out of the hard parts of life.' There's an automatic sense that Amy will be OK. The implication, of course, is that she's beautiful – and with that, comes a certain level of power.

Pop culture offers up plenty of examples where that old 'looks over talent' Hollywood manifesto springs to mind. If you're pretty, there are entire industries open to you that are closed to others, from modelling to whole swathes of the entertainment industry and an increased likelihood of social media or reality TV prominence. In the immortal words of model Kristen Taekman's opening credits from the TV series *The Real Housewives of New York*, Season Six: 'I may not be the sharpest tool in the shed, but I'm pretty!' (There's no prize for anyone who counts the number of reality TV references in this book, sorry.)

As our lives become increasingly dictated by visuals – from the pictures we snap throughout our days to the social media feeds we scroll through – it follows that we are becoming more conscious of the role beauty biases play in society too. In 2021 #Prettyprivilege started trending on TikTok as users posted about how being attractive had benefited them. The long list included receiving extra tips in the service industry, unsolicited discounts, receiving more attention than less attractive people, getting things for free and even obtaining extra credit when being graded on academic work (there are now studies that support the latter). We conflate a *lot* with being pretty.

We're increasingly having more open conversations around where pockets of privilege exist in society and the historical systems of oppression they conceal but being considered attractive – by a rigid and biased set of beauty norms that have been ingrained in us – is often excluded from those discussions. Why? Because it's something we just accept as luck of the draw, genes or the immovable fact: 'those who are seen as attractive do get ahead more easily – and so what?' It goes without saying that those who have this privilege might struggle elsewhere in their lives, but the burden of being shamed for their appearance, or judged negatively on it by a looks-obsessed world doesn't always have a positive side or silver lining. This dividing line – between the haves and the have-nots of pretty privilege – is indicative of the high premium placed on female beauty and can explain our drive to achieve it at all costs.

Our first experiences and encounters of pretty privilege can really stay with us. For some, that can be being praised for their beauty. For others like me, it is seeing the 'golden girls' at school given certain accolades like a smile from a teacher to attracting a string of the most popular suitors when you yourself might have needed to work harder for the same – or not received any of these accolades at all. In the book-turned-TV-series *My Mad Fat Diary* by Rae Earl, there's a golden girl called Chloe. Chloe seems to have everything that's important when you're a teenager: good looks, popularity, good grades, great outfits and no end of romantic admirers. Nothing appears to be that difficult for her – much to the fury of her best friend Rae, who feels she isn't as pretty as Chloe. Rae is fat, she's opinionated, she's a joker, she's into indie bands. She's not seen as 'girlie or feminine': markers of pretty. Growing up, we all had our own version of Chloe – or maybe you were the Chloe in your friendship group. But it's the myriad ways Chloe is treated – and rewarded – by others that speak volumes to Rae and tell her she's not worthy of the same. Chloe, isn't as funny as Rae nor is she as interesting – yet she still seems on the surface at least (we find out later she's jealous of Rae's personality too) to 'have it all'.

A reminder from An Ugly Start (*see also* page 25), our childhoods are pivotal moments for forming our self-esteem and studies on children have shown a direct link between attractiveness and popularity.[1] Early on, we learn that if we're praised for our beauty, it's something we have in our possession and a tool we can wield as part of our appeal to others – hence the recent movement for not telling little girls they're pretty, lest they base their entire worth upon their looks. This is particularly key in adolescence, where we employ 'reflected appraisal' – as Mitch Prinstein, Professor of Psychology and Director of Clinical Psychology at the University of North Carolina and author of *The Popularity Illusion* writes: 'In other words we begin to base our self-esteem not on how we feel but on how we gauge that others approve of us.' Prinstein adds that this can tip into adulthood too when we become increasingly invested in having a 'high status' whether it's wealth, power, fame or beauty.[2]

In a period when our self-esteem is being built, wouldn't it be amazing to show children that our appearance is just a small part of who we are rather than the sum of it? This level of emphasis on looks can work against people in both directions. In 2014 a video emerged of bullies at a school in Russia, forcing a 13-year-old girl to drink from a muddy puddle because she was too pretty – and it's not the only example of someone being bullied for being too attractive.[3] Our appearance is such an ingrained part of our worth in society – and the female experience – that even during our formative educational years, whichever side of it we're on, it can be used against us.

Looking back at diary entries from my teenage years, I can see – and still feel – the anguish of wanting pretty privilege and everything that comes with it, but never attaining it. That's why it's become a fascinating subject to me, simply because I've never had it – I've always felt on the outside of pretty, looking in. But I've seen others appear to benefit from it throughout my life at every stage, from nursery to work. I've always wondered what it would be like to be elevated for your appearance, so that perhaps you wouldn't have to bother being a million lols a minute (as I felt I had to be, growing up, to be valued) or work as hard to be noticed in a room (or to work as hard at all, perhaps? More on that shortly.) A huge part of me envies that, because of the amount of brain space and time that feeling ugly has swallowed during my life so far – but an even bigger part realises that just as ugly can be a societal construct, so too can pretty. That's why pretty privilege, I believe, is a huge, too-often unspoken bias we need to talk about. Being objectified for your looks has disadvantages of course, but it can be the beauty equivalent of being wealthy or born with a 'silver spoon' in your mouth.

It's nice to think that things change when we grow up, or our teenage lens on what's important gets an update, but it doesn't suddenly become a level playing field as we leave education and enter adulthood. The beauty bias in our working lives is so pronounced that it's even become a research field. 'Pulchronomics' was coined by Daniel Hamermesh, a professor of economics at the University of Texas, who has studied the intersection of beauty and economics for decades. Even though it's now financially quantifiable, it's genuinely refreshing to hear it acknowledged that pretty privilege exists. And that maybe – just maybe – it's part of the reason some may have their job, money or associated status. Or that their looks affect how well they're treated and fitting the beauty standard has allowed them the confidence in society to feel attractive – and perhaps to have an easier ride.

In 2012 journalist Samantha Brick penned an infamous viral feature for the *Daily Mail* with the headline: 'There are downsides to looking this pretty, Why women hate me for being beautiful'. Like the women on TikTok, she talked openly about how she was treated specially and out of nowhere given champagne by a steward on a flight, while men paid for her cabs and train tickets. Brick wrote: 'And whenever I've asked what I've done to deserve such treatment, the donors of these gifts have always said the same thing: my pleasing appearance and pretty smile made their day.' She outlines what makes her so attractive: 'While I'm no Elle Macpherson, I'm tall, slim, blonde and, so I'm often told, a good-looking woman. I know how lucky I am.'[4]

Sure, we might automatically behave favourably to people we find attractive. A study on male college students showed that they were more likely to help a woman – donating blood or even a kidney, saving them from a burning building, etc. – if they thought she was attractive.[5]

But that's also *why* we have to be aware of the bias that beauty holds. Why? Because the qualities we associate with being attractive aren't necessarily earned. Why else? Because this is – as ever – largely a female issue, as a result of the premium that a patriarchal society has always placed on female beauty. Because accepting our looks as social currency creates divisions for all of us. And vitally: because what's created our definitions of 'pretty' and 'ugly' is largely the result of a long history of intersectional discrimination that benefits some and disadvantages others. Perhaps that's why pretty privilege has gone relatively unchallenged for so long – there is so much to unpick and it can be tough to know where to begin.

After facing a huge backlash for the feature, a decade later Samantha Brick reflected on the piece, writing: 'Any show of female self-confidence was – and still is – verboten.'[6] That's true, women are conditioned to feel like they must be humble about their appearance, or to deflect compliments. But it was also evidence of how selective the 'prize of beauty' is when it's bestowed upon some and not others. In a time where we are now, finally, talking openly about discrimination of all kinds, the same hasn't always been true of pretty privilege. Instead, those who discuss it are met with cries of jealousy, envy backlash or worse, a surface-level discussion resulting in ambivalence: a collective shrug of the shoulders. It wasn't Brick's self-confidence that made this feature so memorable to me that I could recall it clearly a decade later – we should all be granted that internal certainty as our birthright. For me, it was the lack of acknowledgement of the unearned benefits of pretty privilege that have largely stemmed from beauty standards created by historical systems of oppression. Pretty privilege may be a benefit to some, but it comes at a cost to others. Isn't it time we collectively account for it?

That Brick, a 'proud size 10–12' is still confident in her

beauty in her fifties in an ageist world is applaudable, though equating a clothing size to an achievement is perhaps less so. But reading both pieces a decade apart makes one thing clear: dismantling the narratives around what's ugly and beautiful is a pressing issue. Dismissing pretty privilege under the guise of 'that's just life, sorry you're not me' means we also dismiss the ways people from different marginalised identities have been made to feel ugly. To be nonchalant about it safeguards many ills from ableism and racism to homophobia. That's not to say anyone who is a slim, cisgender, able-bodied, white, heterosexual woman has pretty privilege and others don't – as we know, it's nuanced (and many have worked hard to understand their privilege, and uplift those without it). But that *is* who receives the most beauty privilege in society – both online and offline.

Previous generations were told what was beautiful by TV shows and teen magazines. Our digitally enhanced worlds now mean that our filters or airbrushing apps can give anyone a degree of faux pretty privilege. But rather than functioning as an 'equaliser', they can create a discrepancy between our appearance, online and offline. As psychiatrist Dr Josie Howard told *Instyle*: 'People begin to expect themselves to look like their filtered self and can become obsessed with achieving that in the real world, which leaves them depressed, anxious, lonely, and disappointed.'[7] That partially accounts for how much social media has influenced cosmetic trends across surgery and make-up, as people ask to look like filtered versions of themselves – complete with the more Eurocentric facial features that these filters often prize.

We use the phrase 'never judge a book by its cover' as a cautionary tale, though I think we'd be hard-pressed to find somebody who doesn't do this. Research says that we make a judgement about a person's character within a tenth of a second of seeing their face – which is something to be aware of in every scenario we face.[8] If that person is attractive, all it takes is an instant before we may subconsciously employ the 'attractiveness halo' – when positive attributes are automatically associated with attractive people. Everything from superior health, intelligence, dominance, mental health and competence has been shown to be potentially attributed to a person's attractiveness.[9] Of course, this could also work the other way around with the age-old stereotype of a 'dumb blonde' or airhead used to discredit somebody. That's the very caricature that 'bimbocore' – a recent social media trend – is using to reclaim 'hyper-femininity' through Barbie doll-esque fashion and beauty.[10]

Since the ancient eras – particularly in Ancient Greece – we've seen how appearance and our morality have been linked as interchangeable qualities. We've had it drummed into us from our childhood cartoons through to phrases like 'butter wouldn't melt ...' – most often used to describe a cute but potentially naughty child. I've seen this first-hand in workplaces, when bosses haven't been able to comprehend how the prettiest girl in the office could behave as poorly as was reported. You could see the look on their faces: it's like those two concepts just didn't fit together in their minds and as such, in my experience, they were seldom reprimanded.

Do we have an issue with believing that pretty privilege can go bad sometimes? Society does seem to baulk at those who are considered 'pretty' or handsome being marked as 'immoral' – or even 'evil'. It always seems to come as more of a shock. When American serial killer Ted Bundy confessed to the murder of more than 30 young women and girls, he was still inundated with love letters in prison. 'He just doesn't look like the type to kill somebody,' a young woman told a reporter outside the courtroom at his trial in 1979.[11] There could be other alluring forces at work here too: the exciting pull of a 'bad boy', or the attraction to the notoriety and taboo, perhaps even a sort of fascination with somebody so unfathomably inhumane and how they 'got away with it.' We do have a cultural obsession, from podcasts to films, with serial killers after all. But the fact he was physically attractive certainly added to his fandom.

Though his crimes were far less brutal, this was also the case with Jeremy Meeks. Meeks's mugshot had been posted by the Stockton police in California after he'd served various prison terms for crimes such as grand theft auto and gun possession. The picture went viral and Meeks became known as the 'hot felon', which catapulted him to stardom in 2014 – and even saw him walk in major fashion shows, dating Topshop heiress Chloe Green and reportedly amassing a $4m fortune.[12] Pretty faces behind bars just doesn't make sense to us as a society, or maybe it makes us care less. After all we've been told since we were children that good (beauty) triumphs over evil (ugly), right? This theory could account for the practice of romance scamming in online dating. After matching with somebody, fraudsters with fake profiles ask for money, often to 'visit' their match. Usually, the pictures used to lure people into matching and parting with their cash are of very attractive people taken from elsewhere. It could be that people are so delighted by the match, that the 'attractiveness halo' makes them less likely to question why their match wants the money. Either way, it's working – in 2021 a record $547 million was swindled by romance scammers according to the Federal Trade Commission (FTC).[13]

We even seem to find it easier to believe that attractive people have the capacity to change and overcome their issues. When Cheryl Tweedy (simply Cheryl now) was charged with assaulting toilet attendant Sophie Amogbokpa in 2003, many didn't believe that the pretty girl next door was capable of it. The incident just didn't seem to fit with her pretty 'girl next door' girl-band-member image – and it hasn't stuck. Cole carried on having a successful career in pop and just five years later in 2008 became an *X Factor* judge. She managed to do what so few achieve – to sweep away their pretty serious misdemeanours, as if they'd never happened. We've all made mistakes of course – and deserve to carry on and live our lives – but would the result have been the same for those without pretty privilege? Perhaps it's just easier to forgive a pretty face.

In a much more extreme example, this 'disbelief' occurred when American journalist Amanda Knox was convicted (and later acquitted after almost four years' imprisonment) of the murder of her roommate Meredith Kercher in 2015. Knox is often described as being fresh-faced or youthful in reports, appearing on 'hot killers' listicles ad nauseum and was widely monikered in the media as 'Foxy Knoxy'. One of the books written about her is even called *The Fatal Gift of Beauty*[14] and her own lawyer said she had an 'angel face'.[15] As former senior FBI profiler Mary Ellen O'Toole, author of *Dangerous Instincts: How Gut Feelings Betray Us,* told *Forbes*: 'Attractive people – women in particular – face several dilemmas when accused of a crime. The focus of the case quickly goes to the woman's physical appearance, only to underscore the belief that really pretty women – for whatever reason – cannot also be criminals. Or, if a very attractive woman is in fact guilty, she must be evil.'[16] In court, Knox was also described by the prosecution as a 'she-devil', a 'witch', 'diabolical' and a 'femme-fatale'. O'Toole says looks can potentially be a case of polarity when it comes to standing trial because while the jury might not be able to link a pretty face to a crime, the opposite can also happen, where a jury might think that looks can be used as a device for manipulation.[17] These associations could come from a legacy of Christian attitudes in the early Middle Ages, where being attractive posed a dichotomy – beauty was, on the one hand, 'revered as an image of god's grace' and on the other, 'beauty was feared as a sensual temptation'.[18]

The temptation factor is something to be aware of too. It could employ that 'attractiveness halo', creating a forcefield of protection around those who are attractive, which could sway our decision making and gives pretty privilege a sense of legitimate power beyond getting a free coffee for being hot. Like the romance scammers mentioned, this might be why we might automatically agree unthinkingly to what pretty people want, like the kind of sketch you'd see in an old comedy film, where a stuttering, stunned man tells a beautiful woman – 'um, yeah, sure, take it all, my car, my wallet, my house.' There is the idea that we can't think straight when we find someone attractive – and that 'we can't help it'. Although, it's worth noting that this can also be used to excuse behaviour like cheating and used to justify unjustifiable crimes like sexual assault.

Appearance can also significantly impact our career progression. These criteria are often nuanced (wearing some make-up is generally expected, but not too much, for example), but I heard it quite explicitly once, by accident. At one of the first magazines I worked at, I overheard my seniors discuss their criteria for hiring a beauty editor. The chosen candidate, they said, *must* look the part: perfectly groomed, expensive-looking, well connected and charming. I listened keenly – being a beauty journalist was what I wanted to do for a living, after all – but it astounded me then, as it does now, that there was *never* a mention made of any kind of writing skill or journalistic accolades: what mattered most was physical appearance and the qualities they attributed to that. It confirmed to me – as I'd experienced throughout my life – that being pretty could also get you jobs. It also told me that, if I wanted in, without those privileges, I'd have to go above and beyond to be noticed in another way.

Some sectors or companies do appear to be more 'lookist' – a discrimination based on appearance – than others. Sometimes it's what these companies are *really* selling with their policies that is cause for concern. It doesn't surprise me in the least that multiple hot celebrities were former Abercrombie & Fitch models like Heidi Klum, Jamie Dornan, Emma Roberts and January Jones.[19] I never felt attractive enough to go into an Abercrombie & Fitch store at the height of its popularity in the 2000s – the topless male model-esque staff at the door and their ad campaigns were *far* too intimidating. But I didn't know then that the company was known to be notorious for hiring 'attractive' employees as part of its 'look policy', although a class action lawsuit claimed this was racially discriminatory in 2005.[20] The court found that an 'all-American' look – which falls under the WASP aesthetic (White Anglo-Saxon Protestant) wasn't necessary do the job and the case was settled for $50m. As a result, the company agreed to hire 'attractive people' from other races too.[21]

Because of the nature of appearance bias – like any kind of conscious or unconscious bias – it's hard to say outright that looks are the reason somebody is hired or not. But it did take me ages, and so much despair, to find a beauty journalism role despite my experience. Maybe it was bad luck. Maybe I was too shy? Or maybe it was not having pretty privilege – I'll never really know. But my suspicions were compounded when I got my first beauty journalism role and started attending launches. Seeing the other beauty assistants, it was obvious I didn't fit the mould. The glee of finally getting that first job started to wear off as I realised I'd have to shift my appearance to fit in more and 'look the part'. Often, we don't recognise how much we assimilate or 'code-switch' – adjusting factors like our behaviour, speech and appearance – to fit into our work environments. Until somebody holds up a mirror to us, that is.

Further along in my career, when I met up with a mentor in the industry, she said to me: 'Wow, you *really* look like you work at [insert title here].' She meant that my style and appearance had changed so much, I didn't look like me anymore and I had started dressing like the rest of the office. It would appear I'm not alone – in 2022 a British report called 'Broken Ladders' found that 61 per cent of women of colour said they changed their behaviour, appearance and even their names to fit in at work, compared with 44 per cent of white women.[22] I can confirm that constantly trying to fit in when you so obviously don't – on top of your day job – is *exhausting* work.

Meanwhile, in sectors where you'd think that skill would reign as the number one attribute for being hired and paid fairly, looks still seem to prevail. A study found that attractive male economics professors (using the website Ratemyprofessors.com) actually earned more than their un-rated or less well rated colleagues.[23] One academic review said that: 'Physically attractive individuals are more likely to be interviewed for jobs and hired, they are more likely to advance rapidly in their careers through frequent promotions, and they earn higher wages than unattractive individuals.'[24] But what – pray tell – puts them in the category of unattractive? Those who are obese, dress differently, have tattoos or piercings and don't fit the societal norms of desired appearance, according to the review. Anyone outside the small remit we know to be the beauty norm, anyone who might be considered 'ugly'.[25] [26]

Quantifying this in terms of cold hard cash, researchers found that attractive people could earn 3–4 per cent more than those who aren't as attractive, which adds up to an estimated $230,000 more over a lifetime. An average-looking person too could make $140,000 more in their lifetime than somebody considered unattractive.[27] Our 'beauty premium' is the term used to correlate our attractiveness and our earning potential. But if that wasn't bad enough, there is research to quantify that almost everything that constitutes the conventional beauty standard – from being blonde, the right height, slim, wearing make-up (and also being married) – can mean you'll earn more money.[28]

Attractiveness at work is one area that research supports can be an issue for men, too. An attractive man could make 13 per cent more in his career than a less attractive or 'looks-challenged' colleague.[29] In the US, research found that attractive American Football quarterbacks earned 12 per cent more than their less attractive counterparts – and Harvard University said that men who are 6ft tall and over make on average $5,525 more than their shorter, 5'5 colleagues.[30] The research on this mostly comes down to stereotypes around masculinity and leadership – studies have shown that having a lower-pitched voice can make you seem more trustworthy and make you more money as a result. [31]

There are far fewer studies to show the opposite, that being attractive can affect your career negatively, and sometimes, they're a bit of a backhanded compliment. One study found that if you are 'very unattractive' (their words, not mine), you might feel like you have to work harder to prove yourself and you'll have less distractions (perhaps like a partner or a social life) so you might make more money than an attractive person.[32] Still, research seems to overwhelmingly favour those with pretty privilege in the workplace, especially as building confidence from an early age is said to help you step out of your comfort zone.[33] This could translate as feeling like you are worth more when it comes to work – in terms of salary, progression and treatment – and crucially, having the confidence to ask for it.

It can seem like our appearance is being constantly policed. On the TV show *Curb Your Enthusiasm*, when comedian Larry

David is seated at a table in a restaurant, he looks at another part of the restaurant that's buzzier and sees that everyone seated there is much more attractive. He's perturbed at where he's been seated – 'You know what I think, you have a good-looking section and you have an ugly section,' he tells the maître d. It's a great analogy for so many aspects of life where appearance can dictate our success. So, if some are granted 'exclusive' access and others are denied it, do we ever find out what the rules of admission are?

Nightclubs are renowned for vetting clientele with strict dress codes in a move that says 'this is who we want to be associated with'. But in 2015, the discriminatory door policies at a celebrity-frequented club in London called DSTRKT went a step further and reportedly didn't admit four women, who were deemed 'too fat' and 'too dark'.[34] When the veil that covers the unspoken rules of pretty privilege slips, it is hugely revealing. In 2022, two plus-size models were allegedly denied entry to a club in LA although the rest of their party was allowed to enter. They believe it's due to size-discrimination: 'I was definitely the biggest in the group,' model Alexa Jay said. Speaking of the doorman, she continued: 'He looks me up and down and says, "Yeah, not tonight."'[35] Many clubs are known to use female guests as currency to lure in men to spend money at the bar to impress them. Having 'less attractive' women with a lower currency, wouldn't bring in as many men or as much cash. We could also say there's a metaphorical 'door policy' that's often in use to give or deny us admittance in other areas of life. Clothing with limited sizing tell us who fashion brands want wearing their ranges, as do beauty products with non-inclusive shades – our desirability is monetised on so many levels.

For me, part of the anguish around the ripple effects of pretty privilege is the frequency with which a value is placed on our appearance in different areas of life without our consent. At school in my early teens, 'lists' would circulate: the girls had been ranked by the boys in terms of attractiveness and their physical attributes and given 'ratings'. In a grown-up version of this, psychologist and professor of Northwestern University Renee Engeln wrote in *Beauty Sick*: 'On more than one occasion when I was back in college, I walked by a fraternity house on campus and saw men on the front porch holding up signs with numbers on them, scoring women who walked past.'[36] Being ranked in terms of appearance isn't something that necessarily stops when we leave education either. Often one of our first tests where pretty privilege rears its head is how we find a partner, especially in our digital age.

Modern dating platforms can be explicit about who they want to attract – their branding screams it and sometimes, they're overt about the criteria. Take Beautifulpeople.com, which allows its members to rate 'aspiring' members for their admission, in order to keep out anyone ugly. The aim is to let people date others of a similar level of attractiveness, but there is a way to get in, that is, if you're male and less attractive: 'Men who exude wealth and success in their images, but who may not be that attractive, are often voted in,' MD Greg Hodge told the *Metro* in 2016.[37] As of 2019 they claimed to have rejected 8.5 million people, which speaks to our desire to want to be considered beautiful by applying, but also the reasons the company would reveal this – essentially to show how *selective* they are. Male members of the site revealed the following reasons for rejecting applicants – bad skin, a big or unsightly nose, being obese or overweight, poor figure with no shape or curves, no butt or too much butt, being 'thin fat' (or slim but untoned) made the list. Female members offered a similar criteria, but with factors like bald, short and a thin build thrown in.[38]

When physical beauty isn't openly revealed as the threshold for acceptance, is this automatically implied? Apps like The League – a dating app 'for those very high standards' – can take months to 'vet' a profile. Another 'elite' dating site initially denied me access – until I had to join to write about them for a feature and then they had to let me in (Larry David would be proud!). Luxy, a millionaire and elite dating site launched in 2014 with the initial strapline: 'Tinder, minus the poor people' also has member-voted admission.[39]

Science has repeatedly quantified what it believes to be pretty, but in the dating pool it's not always the most 'beautiful' faces that do well – often it can pay to be average. Pour quoi? Some believe that it's because distinctive facial features are linked to chromosomal disorders – so a preference for average faces is a way to find a mate with 'good genes'.[40] Others like physiologist Johan Koeslag believe our preference for averageness or koinophilia – from the Greek *koinos* (usual) and *philos* (love) – is hardwired into our behaviour. Nature is always looking for a medium, rather than an extreme – for example, human babies who are larger or smaller than average are sadly less likely to survive.[41] Maybe it's also about how approachable people are perceived to be, too. Very attractive people are often assumed to be 'out of the average person's league'. Or if a partner is too hot, that might highlight ones own insecurities too. The middle ground is often the safest bet for many – someone who is attractive, but approachably so.

But what is an average beauty, really? Is it the blonde, all-American girl, or is it the pale-skinned, dark-haired English rose? Either way, it doesn't leave a great deal of scope for much in-between. Often, it's the 'girl next door' trope that is used to evoke a beauty that's commonplace or 'average' in TV and film. She's natural-looking, rarely 'made up' and does indeed live nearby – take Joey Potter, a lead character in the TV series *Dawson's Creek*. Often, she's pure and virginal – she's not been 'corrupted'. In the film *Grease*, she's Sandra

Dee in contrast to Rizzo, the sexually promiscuous bad girl. In 1979, Donald Symons, an anthropologist and one of the founders of evolutionary psychology, proposed the theory that beauty in human faces was based on averageness – and our brains act like 'face averaging devices' that collect images of the faces we encounter and the composite of this becomes our standard of attractiveness.[42] Where this obviously becomes an issue is that it's dependent on the variety of faces we see. So, when it comes to dating and attraction, this is reliant on who makes up the average faces we are exposed to, from our media to our communities. When someone says 'my type is petite brunettes', for example, that could be based on the average of what they've been exposed to. It also means that being an 'average beauty' – known as 'mediocre pretty privilege' on TikTok – is still quite a narrow beauty remit.

It pays to be beautiful, then, and it pays to be average, but what if society won't let you into either category? It's important to reiterate that you can have pretty privilege if you're not white, but racial discrimination is often the unspoken elephant in the room, especially with the visual nature of dating apps and our ever-present Eurocentric standards of beauty. On dating shows like *Married at First Sight Australia*, Season Nine (filmed in 2022), when contestants are asked for their physical preference, 'blue eyes' is a common answer. But when Selina Chhaur (of Chinese/Cambodian heritage) asks her partner why he isn't attracted to her, he confirms her worst fears all along – it's because she's Asian. He said: 'I'm not racist by any means but it's not something I'm familiar with…I do usually go for that blonde, surfy look.' Chhaur, who does actually have dyed blonde hair, reacts to this by saying she was surprised by the comments and didn't know what to do. [43]

We have to recognise that the lack of non-white women as 'celebrated beauties' in the mainstream media has an impact. And if they are there, often it's because they fit in with Eurocentric beauty standards, with smaller noses, light eyes or pale skin, like Beyoncé, Halle Berry or Aishwarya Rai Bachchan. If women dare to resist changing to fit that beauty standard, they're told about it explicitly, as journalist Radhika Sanghani wrote in the *Evening Standard*: 'From a very early age, I knew my nose was ugly, because people told me. Once, while bowling, some teenage boys yelled "big-nosed Indian" at me (a factually correct, if horrible statement). Later in life, men came up to me in bars to tell me they had big nose fetishes. My well-meaning friends, meanwhile, told me I'd be "so, like, pretty, with a smaller nose."'[44]

These attacks can be published under the guise of science too. In 2011, a now-removed feature for *Psychology Today* by Dr Satoshi Kanazawa, an evolutionary psychologist, posed the question: 'Why are Black women less attractive?' using weak scientific claims to justify it.[45] There is no science to explain this, it doesn't exist. What persists is the lack of inclusivity for women of colour (particularly with dark skin) as romantic leads on TV and film, alongside a general lack of people of colour on reality TV and dating shows. All of this constitutes how and what we see as an attractive prospect.

On dating apps, it's clear who has this privilege. Professor Binna Kandola, author of *Racism at Work: The Danger of Indifference*, told the *Independent*: 'As the decision to approach someone on a dating site is largely based on appearance, we also need to be aware of the stereotypes associated with beauty. Unconscious biases held within society dictate that white men, for example, are seen as being analytical and hardworking, while white women are seen as empathetic and caring. Black men, on the other hand, are seen as hyper-masculine, and black women are seen as more aggressive than white women, thanks in part to the "angry black woman" persona that has become prominent in popular culture.'[46] Many Asian women too are filed under the trope of being seen as exotic and submissive.

Having pretty privilege means you could succeed more in dating, not just because of assumptions around race and attractiveness, but due to the bias that exists in our dating tech too. Despite a paper from Cornell University in 2018 already highlighting the inequality in dating apps[47], it wasn't until after the murder of George Floyd in 2020 that Grindr removed its ethnicity filters and other apps followed.[48] Some like Hinge have kept the ethnicity filter to 'support people of color looking to find a partner with shared cultural experiences and background'.[49] Anecdotally, almost all of my non-white friends using dating apps are convinced they receive far fewer matches compared to their white friends and also feel they are placed at a disadvantage in the algorithm hierarchy. But the bias could still be inherent in the tech itself – some dating apps are rumoured to rank users by their 'attractiveness' measured by algorithms.[50]

Of course, if what is held up as an 'ideal' beauty wasn't so narrow, and so tightly gatekept by what we watch on TV (invariably, even the Prince Charming characters in the shows we watch mostly have white men as the 'prize') or the apps we swipe on, then pretty privilege could start to become more inclusive. Likewise, if beauty standards weren't so gendered and binary, then this would make things easier for so many people. But as we know, that's why those parameters exist, to support the majority and to oppress any minorities, and it's also why pretty privilege plays a role in LGBTQ+ history too. As with every piece of research and every study, we are individuals, and our experiences vary hugely. As Autumn Whitefield-Madrano says in *Face Value: The Hidden Ways Beauty Shapes Women's Lives*: 'Researchers have come to varying conclusions about whether queer women are cushioned against conventional beauty standards – where one study says lesbians internalize beauty norms less than straight women, another finds they're at a similar risk for having a poor body image as straight women.'[51]

What is universally true is that the privileges associated with attractiveness elevate some and hurt others. But when those who are marginalised (or sit outside of the mainstream in some way) suffer from it too, it further illuminates the role of appearance bias in our looks-obsessed society. Being able to 'pass' as cisgender shouldn't be a measure of attractiveness, the binary nature of our traditional beauty standards has meant that does affect many in the transgender community. But having or being able to access that privilege comes with a degree of physical safety too. Eva Echo founded the Pass It On campaign with LGBTQ+ platform Unite UK, to break down the barriers of internalised beauty ideals creating a safe space for transgender and non-binary people to be themselves. Echo told *Refinery29*: 'Passing is an important thing, especially at the start of any transition...It's affirming and it makes you realise that you *can* be accepted by society. It's also about safety. When you're going from A to B, it helps, as no one takes any notice and you can move through society easily... cisgender women find it difficult to achieve the beauty standards which the industry sets. It's bad as it is, let alone having gender dysphoria on top of that.'[52]

Producer Janet Mock penned an op ed for *Allure* describing how being attractive benefited her after transitioning, but still had limitations 'I knew very early on that I was not pretty. No one ever called me pretty. It was not the go-to adjective people used to describe me. Throughout elementary and middle school, I was used to hearing other words: Smart. Studious. Well-spoken. Well-read. They became pillars of my self-confidence, enabling me to build myself up on what I contributed rather than what I looked like.' Mock continues to say that she was enamoured by the pretty girls – 'the popular ones who walked into the room and shifted the gaze of the majority without effort, the ones who won class elections, were crowned Miss and voted Most, and who seemed to collect all the trophies and Valentines. I was equally fascinated by the pretty girls and women who were lauded in my favourite films and TV series as well as the ones who took centre stage on MTV.'

After Mock transitioned genders, she said she fitted into the 'pretty' camp but describes how this has limitations: 'Pretty privilege is also conditional and is not often extended to women who are trans, black and brown, disabled, older, and/or fat. Being curvy but not plus size, mixed but not all black, trans but cis-blending, and able-bodied gives me a different experience than many. I am a black and native Hawaiian trans woman (who is often perceived as cis) with brown skin, curly hair, an hourglass size-8 shape. I have symmetrical facial features; a smooth, even complexion; and a white, straight, wide smile. For me, pretty privilege operates in a myriad of ways depending on the spaces I enter, who is in that space, and whether people already know that I am trans.' Being able to pass, and then access a level of pretty privilege, Mock says, 'has contributed to my success and made the road a bit smoother.'[53]

But pretty privilege is a nuanced and delicate topic because – despite the privileges – bad stuff happens to attractive people too, of course it does. Beauty can't stop a giant hailstone falling from the sky and knocking you cold out (Slush Puppy, anyone?) or any of the kind of insecurity issues that affect the rest of us. Pretty doesn't necessarily equate to happily ever after, in the same way that inherited wealth won't automatically guarantee a happier life. Having pretty privilege could even result in harassment, unwanted attention and being seen as 'arm candy' or a commodity rather than being recognised for who you are. There will always be examples where being pretty works against you too. Pretty privilege may hide some 'invisible' disabilities – neurodivergence, for example – making it harder for people to believe you need help, which is informed by, and perpetuates, ableism. Another way it can manifest is when people assume that all you are is a pretty face. Model Emily Ratajkowski told the BBC that when she was considering an acting career: 'agents said to me if you want to be taken serious as an actor you need to stop with the modelling and get ugly for these roles and that you have to prove you're more than a sex object.'[54]

There's also the competition element – another potential downside to being beautiful. Of course, humans want to compete on some level – it's what the animal world does for survival – but when looks are your currency, this can become a source of conflict. Samantha Brick (*see also* page 270) said that she experienced lots of jealousy from other women, so her pretty privilege wasn't always a positive experience. Some studies have shown women are more likely to use 'indirect aggression' like gossiping and exclusion towards a beautiful woman than a less attractive one and evolutionary psychologists have suggested that 'intrasexual competition' or putting other women down is part of a competitive process for a mate.[55] That might be true, but here's an alternative view – maybe that jealousy is due to the unspoken way pretty privilege exists in a society that pits women against each other and elevates beauty as the ultimate female achievement/contest (as it has done for centuries). Above all, we are all diminished when we compete among ourselves for approval from anyone, and in particular the patriarchy, in this way.

So, what happens if our pretty status in society changes for some reason? That could happen to everyone at some point, from men losing their hair to the way women are ignored by society when they're past a certain age and no longer seen as attractive. If you've always been prized for being beautiful and this appears to change, that can be a real jolt to the ego. It can affect how you operate in the world, and going by the research discussed earlier, could even affect your income or ability to get a partner. That change could be a challenge to the status quo: when someone else comes along who is newer and as (or more) attractive, that is threatened. In the film *Mean Girls*, Regina George compliments Cady Heron's looks. She says 'thank you', to which Regina responds: 'So you agree ... you think you're really pretty?' It's a trap to assess just how much Regina's competitor rates herself. And it shows the power and status that prettiness can give you (and in turn, popularity and protection too.) [55]

If something happens to you that changes your appearance drastically with a lasting effect, this could be crushing, especially if you've always been celebrated for your beauty. At the height of her career in 2005, TV presenter Gail Porter was diagnosed with alopecia – an auto immune condition that causes hair loss. She said her career 'just stopped' because she didn't look the same and refused to wear a wig, which resulted in a serious loss of income.[56] Another example is Katie Piper, who was a model, entered beauty pageants and worked as a TV presenter. In 2008, aged 24, she fell victim to an acid attack from a former boyfriend, leaving her face severely burned with visual impairments. Since then, she's campaigned to normalise difference of appearance and the rhetoric that goes alongside being anything other than the conventional 'hot girl' on TV: Piper said: 'I see it as someone who's been burned doesn't have to be put in this box where they can't be glamorous – I try and live that vision all the time and push those stereotypes away.'[57]

That a woman loses her pretty privilege as she ages is undoubtedly part of the same, patriarchal gaze that's defined female beauty throughout history. The examples we see most often are celebrities famed for their beauty going 'too far' to keep their looks. Cosmetic surgeries and 'tweakments' might also feel like they equalise the playing field, both in terms of hiding our ageing and giving us access to 'pretty privilege' if we felt like we didn't have it before. Or, at least, that's how it's been marketed to us. That these outdated and deeply damaging stereotypes around beauty keep damaging and defining us are the real travesty here, though.

But it doesn't necessarily correlate to mega-confidence if you 'become' hot in some way later in life, either. When I lost a huge amount of weight, it felt novel to walk into Topshop and find jeans that (almost) fit, but I also felt unstable after basing so much of my self-worth on my appearance for so long. I felt so uneasy in my body, that I almost felt more vulnerable.

On the second season of the dating reality series *Love Is Blind* a participant called Danielle Ruhl has a familiar dating show backstory – she's lost a lot of weight, 70lb in fact. Despite now being slim, her insecurities are painfully obvious; she alludes that they are the result of being made to feel unattractive when younger.[58] Just as those who spend eternity chasing being beautiful with successive cosmetic surgery procedures, Ruhl's software didn't get the confidence update that said she was now 'hotter' – nothing is ever enough. It doesn't seem to match the innate confidence of being attractive from birth either. But then who would create those ugly duckling makeover moments that reality TV *loves* so much if we didn't have these people? Although, to note, they're often just fat-shaming in a covert guise, celebrating the hero's journey – and anchoring being worthy of a good relationship to body size/appearance.

Actor Rebel Wilson was famous for (alongside other roles) playing Fat Amy in the comedy film *Pitch Perfect* (2012) and received significant media attention for her weight loss. But she's also been vocal about wanting people to focus on her career, rather than her appearance. 'Is that what a woman has to do in the world, lose weight to get attention?' she said. 'It's fascinating, why are people so obsessed with it? Like, with women in particular about their looks? I know what it's like to be a woman who is essentially invisible to most people because of not being seen as traditionally beautiful or whatever. It's crazy to try to fit that,' she told *BBC Breakfast*.[59] When celebrities lose weight and access pretty privilege it can feel like a betrayal to those who saw them as a role model for sitting outside of beauty norms in some way. But rather than berate said celebrity for their personal choices and the pressure they may be under – which could be anything from the pressure to fit into sample clothes, or public scrutiny about their weight, for example – ultimately unless we take control of and equalise the narrative around 'pretty', it will always have the power to define us.

Pretty privilege somehow feels like the final beauty taboo in a world that talks *constantly* about beauty. Why is it taboo? Because we accept that beauty standards are just a case of winning a genetic lottery, without being given the space to discuss them openly. Perhaps we avoid discussing it because, firstly, it feels uncomfortable in polite society to talk about things like appearance and to really deconstruct the mechanisms underpinning them. That's challenging on all accounts. Secondly, we feel awkward about it, so we accept pretty is a privilege and just move on. And finally, it feels too darn obvious. Neither do we want to appear jealous or provoke some kind of 'pretty fragility' in response, or to diminish others' experiences too – that's not the point here. While also acknowledging this side, we can – and should – talk about and recognise the privileges that being conventionally pretty have often conferred on people because of what those beauty standards really conceal.

I've certainly been guilty of thinking 'if only I was [Insert beauty woe of your choice], everything in my life would be perfect'. So, maybe it's worth remembering that being pretty or achieving it in some way doesn't always give us the fairy-tale ending. In a 2013 TED talk Cameron Russell said that despite her work as a model and all the benefits she's received from that, she's still insecure: 'You just need to meet a group of models because they have the thinnest thighs, the shiniest hair and the coolest clothes and they're the most physically insecure women on the planet.'[60] The thing about being 'pretty' is that it so often comes from outside us when somebody defines us as 'pretty' or 'ugly' in some way. It's an external validation, which means it needs reinforcing. If it doesn't or it's inconsistent, or as above, our entire career hangs on it, it's easy to see how this could become a source of anguish. And the moral of the story? We have to root our self-worth elsewhere.

We can build self-esteem in other ways than appearance using self-compassion. This might mean taking a less critical view of any of our perceived physical flaws and pinpointing where and who that critical voice comes from. But we can also use the ever-popular gratitude method of counting our blessings – but about ourselves. It might sound a little self-centred, but if you can think of a few qualities you possess every day that are non-appearance based that you're grateful for – like being creative, or always remembering birthdays – then it reminds us that despite societal pressures we're worth more than just our appearance. Likewise, for me it's been about stepping back in areas of my life where I've felt I've had to make up for my lack of pretty privilege. I try not to work so hard to prove myself that it supersedes everything else in my life and makes me ill. I accept that some days I'm comedy value, and others I'm just not, and I'm still valuable either way.

What's also crucial is examining where we might hold implicit biases against ourselves or others and the value we place on 'pretty' or 'ugly'. Patricia Devine, a professor of psychology at the University of Wisconsin, and her colleagues developed a form of unconscious bias training called 'prejudice habit-breaking'.[61] Firstly, we need to be *aware* of our beauty bias – TV shows are a great one to test this out on – what judgements do you make based solely on appearance? Now think about what that bias means – what are the consequences of having this bias, for yourself and others? Finally, replace your immediate response with one that's in line with the non-prejudiced way you'd much rather be thinking. You could even go a step further and try to build that into your life somehow, following new people on social media or watching different TV shows to re-wire your thinking. Over time, it could even help us retrain ourselves to think about appearance in a bold new way – and start to dismantle the power being pretty or ugly has over us.

THE END OF UGLY

BEAUTY IS A WONDERFUL thing. I do want to make that clear, otherwise I wouldn't still be writing about it, or care about how it's affecting us. But if you take away one thing from reading this book, let it be this: our beauty standards don't just 'appear', whether they're on TikTok as a fun new trend, a celebrity on our TVs or as a product in our bathrooms. The beauty culture we currently exist in is the result of a long and complex history that could fill multiple volumes. Because their origins come from a legacy of power imbalance, they still continue to reflect the power dynamics and struggle of our current society.

We have to be aware of that to be able to pinpoint them, notice when they're exerting control over us and to reclaim beauty on our own terms. It's never been more pressing because the pressure to be 'perfect' still exists, just as the pressure to 'love yourself as you are' does too. Crucially, there are industries that profit from upholding beauty standards and they are so colossal, and so powerful, that they exert an invisible dominance over us that we need to be able to see and contextualise.

It's my hope that by dissecting our beauty norms, we will also start to make things click for us on a personal level. Those clicks could feel like watching reality TV and realising that the normalisation of cosmetic surgery is actively making you feel ugly and sends you scrolling for the nearest injectables clinic. *Click*. You go to put on your make-up and notice how much you focus on concealing your 'flaws' like dark circles and that you have an inner monologue that berates your appearance as you do so. *Click*. You look in the mirror each day and clock that rather than dressing for yourself, you're trying to look 'flattering' or hide yourself away. Your brain does a roll call of what you dislike about your appearance. *Click Click Click*.

Far from being one giant epiphany, those little clicks add

up. They're small, cognitive changes that mean the beauty standards we're currently living by start to become less potent and all-consuming – and recognisable. Hopefully, they'll mean that when you buy a beauty product/start a new wellness regime/buy some new clothes it's from a neutral place, one where we're not outsourcing all our self-esteem to something external. And of course, over time, hopefully, with some of the suggestions here, further exploration, therapy, whatever it takes, you'll be able to start interrupting those patterns and turn the dial down on the voices telling you you're ugly and offering you the fix.

Writing this book has been illuminating, sometimes shocking and deeply healing, even to somebody who thought they were well versed in beauty standards and feminist theory. It's also been confronting – you might feel that too. We can feel sad about the way beauty standards were imposed on us and mourn for our younger selves, who were journalling about how ugly we thought we felt. We can mourn that so many of us were never allowed to really *be*, or got to love ourselves as we should have. It's as though our bodies were like a temporary home that needed to be patched up and rebuilt in order to make it even vaguely liveable. Beauty standards did that to us, however we received them. Many of us spent our teens wishing we had bigger boobs/smaller boobs, thigh gap, clear skin, straight hair, a flat stomach. At every stage in life, we've been sold something new to hate about our appearance. We're taught to fear ageing in our twenties; by the time we reach our fifties, we'll regret that we didn't get to truly appreciate how great we looked in the past or accept how our beauty is evolving. That's why it's imperative that we do something to reclaim our own definition of beauty now. Just as previous generations, new generations continue to fall prey of the sicknesses that can come with beauty standards. It's easy to dismiss the world of beauty as skin-deep, or superficial, but it's anything but. The suffering from eating disorders, anxiety, depression, bullying, low self-esteem and poor self-worth can be a matter of life or death.

Beauty culture should make us feel joyful, not panicky. Embracing our evolving beauty should feel peaceful, not a constant battle against time and other factors. Wellness should be making us healthier, not sicker and sadder. That the same tired beauty standards we've had for centuries keep shapeshifting into new tyrannical forms is indicative of how badly we need to take control of them.

So, what do we do? The knee-jerk response might be to renounce beauty standards altogether – throw away your products, tell wellness to go choke on a protein ball and write an email that starts: 'Dear Hollywood/social media/patriarchy/capitalism, go f*ck yourself.' Tempting (if you find any addresses, let me know) but perhaps we can imagine a new version of beauty. One that looks completely different, if we can manage to break free of just a few of the ways it's had us caged. We do have choices that don't boil down to a binary of 'beautiful or ugly'; there are ways to love or feel neutral about ourselves not dependent on how visible our frown lines are or whether we've gained or lost weight that week.

Part of that journey begins with getting angry or feeling fed up enough to do something about it. Sure, we've come a long way from when I was buying beauty products in my teens. And our current discussions around deconstructing gender, sexuality, race and structure of privilege have played a huge part in this progress. Let's absolutely celebrate that. But let's also be aware that there is a strong pattern that history has shown us repeatedly. Beauty standards become more extreme when patriarchal power is questioned or threatened in some way. We saw that in the 1980s when more women entered traditionally male industries, in the 1950s when we gained more reproductive freedom and in the 1920s when we attained a degree of sexual liberation and now, as we try to reclaim autonomy over our bodies, beauty standards and more. So what can we do to protect ourselves?

Reclaim your tech ...

Look at every significant progress milestone in history – for each positive there's always a negative flipside. Television was a brilliant technological invention, but it also spread patriarchal gender norms via TV shows and advertisements, controlled beauty standards and was used to sell us everything from shampoo to political ideology. Mobile phones revolutionised communication (and 'Snakes' was an epic game) but now we're addicted to their dopamine boosts because the tech industry designed them that way. Social media was a game-changing way to embrace the body-positivity movement, but it also elevated one form of ideal beauty and normalised using as much retouching as a magazine photo shoot.

Social media (and reality TV, they're very much bedfellows) is instrumental in creating the constructs of 'ugly' and 'pretty' that are hurting so many people in society; the research on the effects on our self-esteem just keep coming. Unless we police that for ourselves and make it a more positive experience we'll look back on this period with the same dismay as plucking hairlines and lashes in the Middle Ages, or the Victorians aiming for tuberculosis-chic. Future generations might think of us – *'what the hell were they on?'* Let's make sure we're gaining from using social media, not losing. That might involve unfollowing – or muting – anyone who makes you feel like you're ugly or who triggers comparison. Following a much wider cross section of beauty influencers, across every intersection, can also really expand your limited definitions of what's beautiful and helps support those the biased algorithms hides. When scrolling, aim to do so intentionally rather than mindlessly – that tends to be when we're caught off guard and think less about what the arbitrary definitions of 'perfection' conceal.

Celebrate yourself away from beauty

Women have always been defined by their appearance first in society, so it stands to reason that we largely do that to ourselves too. But if we can define ourselves in ways that aren't appearance based, it might make factors like ageing or changes with pregnancy easier to cope with – and crucially, it can set us up to value ourselves as being more than just decorative. You could take that self gratitude list from the last chapter a step further. Have a list of what you do like about yourself physically, alongside practical explanations of why – for example, 'I love how strong my thighs are, they allow me to walk miles every day.' This can help ease into body neutrality.

Another way to celebrate yourself is to have some 'step away days'. Can you gradually work in a day a month where you 'step away' from things you rely on for beauty validation? That might be your phone or social media. Maybe it's not to look in a mirror after you get ready in the morning. That means no shop windows or wing mirrors either – just focus on how you *feel* instead (I know, radical concept, right?). Step aways days could be going outside without your hair/make-up done and seeing what comes up when you do that. How does it make you feel? Was it so bad? Can you think about why it might feel like that? Gradually work up your tolerance so it feels less scary to feel valuable for who you are, as you are and not just what you look like.

Buy and use beauty products consciously and slowly

We can still love reading about, trying and buying beauty products, but doing so in a conscious way is so much more joyful. Try keep a tab on your mindset whon beauty shopping: are you in beauty anxiety mode, or do you feel neutral about what you're buying and just need a replacement? When shopping in a place of neutrality, you're less likely to impulse buy and regret it, or pin your hopes on something that might not deliver. There's a sustainability element to this too – you can't use 30 face creams at a time. They do have shelf lives; using and buying one at a time is better all round. There's a huge issue with beauty packaging and excess products being wasted; it's better for our purses and the planet to shop slowly. When surrounded by piles of products, we don't value them, they don't feel special and we lose the joy of experimenting with beauty for fun – it just becomes *stuff*.

What makes you buy a product? The next time you're beauty shopping, choose the items that fill up your senses in some way. Maybe that's the fragrance of a certain lipstick, the charm of the packaging, an incredible scented candle, or using a hair oil evocative of your childhood (it's Dabur Jasmine oil for me). That's just some of the joy beauty products can bring us on a multi-sensory level. To notice that, we have to slow down. I'm not suggesting we make our routine mindful as such – that phrase has been commodified enough – but we can focus on applying products from a mindset where we're celebrating ourselves and enjoying the experience rather than just aiming for the outcome and covering things up.

Give beauty standards back to others ...

You can be a feminist and enjoy beauty in its many forms. But we *all* deserve to enjoy a beauty and wellness culture from a neutral place without it making anyone feel terrible. One way to enact this is by engaging with beauty and wellness consciously, to notice who isn't in the room. That room might be a physical yoga class (does it feel inclusive, is it accessible?) or the room could be a beauty shelf you're looking at in a shop (and noticing that it doesn't have many shades for dark skin tones).

Giving beauty back to others might include using some of what you've read in this book to have more challenging conversations with friends and family when comments are made about topics like ageing, or weight for example (a huge number of female friends have this issue with their mothers, who were influenced by toxic 1970s/80s diet culture). This might also involve having those conversations with clothing brands if you see that they have limited sizing, or challenging a beauty advert that doesn't feature older women. Even if those things don't affect us directly, we have to start noticing them and supporting the expansion of beauty standards for everyone. This might entail challenging your own assumptions about beauty to help dismantle them for other people's benefit as well as your own too. But with kindness, civility and a realisation that we're all at different stages of this journey and these things take time – this isn't me supporting 'call out' culture – I don't. Something to note too: whenever somebody tries to challenge a beauty norm, there is always a backlash of some kind. But that also proves that there are societal forces (like patriarchy, white supremacy, classism, et al.) that are alive and active with a vested interest in keeping beauty standards narrow, admitting some in and keeping others out. What we do and say matters, whether we're in a position of influence with millions of followers, or just in our own communities.

Create your own beauty rules ...

Hopefully there will be elements in this book that have been a bit of a lightbulb moment – perhaps you've marked them in some way or can list them now. Use them to create a list of your own 'beauty rules' detailing all your boundaries around how you want to feel and what you love about beauty to help keep the negative influences out. It could read something like: 'I apply my make-up to express myself, not hide. I wear clothes that make me feel happy, not to cover myself up. I only buy something new when I've finished what I have. I give myself time and space to think carefully before cosmetic procedures'. Creating our own beauty rules is never going to be easy when so much feels out of our control, but that's why we have to redefine what beauty is for ourselves. Put that list wherever you get ready – in multiple locations if you can – and think of it as a list of affirmations. Keep adding to it as you go along.

This book is a snapshot of the vast history of our beauty standards, the complexities that have fed into it and the enduring legacy we now live with as a result. It's challenging – it picks at wounds that society – or more specifically, the businesses that profit from our insecurities – would rather we didn't address. But ultimately, *Ugly* is about reclaiming ourselves from the beauty standards that are holding us back and spreading that effect as widely as possible. Together, this ripple effect could help shift the unhappiness surrounding our looks that has plagued women for centuries. Our beauty culture and standards can feel like a hall of mirrors at a funfair. No matter what mirror you peer into, the message consistently says 'you're ugly, you don't deserve to value yourself and you must change'. What if there was one that said – 'you're amazing as you are'? That's the mirror we need to create now – and in our new reality ugly doesn't exist.

ENDNOTES

BEFORE UGLY

1 https://pubmed.ncbi.nlm.nih.gov/21271817/

2 https://royalsociety.org/news/2014/symmetrical-faces-dont-mean-better-health/

3 https://www.nineteenthcenturydisability.org/items/show/48

4 https://www.christopherreeve.org/blog/life-after-paralysis/ugly-laws

5 https://lordslibrary.parliament.uk/disability-discrimination-act-1995-and-now/

6 Gretchen, E. Henderson. *Ugliness: A Cultural Anthology*, Reaktion Books (2015), p52

7 https://www.independent.co.uk/news/uk/home-news/my-dear-you-are-ugly-but-tomorrow-i-shall-be-sober-and-you-will-still-be-ugly-winston-churchill-tops-poll-of-history-s-funniest-insults-8878622.html

8 https://overland.org.au/previous-issues/issue-237/feature-look-good-feel-good/

9 https://publications.parliament.uk/pa/cm5801/cmselect/cmwomeq/805/80502.htm

10 https://www.bbc.co.uk/news/uk-wales-politics-56594309

11 https://www.dove.com/uk/stories/about-dove/ending-hair-discrimination.html

12 https://www.theguardian.com/society/2018/feb/28/more-than-half-of-children-in-england-and-wales-bullied-about-appearance

13 https://www.theguardian.com/society/2018/feb/28/more-than-half-of-children-in-england-and-wales-bullied-about-appearance

14 https://bmcpsychiatry.biomedcentral.com/articles/10.1186/s12888-020-2433-8]

AN UGLY START

1 https://www.reddit.com/r/AskReddit/comments/3lpe39/parents_of_ugly_children_when_did_you_first/

2 https://variety.com/video/lady-gaga-bradley-cooper-star-is-born-bullied/

3 https://www.thecut.com/2018/04/25-celebrities-on-their-ugly-duckling-phase.html

4 https://www.seventeen.com/celebrity/a40906/how-leaving-her-small-town-helped-uzo-aduba-embrace-the-gap-in-her-teeth/

5 https://www.stuff.co.nz/entertainment/celebrities/2396524/I-used-to-be-fat-Beyonce

6 https://www.psychologytoday.com/gb/blog/the-main-ingredient/202109/are-negative-core-beliefs-wrecking-your-life

7 https://www.psychologytoday.com/us/blog/great-kids-great-parents/201211/self-awareness.

8 https://www.washington.edu/news/2015/11/02/childrens-self-esteem-already-established-by-age-5-new-study-finds/#:~:text=By%20age%205%20children%20have,by%20University%20of%20Washington%20researchers.

9 https://www.verywellmind.com/piagets-stages-of-cognitive-development-2795457

10 https://www.verywellmind.com/piagets-stages-of-cognitive-development-2795457

11 https://www.verywellfamily.com/causes-of-low-self-esteem-in-kids-3288009

12 https://www.eurekalert.org/pub_releases/2006-01/asu-cpr012406.php

13 https://www.today.com/health/children-young-3-have-poor-body-image-talk-dieting-says-t102453

14 https://www.pacey.org.uk/news-and-views/news/archive/2016-news/august-2016/children-as-young-as-3-unhappy-with-their-bodies/

15 https://www.today.com/health/children-young-3-have-poor-body-image-talk-dieting-says-t102453

16 https://www.pacey.org.uk/news-and-views/news/archive/2016-news/august-2016/children-as-young-as-3-unhappy-with-their-bodies/

17 https://www.fastcompany.com/3060491/what-happened-to-my-brain-after-a-month-without-watching-tv

18 https://www.addicta.com.tr/Content/files/sayilar/12/1.pdf

19 https://www.theguardian.com/tv-and-radio/2020/apr/07/wide-awoke-club-childrens-tv-that-represents-britains-diversity

20 https://www.televisual.com/news/less-than-25-of-kids-say-uk-tv-represents-them/

21 https://clpe.org.uk/research/clpe-reflecting-realities-survey-ethnic-representation-within-uk-childrens-literature

22 https://www.ferris.edu/HTMLS/news/jimcrow/coon/homepage.htm

23 https://news.sky.com/story/enid-blyton-blue-plaque-bio-by-english-heritage-includes-racist-and-xenophobic-criticism-12334601

24 http://revealinghistories.org.uk/legacies-stereotypes-racism-and-the-civil-rights-movement/objects/robertson-s-golliwogs.html

25 http://news.bbc.co.uk/1/hi/magazine/7920962.stm

26 https://newsfeed.time.com/2014/02/06/barbie-lead-designer-blames-moms-not-dolls-crazy-proportions-for-girls-body-issues/

27 https://psmag.com/social-justice/i-am-a-barbie-girl-in-what-is-not-a-barbie-world

28 https://www.naacpldf.org/ldf-celebrates-60th-anniversary-brown-v-board-education/significance-doll-test/

29 https://theconversation.com/what-i-learned-when-i-recreated-the-famous-doll-test-that-looked-at-how-black-kids-see-race-153780

30 https://www.kiro7.com/news/trending/all-children-should-have-toys-that-reflect-individuals-with-disabilities-michigan-mom-says/KJ3MALVY2FHI5ANTY7ZZX4NB4Q/

31 https://bpspsychub.onlinelibrary.wiley.com/doi/10.1111/j.2044-835X.2011.02027.x

32 https://www.bbc.com/future/article/20210524-the-gender-biases-that-shape-our-brains

33 https://www.bbc.com/future/article/20210524-the-gender-biases-that-shape-our-brains

34 https://www.nytimes.com/roomfordebate/2014/12/22/why-should-toys-come-in-pink-and-blue/how-did-toys-get-stereotyped-by-sex

35 https://www.forbes.com/sites/danidiplacido/2022/09/14/disneys-little-mermaid-backlash-has-reached-insane-heights/?sh=31798ef25592

A CULTURE OF UGLY

1 https://archive.archaeology.org/0007/newsbriefs/zambia.html

2 Stewart, Susan. *Painted Faces*, Amberley Publishing (2020), p16

3 https://www.history.com/topics/pre-history/bronze-age

4 Stewart, Susan. *Painted Faces*, Amberley Publishing (2020), p16

5 https://www.inbmedical.com/the-evolving-role-of-skincare

6 https://www.newscientist.com/article/dn20809-ancient-egyptians-believed-in-coiffure-after-death/

7 https://greekreporter.com/2021/11/13/ancient-greek-beauty-standards-beautiful-greece/

8 https://www.bbc.co.uk/news/magazine-30746985

9 https://greekerthanthegreeks.com/2017/09/20-weird-crazy-and-incredible-facts.html

10 https://listverse.com/2017/01/03/10-disgusting-facts-about-ancient-greek-life/

11 https://www.jstor.org/stable/3719759

12 Stewart, Susan. *Painted Faces*, Amberley Publishing (2020), p30

13 https://www.racked.com/2017/3/30/14988124/makeup-trickery-viral-news

14 https://www.thesun.co.uk/news/2012161/husband-divorces-his-wife-after-seeing-her-without-makeup-for-the-first-time-days-after-their-wedding/

15 https://www.etymonline.com/word/pretty#:~:text=1300 per cent20as per cent20a per cent20surname) per cent2C per cent20from,Middle per cent20Dutch per cent20perte per cent2C per cent20Dutch per cent20pret per cent20 per cent22

16 Stewart, Susan. *Painted Faces*, Amberley Publishing (2020), p24

17 https://www.pblmagazine.co.uk/news/history-of-nail-art

18 https://bust.com/style/15479-tk-totally-weird-beauty-trends-in-history.html

19 https://www.phrases.org.uk/meanings/blue-blood.html

20 Hernandez, Gabriela. *Classic Beauty*, Schiffer (2011)

21 Hernandez, Gabriela. *Classic Beauty*, Schiffer (2011)

22 Downing, Sarah Jane. Beauty and Cosmetics 1550-1950, Shire Publications (2012), p13

23 Kendall, Mikki. *Hood Feminism*, p.256, Bloomsbury (2020), p256

24 https://www.theguardian.com/books/2008/dec/20/women-pressandpublishing

25 https://www.atlasobscura.com/articles/the-poisonous-beauty-advice-columns-of-victorian-england

26 https://talks.ox.ac.uk/talks/id/a6af8ca2-c277-4ef5-a579-c705381df3d4/

27 https://hyperallergic.com/415421/consumptive-chic-a-history-of-beaty-fashion-disease/

28 https://dirtysexyhistory.com/tag/the-ugly-girl-papers/

29 https://medium.com/history-of-women/ugly-girl-papers-advice-for-women-from-an-1870s-magazine-31fb73785773)

30 Downing, Sarah Jane. Beauty and Cosmetics 1550-1950, Shire Publications (2012)

31 https://www.nationalgeographic.com/science/article/ingredients-lipstick-makeup-cosmetics-science-history

32 https://www.atlasobscura.com/articles/who-was-madame-rachel-scam

33 https://www.biography.com/business-figure/helena-rubinstein

34 https://www.biography.com/business-figure/estee-lauder

35 https://www.infoplease.com/biographies/society-culture/charles-revson

36 https://www.makeupinbusiness.co.uk/avon-history/brief-view-of-the-history-of-avon-cosmetics/

37 https://www.selfridges.com/GB/en/features/int/in-bloom-the-selfridgesstory

38 https://exhibition.mixedmuseum.org.uk/museum/timeline/presence-of-minority-ethnic-populations-in-britain

39 https://www.harpersbazaar.com/uk/beauty/a38010209/black-beauty-evolution/

40 https://www.racked.com/2018/1/23/16901594/black-makeup-brands-history

41 https://www.racked.com/2018/1/23/16901594/black-makeup-brands-history

42 https://metro.co.uk/2022/02/01/i-can-never-find-a-shade-deep-enough-black-women-on-beauty-shopping-16020265/

43 https://www.bustle.com/articles/196747-the-sneaky-manipulative-history-of-why-women-started-shaving

44 Tungate, Mark. *Branded Beauty: How Marketing Changed the Way We Look.* Kogan Page (2011)

45 https://www.hollywoodreporter.com/news/loreal-fetes-40th-anniversary-because-youre-worth-it-paris-261216

46 https://customdirectpromo.com/the-history-of-the-beauty-industrys-most-salient-sales-strategy/

47 Downing, Sarah Jane. Beauty and Cosmetics 1550-1950, Shire Publications (2012)

48 https://www.thoughtco.com/1970s-feminist-activities-3529001 https://www.thoughtco.com/1970s-feminist-activities-3529001

49 https://hair-and-makeup-artist.com/womens-1970s-makeup/

50 https://yesterdaysperfume.typepad.com/yesterdays_perfume/2010/07/charlie-by-revlon-1973.html

51 https://historyofcosmetics.weebly.com/blog/america-1970s

52 https://www.theguardian.com/artanddesign/2016/jul/03/miss-black-and-beautiful-the-pageants-where-curves-and-afros-ruled

53 Downing, Sarah Jane. Beauty and Cosmetics 1550-1950, Shire Publications (2012)

54 https://www.collectorsweekly.com/articles/selling-shame-40-outrageous-vintage-ads-any-woman-would-find-offensive/

55 Faludi, Susan. *Backlash: The Undeclared War Against American Women,* Crown Publishing (1991) p83

56 https://www.theguardian.com/lifeandstyle/2018/jan/31/as-a-1990s-teenager-the-world-gave-us-girl-power-and-pornification

57 https://time.com/5310256/90s-gender-equality-progress/

58 https://www.mirror.co.uk/tv/tv-news/simon-cowell-cruelly-fat-shamed-22511661

59 https://graziadaily.co.uk/life/in-the-news/what-is-mid-size/

60 https://yougov.co.uk/topics/lifestyle/articles-reports/2020/01/23/nearly-half-brits-are-unhappy-their-body

WHITE AND UGLY

1 https://www.theguardian.com/education/2021/mar/28/uk-schools-record-more-than-60000-racist-incidents-five-years

2 https://www.bbc.co.uk/news/uk-wales-49036798

3 https://www.pcc.edu/diversity-councils/cascade/whiteness-history-month/whiteness

4 https://www.huffingtonpost.co.uk/entry/iman-racism-fashion-industry_n_55f02b31e4b002d5c0775000

5 https://link.springer.com/article/10.1023/A:1020683720636

6 https://www.bbc.com/future/article/20200818-colourism-in-india-the-people-fighting-light-skin-bias

7 https://www.bbc.co.uk/news/entertainment-arts-49976837

8 https://www.allure.com/story/charithra-chandran-favorite-beauty-spots-london

9 https://www.sciencedaily.com/releases/2017/10/171012143324.htm

10 https://www.thetech.org/ask-a-geneticist/ask330

11 Etcoff, Nancy. *Survival of the Prettiest*, Doubleday (1999)

12 Etcoff, Nancy. *Survival of the Prettiest*, Doubleday (1999), p105

13 https://www.independent.co.uk/news/science/men-women-the-secrets-of-skin-colour-796610.htmL

14 Gabriel, Deborah. *Layers of Blackness: Colourism in the African Diaspora*. Imani Media (2007)

15 https://en.wikipedia.org/wiki/Columbus%27s_letter_on_the_first_voyage

16 https://www.etymonline.com/search?q=race

17 https://www.britannica.com/topic/race-human/The-history-of-the-idea-of-race

18 C. Loring, Brace. *"Race" is a Four-Letter Word: the Genesis of the Concept*. New York: Oxford University Press, 2005.

19 Dabiri, Emma. *Don't Touch My Hair*, Penguin (2020), p. 67

20 Dabiri, Emma. *Don't Touch My Hair*, Penguin (2020), p. 68

21 Dabiri, Emma. *Don't Touch My Hair*, Penguin (2020), referencing A New General Collection of Voyages and Travels, Vol. II, p. 319, p. 71

22 https://ldhi.library.cofc.edu/exhibits/show/africanpassageslowcountryadapt/introductionatlanticworld/europnea_christianity_and_slav

23 https://www.essence.com/celebrity/viola-davis-less-classically-beautiful-ny-times/

24 https://www.bbc.co.uk/news/newsbeat-43879480

25 https://www.washingtonpost.com/news/morning-mix/wp/2018/02/05/beyonces-father-airs-colorism-he-dated-her-mother-because-he-thought-she-was-white/

26 https://www.washingtonpost.com/news/wonk/wp/2015/12/29/obamas-skin-looks-a-little-different-in-these-gop-campaign-ads/

27 https://www.scientificamerican.com/article/the-bad-is-black-effect/

28 https://eu.usatoday.com/story/life/people/2013/09/12/julie-chen-plastic-eye-surgery-less-chinese/2803049/

29 https://quillette.com/2019/02/13/the-origins-of-colourism/

30 https://www.byrdie.com/skin-bleaching

31 https://www.allure.com/story/aesthetic-trauma-generational-beauty-standards

32 https://www.sciencedaily.com/releases/2019/07/190708112419.htm

33 https://www.wired.co.uk/article/inclusive-cameras-apple-google. https://www.obeducators.com/reflections/do-you-know-how-chocolate-and-furniture-impacted-the-film-industry-jg33j

34 https://www.theguardian.com/technology/2016/sep/08/artificial-intelligence-beauty-contest-doesnt-like-black-people

35 https://www.cnbc.com/2020/06/02/tiktok-blacklivesmatter-censorship.html)

36 https://www.theverge.com/2018/1/12/16882408/google-racist-gorillas-photo-recognition-algorithm-ai

37 https://www.media.mit.edu/posts/how-i-m-fighting-bias-in-algorithms/

38 https://theintercept.com/2020/03/16/tiktok-app-moderators-users-discrimination/

39 https://edition.cnn.com/style/article/fox-eye-trend-asian-cultural-appropriation-trnd/index.html

40 https://www.standard.co.uk/showbiz/hailey-bieber-accused-cultural-appropriation-tiktok-makeup-tutorial-brownie-glazed-lips-b1028878.html

41 https://www.theguardian.com/commentisfree/2014/sep/23/why-black-bum-only-good-white-skin-cultural-appropriation

42 https://www.theweek.co.uk/98291/what-is-blackfishing

43 https://www.insider.com/black-texas-teen-suspended-from-school-over-hair-length-2022-5

44 https://www.essence.com/news/judge-ban-dreadlocks-workplace-discrimination/

45 https://edition.cnn.com/2022/09/01/business/uk-workplace-racism/index.html

THE WEIGHT OF UGLY

1 https://www.verywellfit.com/what-is-the-sacred-heart-diet-4109189

2 https://digitalcommons.wou.edu/pure/vol4/iss1/7

3 https://www.theguardian.com/commentisfree/2015/mar/27/ancient-greece-physical-pressure-hercules-body-image

4 https://www.medievalists.net/2020/06/fatness-thinness-middle-ages/

5 Strings, Sabrina. *Fearing the Black Body: The Racial Origins of Fat Phobia*, NYU Press (2019), p104

6 Strings, Sabrina. *Fearing the Black Body: The Racial Origins of Fat Phobia*, NYU Press (2019), p109

7 https://daily.jstor.org/how-colonialism-shaped-body-shaming/

8 Strings, Sabrina. *Fearing the Black Body: The Racial Origins of Fat Phobia*, NYU Press (2019), p149

9 https://www.npr.org/transcripts/893006538

10 https://onlinebooks.library.upenn.edu/webbin/book/lookupid?key=ha000782202

11 https://www.mimimatthews.com/2016/04/25/victorian-fat-shaming-harsh-words-on-weight-from-the-19th-century/

12 https://www.historyextra.com/period/victorian/queen-victoria-favourite-food-eating-sex-appetites-guilty-pleasures/

13 https://www.mimimatthews.com/2016/04/25/victorian-fat-shaming-harsh-words-on-weight-from-the-19th-century/

14 https://www.mimimatthews.com/2016/04/25/victorian-fat-shaming-harsh-words-on-weight-from-the-19th-century/

15 https://www.mimimatthews.com/2016/04/25/victorian-fat-shaming-harsh-words-on-weight-from-the-19th-century/

16 https://www.researchgate.net/publication/265497563_The_Development_of_Muscular_Christianity_in_Victorian_Britain_and_Beyond

17 https://www.verywellmind.com/history-of-eating-disorders-4768486

18 [illegible]story.co.uk/blogs/news/corsets-in-fashion-a-full-history

19 https://www.atlasobscura.com/articles/1920s-food-flapper-diet

20 https://www.goodhousekeeping.com/health/diet-nutrition/g3912/worst-weight-loss-advice/?slide=2

21 https://www.goodhousekeeping.com/health/diet-nutrition/g3912/worst-weight-loss-advice/?slide=2

22 http://www.youmustrememberthispodcast.com/episodes/2020/1/20/hollywoods-first-weight-loss-guru-madame-sylvia-make-me-over-episode-2

23 https://www.independent.co.uk/arts-entertainment/obituary-molly-o-day-1181071.html

24 https://www.independent.co.uk/arts-entertainment/obituary-molly-o-day-1181071.html

25 https://www.jstor.org/stable/24632111

26 https://www.goodhousekeeping.com/beauty/a32787/ideal-woman-body-type-1930s/

27 https://www.foodingredientsfirst.com/news/sweet-survey-who-are-the-worlds-biggest-sugar-consumers.html

28 https://www.striking-women.org/module/women-and-work/world-war-ii-1939-1945

29 https://greatist.com/grow/100-years-womens-body-image#4

30 https://www.royalalberthall.com/about-the-hall/news/2020/october/unstoppable-voices-how-the-1970-miss-world-contest-sparked-a-revolution/

31 https://www.legislation.gov.uk/ukpga/1975/65/enacted

32 https://www.newyorker.com/magazine/2019/03/18/kwame-brathwaites-grandassa-models

33 Orbach, Susie. *Fat is a Feminist Issue*, Arrow (1978)

34 https://www.vogue.co.uk/arts-and-lifestyle/article/monica-lewinsky-fat-shaming

35 Pausé, Cat and Renee Taylor, Sonya. *The Routledge International Handbook of Fat Studies*. Routledge (2021)

36 https://www.newstatesman.com/culture/tv-radio/2018/08/how-triggering-noughties-show-supersize-vs-superskinny-troubling-new

37 https://www.theguardian.com/lifeandstyle/2018/jul/23/the-rise-of-the-body-neutrality-movement-if-youre-fat-you-dont-have-to-hate-yourself

38 https://www.nytimes.com/1985/12/08/style/anorexia-it-s-not-a-new-disease.html

39 https://www.theguardian.com/lifeandstyle/2018/jul/23/the-rise-of-the-body-neutrality-movement-if-youre-fat-you-dont-have-to-hate-yourself

40 https://publications.parliament.uk/pa/cm5801/cmselect/cmwomeq/805/80502.htm

41 https://time.com/4538376/weight-watchers-sex-ad-offensive/

42 https://www.dazeddigital.com/beauty/article/55411/1/[illegible]-are-in-smoking-is-back-is-heroin-chic-next

FIXING UGLY

1 https://www.theguardian.com/fashion/2021/mar/03/zoom-ready-male-demand-for-cosmetic-procedures-rising

2 https://www.theguardian.com/fashion/2021/mar/03/zoom-ready-male-demand-for-cosmetic-procedures-rising

3 https://happiful.com/almost-half-of-the-uk-experience-low-body-confidence/

4 https://www.nhs.uk/mental-health/conditions/body-dysmorphia/

5 https://www.epsteinplasticsurgery.com/procedures/breast-procedures/breast-augmentation/one-day-rapid/

6 https://www.huffingtonpost.co.uk/entry/people-regret-plastic-surgery_l_6259cc86e4b052d2bd61d91c

7 https://www.huffingtonpost.co.uk/entry/bella-hadid-regret-nose-job-14_n_62309893e4b0b6282028961a

8 Haiken, Elizabeth. *Venus Envy: A History of Cosmetic Surgery*, The Johns Hopkins University Press (1999,) p1

9 https://www.verywellhealth.com/the-history-of-plastic-surgery-2710193

10 Haiken, Elizabeth. *Venus Envy: A History of Cosmetic Surgery*, The Johns Hopkins University Press (1999), p5

11 https://www.independent.co.uk/life-style/health-and-families/health-news/ugly-history-cosmetic-surgery-a7072216.html

12 Haiken, Elizabeth. *Venus Envy: A History of Cosmetic Surgery*, The Johns Hopkins University Press (1999), p20

13 Haiken, Elizabeth. *Venus Envy: A History of Cosmetic Surgery*, The Johns Hopkins University Press (1999), p21

14 https://www.verywellhealth.com/the-history-of-plastic-surgery-2710193

15 https://history.house.gov/Exhibitions-and-Publications/BAIC/Historical-Essays/Temporary-Farewell/World-War-I-And-Great-Migration/

16 https://www.nytimes.com/1926/03/30/archives/had-her-face-lifted-now-sues-for-100000-woman-asking-damages-from.html

17 https://www.history.com/news/10-things-you-may-not-know-about-john-dillinger

18 Haiken, Elizabeth. *Venus Envy: A History of Cosmetic Surgery*, The Johns Hopkins University Press (1999), p181

19 Haiken, Elizabeth. *Venus Envy: A History of Cosmetic Surgery*, The Johns Hopkins University Press (1991), p182

20 Haiken, Elizabeth. *Venus Envy: A History of Cosmetic Surgery*, The Johns Hopkins University Press (1999), p184

21 Haiken, Elizabeth. *Venus Envy: A History of Cosmetic Surgery*, The Johns Hopkins University Press (1999), p185

22 https://pubmed.ncbi.nlm.nih.gov/9047184

23 Haiken, Elizabeth. *Venus Envy: A History of Cosmetic Surgery*, The Johns Hopkins University Press (1999), p201

24 https://www.thecut.com/2021/08/how-to-treat-keloids-on-black-skin.html

25 Haiken, Elizabeth. *Venus Envy: A History of Cosmetic Surgery*, The Johns Hopkins University Press (1999), p214

26 https://www.theguardian.com/lifeandstyle/2015/jan/25/beauty-breast-the-sun-female-form

27 Haiken, Elizabeth. *Venus Envy: A History of Cosmetic Surgery*, The Johns Hopkins University Press (1999), p235

28 https://www.biography.com/news/marilyn-monroe-playboy-first-issue-didnt-pose

29 https://www.history.com/this-day-in-history/barbie-makes-her-debut

30 Haiken, Elizabeth. *Venus Envy: A History of Cosmetic Surgery*, The Johns Hopkins University Press (1991), p249

31 Haiken, Elizabeth. *Venus Envy: A History of Cosmetic Surgery*, The Johns Hopkins University Press (1991), p242

32 Haiken, Elizabeth. *Venus Envy: A History of Cosmetic Surgery*, The Johns Hopkins University Press (1999), p237

33 Haiken, Elizabeth. *Venus Envy: A History of Cosmetic Surgery*, The Johns Hopkins University Press (1999), p242

34 Haiken, Elizabeth. *Venus Envy: A History of Cosmetic Surgery*, The Johns Hopkins University Press (1999), p249

35 https://www.bbc.co.uk/news/magazine-17511491

36 https://www.bbc.co.uk/news/magazine-17511491

37 https://www.allure.com/story/breast-implant-history

38 https://www.allure.com/story/breast-implant-history

39 www.theguardian.com/society/2021/dec/25/implants-must-carry-stronger-warnings-about-cancer-risk

40 https://www.forbes.com/sites/angelalei/2022/01/20/how-to-achieve-the-best-snatched-jawline-according-to-top-medical-aesthetic-professionals/?sh=5cf57c23e53a

41 Haiken, Elizabeth. *Venus Envy: A History of Cosmetic Surgery*, The Johns Hopkins University Press (1999), p10

42 Haiken, Elizabeth. *Venus Envy: A History of Cosmetic Surgery*, The Johns Hopkins University Press (1999), p145

43 https://www.vintag.es/2017/10/11-classic-hollywood-stars-who-had.html

44 https://www.independent.ie/entertainment/books/the-truth-behind-the-wallis-myths-26766286.html

45 https://www.tatler.com/article/happy-100th-birthday-to-the-facelift

46 Haiken, Elizabeth. *Venus Envy: A History of Cosmetic Surgery*, The Johns Hopkins University Press (1999), p151

47 Haiken, Elizabeth. *Venus Envy: A History of Cosmetic Surgery*, The Johns Hopkins University Press (1999), p15

48 https://www.allure.com/story/birth-of-botox

49 https://www.researchandmarkets.com/reports/5675579/global-botulinum-toxin-market-by-product-by-end

50 https://www.womenshealthmag.com/beauty/g35593008/celebrities-who-have-botox-fillers/

51 https://www.dailymail.co.uk/femail/article-7935367/Gwen-Stefani-fans-insist-looks-unrecognizable-Grammys-accuse-plastic-surgery.html

52 https://www.newbeauty.com/kristin-davis-cover-story/

53 https://www.fortunebusinessinsights.com/industry-reports/dermal-fillers-market-100939

54 https://www.diyphotography.net/55-plastic-surgery-patients-want-look-better-selfies-study-finds/

OLD AND UGLY

1 https://www.nytimes.com/2005/08/02/science/your-body-is-younger-than-you-think.html

2 https://abcnews.go.com/Politics/Vote2008/story?id=4193461&page=1

3 https://www.simonandschuster.com/authors/Hannah-Pool/47875433

4 https://journals.sagepub.com/doi/abs/10.1177/105960117700200422

5 https://www.harpersbazaar.com/beauty/skin-care/a14980/history-of-anti-aging/

6 https://www.historyhit.com/the-blood-countess-facts-about-elizabeth-bathory/

7 https://www.womenshealthmag.com/health/a37528827/fertility-cliff-myth/

8 https://www.britannica.com/topic/witchcraft/The-witch-hunts

9 https://www.thecollector.com/european-witch-hunting

10 https://www.britannica.com/topic/Malleus-maleficarum

11 https://www.heraldscotland.com/opinion/13114676.witch-myth/

12 https://www.heraldscotland.com/opinion/13114676.witch-myth/

13 https://en.wikipedia.org/wiki/Cailleach

14 https://www.cronescounsel.org/the-ancient-crone/#:~:text=Crone%2C%20hag%2C%20and%20witch%20once,and%20healers%20in%20their%20communities

15 https://pursuit.unimelb.edu.au/articles/it-s-a-fact-women-get-better-with-age

16 https://www.globenewswire.com/en/news-release/2022/03/29/2412093/0/en/Anti-aging-Market-Size-to-Worth-Around-US-119-6-Bn-by-2030.html

17 https://www.gcimagazine.com/consumers-markets/article/22302117/the-return-of-antiaging

18 https://frownies.co.uk/pages/the-history-of-frownies-est-1889

19 https://theconversation.com/how-20th-century-rejuvenation-techniques-gave-rise-to-the-modern-anti-ageing-industry-133569

20 https://theconversation.com/how-20th-century-rejuvenation-techniques-gave-rise-to-the-modern-anti-ageing-industry-133569

21 https://theconversation.com/how-20th-century-rejuvenation-techniques-gave-rise-to-the-modern-anti-ageing-industry-133569

22 https://embryo.asu.edu/pages/eugen-steinach-1861-1944

23 https://www.cracked.com/article_24278_forced-abortions-5-insane-ways-old-hollywood-tortured-stars.html

24 https://www.ranker.com/list/how-old-hollywood-studio-system-worked/lisa-waugh

25 https://www.ranker.com/list/how-old-hollywood-studio-system-worked/lisa-waugh

26 https://www.harpersbazaar.com/uk/beauty/skincare/a18672934/isabella-rossellini-on-ageing-beauty-and-her-return-to-lancome/

27 https://eu.usatoday.com/story/entertainment/movies/2021/04/13/women-film-study-highlights-ageism-concerns-hollywood/7201257002/

28 https://womenintvfilm.sdsu.edu/research/

29 https://eu.usatoday.com/story/entertainment/movies/2021/04/13/women-film-study-highlights-ageism-concerns-hollywood/7201257002/

30 https://www.nowtolove.com.au/news/local-news/rebel-wilson-reveals-why-she-lied-about-her-age-7370

31 https://www.theguardian.com/film/2015/may/21/maggie-gyllenhaal-too-old-hollywood

32 https://www.dailymail.co.uk/femail/article-7723827/The-gender-age-gap-British-TV.html

33 https://fashionweekdaily.com/ysl-catherine-deneuve-ss21/

34 https://www.dailymail.co.uk/femail/article-10499443/Former-French-lady-Carla-Bruni-54-sizzles-campaign-Balmain.html

35 https://www.mirror.co.uk/3am/celebrity-news/madonnas-bitter-feud-piers-morgan-26234274

36 https://www.thetimes.co.uk/article/paulina-porizkova-the-supermodel-who-dared-to-look-her-age-nfhz8c6kn

37 https://www.nationalgeographic.com/history/article/fountain-of-youth

38 https://www.dailymail.co.uk/video/tvshowbiz/video-1370895/Put-away-Piers-Morgan-says-Madonna-act-age.html

39 https://www.usmagazine.com/celebrity-news/news/jane-fonda-turns-75-credits-youthful-looks-to-good-genes-and-money-20122112/

40 https://www.theartnewspaper.com/2007/10/01/illuminating-lacquer-maker-onishi-isao-one-of-japans-living-national-treasures

41 https://www.newscientist.com/article/dn13874-how-the-brain-detects-the-emotions-of-others/

42 https://www.bacp.co.uk/news/news-from-bacp/2018/7-november-stress-can-be-contagious/

43 https://ideas.ted.com/5-ways-to-build-lasting-self-esteem/

THE UGLY SIDE OF WELLNESS

1 https://www.fiercehealthcare.com/tech/headspace-ginger-finalize-3b-merger-to-offer-meditation-mindfulness-and-tele-therapy

2 https://mashable.com/article/hinge-headspace-dating-meditation

3 https://theconversation.com/how-children-who-dread-pe-lessons-at-school-can-be-given-a-sporting-chance-122565

4 https://www.theatlantic.com/education/archive/2019/01/why-pe-is-terrible/581467/

5 Bell, Poorna. *Stronger*, Pan Macmillan (2021), p101

6 https://www.teenvogue.com/story/nike-london-flagship-plus-sized-mannequins

7 https://www.newsweek.com/wimbledon-mihaela-buzarnescu-forced-change-bra-court-1722178

8 https://www.theguardian.com/sport/2014/oct/21/shamil-tarpischev-forced-apology-williams-sisters-slur

9 https://www.theguardian.com/sport/2014/oct/18/russian-president-williams-brothers-banned

10 https://metro.co.uk/2022/08/31/why-the-fitness-industry-is-not-as-accessible-as-it-should-be-17273798/

11 https://www.theguardian.com/environment/2018/jul/13/hiking-african-american-racism-nature

12 https://www.ethnicity-facts-figures.service.gov.uk/culture-and-community/culture-and-heritage/visits-to-the-natural-environment/latest

13 https://www.spectator.co.uk/article/countryfile-countryside

14 https://www.walesonline.co.uk/lifestyle/tv/who-masterchef-2022-finalists-23870206

15 https://www.thesun.co.uk/tvandshowbiz/12090557/bbc-complaints-inaccurate-countryfile-bame-people-countryside/

16 https://globalwellnessinstitute.org

17 https://depts.washington.edu/hrome/Authors/kjw2/BathsBathinginAncientRome/pub_zbarticle_view_printable.html

18 https://www.thoughtco.com/hygiene-in-ancient-rome-and-baths-119136

19 https://www.parkhallhotelandspa.co.uk/history-english-spa/

20 https://ard.bmj.com/content/61/3/273

21 https://bathmedicalmuseum.org/did-the-bath-waters-really-cure-patients/

22 https://goodspaguide.co.uk/features/spa-through-the-ages

23 https://bathmedicalmuseum.org/did-the-bath-waters-really-cure-patients/

24 https://goodspaguide.co.uk/features/spa-through-the-ages

25 https://www.francisfrith.com/uk/cheltenham/history

26 https://www.etymonline.com/word/well-meaning

27 https://goodspaguide.co.uk/features/spa-through-the-ages

28 https://goodspaguide.co.uk/features/spa-through-the-ages

29 https://www.swimming.org/swimengland/decade-decline-report/

30 https://goodspaguide.co.uk/features/wheelchair-access-and-support-for-disabled-spa-guests

31 https://goodspaguide.co.uk/features/wheelchair-access-and-support-for-disabled-spa-guests

32 https://www.wellnesscreatives.com/yoga-industry-trends

33 https://www.finder.com/uk/yoga-statistics

34 https://www.34st.com/article/2021/09/wellness-yoga-gua-sha-beauty-smudging-cultural-appropriation

35 https://www.huffingtonpost.co.uk/entry/gwyneth-paltrow-yoga_n_5c07b347e4b0680a7ecabe40

36 https://positivepsychology.com/history-of-meditation/

37 https://www.theguardian.com/lifeandstyle/2017/oct/22/mindfulness-jon-ka-bat-zinn-depression-trump-grenfell

38 https://www.theguardian.com/lifeandstyle/2017/oct/22/mindfulness-jon-kabat-zinn-depression-trump-grenfell

39 https://www.ncbi.nlm.nih.gov/books/NBK210143/

40 https://jothivita.com/what-is-ayurveda/history/

41 https://www.glamourmagazine.co.uk/article/wellness-whitewashing

42 https://jothivita.com/what-is-ayurveda/history/

43 https://metro.co.uk/2020/07/11/sweaty-betty-ditches-insensitive-sanskrit-product-names-12975262/

44 La Pompe-Moore, Giselle. Take It In, Rider (2002), p204

45 https://www.slimmingworld.co.uk/what-can-i-eat

46 https://www.vice.com/en/article/jm5nvp/ruby-tandoh-eat-clean-wellness

47 https://www.bbc.co.uk/bbcthree/article/9fe47476-ad1f-414c-a925-cf078a2145a8

48 https://www.theguardian.com/lifeandstyle/2017/oct/22/mindfulness-jon-kabat-zinn-depression-trump-grenfell

49 https://www.theguardian.com/commentisfree/2020/jan/31/we-need-to-move-on-from-self-care-to-something-that-cannot-be-captured-by-capitalism

50 https://www.bluezones.com/2018/08/moai-this-tradition-is-why-okinawan-people-live-longer-better/

51 https://www.simplypsychology.org/maslow.html

PRETTY UGLY

1 Prinstein, Mitch. *The Popularity Illusion: Why Status is Toxic But Likeability Wins All*, Ebury Digital, (2018), p187

2 Prinstein, Mitch. *The Popularity Illusion: Why Status is Toxic But Likeability Wins All*, Ebury Digital, (2018), p65

3 https://www.dailymail.co.uk/video/news/video-1101302/School-bullies-force-girl-drink-puddle-water-pretty.html

4 https://www.dailymail.co.uk/femail/article-2124246/Samantha-Brick-downsides-looking-pretty-Why-women-hate-beautiful.html

5 Etcoff, Nancy. *Survival of the Prettiest: The Science of Beauty*, Little, Brown (1999), p44

6 https://www.dailymail.co.uk/femail/article-10701053/SAMANTHA-BRICK-Ten-years-think-Im-beautiful-women-hate-me.html

7 https://www.instyle.com/beauty/social-media-filters-mental-health

8 https://journals.sagepub.com/doi/10.1111/j.1467-9280.2006.01750.x

9 https://www.wired.co.uk/article/prettier-people-more-intelligent

10 https://hypebae.com/2022/3/tiktok-bimbocore-trend-feminism-op-ed-elle-woods-kim-kardashian-paris-hilton

11 https://www.abc.net.au/news/2019-02-01/ted-bundy-why-the-serial-killer-attracted-female-fans/10763676

12 https://www.thesun.co.uk/tvandshowbiz/3408090/jeremy-meeks-chloe-green-baby-hot-felon-wife-melissa/

13 https://www.cnbc.com/2022/03/08/online-daters-lost-a-record-547-million-to-scams-in-2021.html

14 https://www.amazon.co.uk/Fatal-Gift-Beauty-Nina-Burleigh/dp/0307588599

15 https://www.forbes.com/sites/kiriblakeley/2011/09/29/good-looks-on-trial-the-amanda-knox-case/?sh=71356f983e9b

16 https://www.forbes.com/sites/kiriblakeley/2011/09/29/good-looks-on-trial-the-amanda-knox-case/?sh=44f73fe73e9b

17 https://www.forbes.com/sites/kiriblakeley/2011/09/29/good-looks-on-trial-the-amanda-knox-case/?sh=5f6038cf3e9b

18 Etcoff, Nancy. *Survival of the Prettiest: The Science of Beauty*, Little, Brown (1999), p19

19 https://www.cosmopolitan.com/style-beauty/fashion/advice/a5968/celebs-abercrombie-models/

20 https://graziadaily.co.uk/fashion/news/s-another-elitist-tale-ex-abercrombie-fitch-employee/

21 https://www.yourerc.com/blog/post/the-beauty-bias-can-you-hire-based-on-looks_

22 https://www.bbc.co.uk/news/business-61514430

23 https://newsroom.carleton.ca/archives/2010/11/02/the-hottie-factor-why-some-profs-out-earn-others/

24 https://www.forbes.com/sites/tomaspremuzic/2019/07/17/its-time-to-expose-the-attractiveness-bias-at-work/?sh=3bee13071324

25 https://pubmed.ncbi.nlm.nih.gov/27283466/

26 https://www.wsj.com/articles/SB10001424052970203687504576655331418204842

27 https://www.businessinsider.com/if-you-have-any-of-these-20-physical-features-your-pay-check-will-probably-be-higher-2011-2?r=US&IR=T&utm_source=copy-link&utm_medium=referral&utm_content=topbar

28 https://www.businessinsider.com/if-you-have-any-of-these-20-physical-features-your-pay-check-will-probably-be-higher-2011-2?r=US&IR=T&utm_source=copy-link&utm_medium=referral&utm_content=topbar

29 https://www.businessinsider.com/15-signs-you-will-be-rich-2010 10?r=US&IR=T#being-married-and-staying-married-increases-your-net-worth-by-77-percent-6

30 https://www.businessinsider.com/if-you-have-any-of-these-20-physical-features-your-pay-check-will-probably-be-higher-2011-2?r=US&IR=T&utm_source=copy-link&utm_medium=referral&utm_content=topbar

31 https://www.insuredsolutions.net/blog/pitch-wars-the-gender-bias-behind-the-idea-of-a-professional-voice/

32 https://www.dailymail.co.uk/sciencetech/article-5647049/Very-unattractive-people-open-new-experiences-devoted-careers.html

33 Etcoff, Nancy. *Survival of the Prettiest: The Science of Beauty*, Little, Brown (1999), p144

34 https://www.independent.co.uk/news/uk/london-club-accused-of-refusing-women-entry-for-being-too-dark-and-too-fat-a6672071.html

35 https://www.thesun.co.uk/fabulous/20391604/plus-size-model-nightclub-body-shaming-controversy/

36 Engeln, Renee, PhD. *Beauty Sick: How the Cultural Obsession with Appearance Hurts Girls and Women*, Harper (2017), p170

37 https://www.beautifulpeople.com/en-UK. https://metro.co.uk/2016/10/07/theres-a-bar-opening-which-only-admits-beautiful-people-because-thats-the-world-we-live-in-6175469/

38 https://www.mirror.co.uk/news/beautifulpeople-dating-site-members-share-15003980

39 https://www.businessinsider.com/luxy-dating-app-is-tinder-minus-the-poor-people-2014-10?r=US&IR=T

40 https://www.businessinsider.com/studies-show-the-advantages-of-being-beautiful-2013-6?r=US&IR=T

41 Etcoff, Nancy. *Survival of the Prettiest: The Science of Beauty*, Little, Brown (1999), p145

42 Etcoff, Nancy. *Survival of the Prettiest: The Science of Beauty*, Little, Brown (1999), p145

43 https://www.dailymail.co.uk/tvshowbiz/article-10496111/MAFS-AU-Selina-wearing-wedding-ring-Asian-bombshell.html

44 https://www.standard.co.uk/esmagazine/how-radhika-sanghani-learned-to-stop-worrying-and-love-her-nose-a3814731.html

45 https://www.salon.com/2011/05/17/psychology_today_racist_black_women_attractive/

46 https://www.independent.co.uk/life-style/love-sex/dating-apps-racism-tinder-bumble-grindr-online-dating-a8504996.html

47 https://news.cornell.edu/stories/2018/09/redesign-dating-apps-lessen-racial-bias-study-recommends

48 https://www.bbc.co.uk/news/technology-52886167

49 https://hingeapp.zendesk.com/hc/en-us/articles/360049436394-Why-does-Hinge-have-an-ethnicity-preference-

50 https://www.wired.co.uk/article/racial-bias-dating-apps

51 Whitefield-Madrano, Autumn. Face Value, *The Hidden Way Beauty Shapes Women's Lives*. Simon & Schuster (2016), p104

52 https://www.refinery29.com/en-gb/passing-as-a-trans-woman

53 https://www.allure.com/story/pretty-privilege

54 https://www.bbc.co.uk/news/av/entertainment-arts-59225576

55 Whitefield-Madrano, Autumn. *Face Value, The Hidden Way Beauty Shapes Women's Lives*. Simon & Schuster (2016), p104

56 https://www.dailymail.co.uk/tvshowbiz/article-9333747/Gail-Porter-reveals-left-homeless-TV-career-just-stopped.html

57 https://www.brainyquote.com/authors/katie-piper-quotes

58 https://www.cheatsheet.com/entertainment/love-is-blind-danielle-ruhl-reveals-old-photos-weight-changes-filming-season-2.html/

59 https://www.theguardian.com/film/2021/dec/07/funny-fat-girl-rebel-wilson-says-her-team-were-against-her-losing-weight

60 https://www.ted.com/talks/cameron_russell_looks_aren_t_everything_believe_me_i_m_a_model?language=en

61 https://www.apa.org/monitor/2011/10/biased-brain

FURTHER READING

Bell, Poorna. *Stronger*, Pan Macmillan (2021)

Dabiri, Emma. *Don't Touch My Hair*, Penguin (2020)

Downing, Sarah Jane. *Beauty and Cosmetics 1550-1950*, Shire Publications (2012)

Engeln, Renee, PhD. *Beauty Sick: How the Cultural Obsession with Appearance Hurts Girls and Women*, Harper (2017)

Etcoff, Nancy. *Survival of the Prettiest: The Science of Beauty*, Little, Brown (1999)

Faludi, Susan. *Backlash: The Undeclared War Against American Women*, Crown Publishing (1991)

Gretchen, E. Henderson. *Ugliness: A Cultural Anthology*, Reaktion Books (2015)

Haiken, Elizabeth. *Venus Envy: A History of Cosmetic Surgery*, The Johns Hopkins University Press (1999)

Hernandez, Gabriela. *Classic Beauty*, Schiffer (2011)

Kendall, Mikki. *Hood Feminism: Notes From the Women White Feminists Forgot*, Bloomsbury (2020)

La Pompe-Moore, Giselle. *Take It In*, Rider (2002)

Orbach, Susie. *Fat is a Feminist Issue*, Arrow (1978)

Oyěwùmí, Oyèrónkẹ́. *The Invention of Women: Making an African Sense of Western Gender Discourses*. University of Minnesota Press (1997)

Prinstein, Mitch. *The Popularity Illusion: Why status is toxic but likeability wins all*. Vermilion (2008)

Stewart, Susan. *Painted Faces: A Colourful History of Cosmetics*, Amberley Publishing (2020)

Strings, Sabrina. *Fearing the Black Body: The Racial Origins of Fat Phobia*, NYU Press (2019)

Tungate, Mark. *Branded Beauty: How Marketing Changed the Way We Look*. Kogan Page (2011)

Whitefield-Madrano, Autumn. *Face Value: The Hidden Ways Beauty Shapes Women's Lives*. Simon & Schuster (2017)

Woolf, Naomi. *The Beauty Myth: How Images of Beauty Are Used Against Women*, Vintage (1990)

Yeboah, Stephanie. *Fattily Ever After: A Black Fat Girl's Guide to Living Life Unapologetically*. Hardie Grant (2020)

Zeitz, Joshua. *Flapper: A Madcap Story of Sex, Style, Celebrity, and the Women Who Made America Modern*. Crown Publishing (2006)

For further reading around disability, please see Leah Lakshmi Piepzna-Samarasinha's writing, and Mikaela Moody's work on disfiguremisia.

ACKNOWLEDGEMENTS

To say writing this book has been stressful is an understatement. So, this is a bit of a mix of 'thank you's' and 'sorry's' to everyone who has been on the journey with me – books are seldom written alone.

A huge thank you firstly to my parents who told all their friends to buy this book without knowing that it is, essentially, one big long overshare and now they have to deal with that. Sorry. Thank you for all your unconditional love and support. I'm very lucky to have you and I don't say it enough. We don't have much family in the UK, but we have lots of chosen family – thanks to Auntie Della, Auntie Pat and Uncle Mick, Wendy and Phillip and Auntie Babs for being wonderful. Thank you to my family in India, cousins and chinna thatha.

Next up (this feels like the Oscars, but like, not), thanks to my brilliant publishing team: my agent Emma Finn at C&W agency for believing in *Ugly*, your incredible eye for detail and getting it off the ground and to the end. To my editors, Susannah Otter and Madiya Altaf, all I can say is I'm so sorry for all the over researching. Thank you for all your guidance, flexibility, handholding, words of wisdom, time and attention. It's been a longer journey than anticipated but it's finally here

(Susannah… I'm sorry if this felt in any way like your second baby). Liz Marvin – thank you for your amazing line edits, it made all the difference. Nicky Watkinson – thank you for all your helpful comments on the text. Thanks to everyone else at Blink and Bonnier Books too, including Eleanor Stammeijer and Jessica Tackie for all your PR and marketing wizardry, I super appreciate it. Thanks to anyone else who worked on it. I couldn't have wished for a better team.

So many friends were mega pillars of support and reassurance during this process. Lizzie Pook, your sage advice and pep talks were just what I needed every time, thank you, pal. Grace Timothy, your kindness and brilliance extend way beyond the support you gave me while writing this book – you are a magical human. Maggie Hitchins, for being my rock during this and for being on the receiving end of many panicky voice notes – love you. Giselle La Pompe-Moore, your podcasts/voice notes are a daily highlight and inspiration, thanks for all your wonderful words. Rebecca Denne, thank you for all your support, chapter reading, and lols along the way. Eloise Kerr, thanks for always being the Panda to my Shoe, even though you're far way. Alix Fox, for being a wonderful, inspirational pal and sounding board. Rachael Hattan, you're everyone's rock, thank you (and Oscar) for all your support. Caroline Hirons, thank you for your support on this book, pal, I'm super grateful. Poorna Bell, thanks for your endless lols, inspiration and advice on this process. Zoe Moore, thanks for your support, love you long-time and to my sister Natasha Asghar, we'll always be the 'zinc' girls together.

Thank you to all my wonderful friends for just being there including Sally Stevenson, Lucy Sheridan, Simon Gallagher, Alex Popoff, my Stokey girls – Tani, Tools, Simpo, Jeff, Poppy, Nat, you're the best. Lots of wonderful people helped quell my panic by reading chapters or giving me advice too, so a big thank you also to: Annie Davies, Daksha Chikhal, Cemo Imamzade, Natasha Tomalin-Hall, Emma Guns, Fiona Embleton, Amy Grier, Laura Millar, Cassie Steer and to my brilliant fact-checking crew: Alice Snape, Amy Davies-Adams, Emma Nicklin and Tom Stevens.

A big 'diolch' (I've gone Welsh for variation) to my support systems: Steph Camilleri aka ADHD Advocate for all your help getting me through this (and life), Michelle Beckett, Holly Paton and everyone at ADHD Collective for being a wonderful community. Judith Quinn, for always believing in me and my voice. Luke Goulden, part PT/part comedy meerkat – you're the best. If I'm not your favourite client now, then there's nothing more I can do.

My career path hasn't always been easy, but so many people helped me get to the place I am today. James Mclaren, I miss you every day, thank you for believing in me. Nicola Down and Charlotte Haigh – I learned so much from you both, it was the best career start and so much fun. All of my *Stylist* family particularly Lisa Smosarski – thanks for letting me run with my wild ideas, and for your support when I was honing my skills. Deborah Joseph, for all your kindness and beyond. You, Camilla Kay (and team *Glamour*), restored my faith in this industry. Farrah Storr, for being my work mum, helping me through the process and always having sage advice – now please reply to your texts (love you). A huge thanks to the wonderful Divia Thani, for your kindness and Louisa Parker-Bowles, Lydia Bell and crew at *Conde Nast Traveller* for being so supportive during this process. Big love to the team at the *Guardian*, including Morwenna Ferrier, Hannah Booth and Abigail Radnor. And sorry if I've missed anyone else in this list. I've been worried about that since I got the book deal – no joke. A big thanks to anyone I've quoted and mentioned in the book too.

Much love to all my beauty industry family, to the wonderful beauty PRs (honestly you guys are *top* of the game) and sorry you've not seen me in two years. And a big thank you to all the brands who have supported this book. A huge thanks to Firdaous El Honsali, Sarah Potter and all at Dove.

A final mega thank you to everyone who has bought *Ugly*, who recommended it to somebody and the readers who have been with me through my career. Your lovely words are so appreciated and make all the difference – I save them all.

And, thanks to the troll who called me ugly in the first place and set this train in motion – I owe you a pint.